Improving the Quality
of Reference Service
for Government Publications

ALA STUDIES IN
LIBRARIANSHIP
NO. 10

Improving the Quality
of Reference Service
for Government Publications

CHARLES R. McCLURE

PETER HERNON

AMERICAN LIBRARY ASSOCIATION

CHICAGO 1983

Library of Congress Cataloging in Publication Data

McClure, Charles R.
  Improving the quality of reference service for   *025.5*
government publications.   *M128i*

  (ALA studies in librarianship ; no. 10)
  Bibliography: p.
  Includes index
  1. Libraries, Depository—United States—Reference
services. 2. Libraries—Special collections—
Government publications. 3. Reference services
(Libraries)—United States. 4. United States—
Government publications. 5. Government information—
United States. I. Hernon, Peter. II. American
Library Association. III. Title. IV. Series.
Z675.D4M37 1983   025.5′2   83–3754
ISBN 0–8389–0388–6

85-3371

Contents

Tables

Figures

Preface

All phases of document activities, from the production and distribution of government publications to their servicing and use in libraries, present problems and issues amenable to research and investigation. However, in many instances, the operating principles and conventions accepted by practicing librarians are based on opinions and assumptions rather than on scientific investigation. Complicating matters is the fact that many of the currently debated issues, including those relating to depository programs and access to government information, have been discussed for years and are apparently no closer to resolution than they were when they first arose.

For example, the arguments assessing the value of separate documents collections versus integrated collections were formulated and solidified by the decade of the 1940s. However, it seems that the apparent advantages and disadvantages of each organizational arrangement are based on supposition and practice rather than scientific investigation. A commonly accepted advantage of the separate collection is that experienced library personnel could provide the type of assistance needed by clientele. However, the historical record suggests that provision of a better quality of reference service was, in large part, a rationale after the fact for the trend toward separate collections.[1] Government publications have been a resource which libraries still are unsure how to handle. Libraries receive an increasing volume of government publications and, as in the past, often lack sufficient time and staff to process them as fully as other materials.

Research enables the library profession to add to knowledge by making new discoveries. It also enables a better and more complete understanding of current phenomena. The documents field, unfortunately, has not developed a sufficient body of descriptive research from which other types of research can build. As noted in one study,

> given the dearth of reliable information, it is difficult for senior policy makers to determine what should constitute rational standards of service for government publications or a national program

for library and information services in this area; nor can front-line practitioners determine where their institution stands in comparison to other depository libraries or to accepted standards.[2]

Except for the literature describing reference sources or the value of documents in reference work, documents reference service in academic depository libraries is one area that has received little scholarly attention. Coverage of reference work in *Guidelines for the Depository Library System*[3] lacks the detail found in other sections of the document. It may be that practicing librarians and government officials who administer the depository library program assume that library clientele receive documents reference service of a high quality.

Research topics abound in the area of documents reference service. One of the most fundamental issues deals with the accuracy of the reference assistance provided by depository staff members and their willingness to provide referral service. This book reports data gathered from an unobtrusive study of the quality of reference service provided by academic depository libraries in the northeastern and southwestern parts of the United States. A set of twenty typical documents-related questions were administered to preselected depository libraries and the accuracy of the responses, staff willingness to engage in referral, and the characteristics of the reference interview were recorded.

The study reported in this book is based on *exploratory* research. Exploratory studies emphasize the "discovery of ideas and insights. Therefore, the research design must be flexible enough to permit the consideration of many different aspects of a phenomenon."[4] Consistent with the purpose of exploratory research, this study tests the application of a methodology (based upon unobtrusive testing) to the documents field and finds that it can produce new insights. The study also identifies areas for further research and suggests that more precise investigations can be undertaken. These other studies can build upon the research questions listed in chapter 1, and develop and test hypotheses. Further, these studies should be able to expand greatly upon the institutional variables studied here. To aid in the development of hypotheses, the authors have identified a range of other variables that merit examination. Still, the empirically derived data are presented in practical terms and placed in the context of the published literature in and outside library and information science. The results of this study should therefore be accessible and useful to everyone with a stake in their implications.

In the following chapters, the authors discuss the success of depository library personnel in answering the test questions, the impact of asking the questions over the telephone versus in person, and the impact of the characteristics of the reference interview on the ultimate answer given to the proxy. Further, an analysis of the referral process is provided in terms of what types of questions tend to be referred. The relationships between institutional and library variables such as budget, number of volumes held, staffing, and highest degree granted on the quality of reference service provided are also explored.

The study presents some major findings of interest to anyone who is concerned with reference service and its effective administration. The findings suggest that the general public will experience problems in gaining access to some depository collections and that documents staff members correctly answer a low percentage of test questions and infrequently engage in referral. Further, a library user has a better chance of receiving a correct response to a telephone rather than an in-person request, and the length of the search process does not increase the likelihood of a correct answer. Two other points should be noted: (1) in a number of instances documents personnel admitted that they did not know the answer to the question but were unwilling to suggest referral, even to someone else on the library staff, and (2) the interpersonal communications skills of some documents personnel are limited and these people can be abrasive in their dealings with the public.

These findings are detrimental to the depository library program and, presumably, the public service goals of many libraries. However, they can be rectified if the Government Printing Office, libraries, and practicing librarians are willing to address them. To this end, the authors make specific recommendations whereby documents reference services can be improved and the overall depository library program made more cost-effective.

The emphasis of the book is on the process of better integrating documents reference service with the library as a whole. Even if they are located in separate collections, government publications should not be regarded as a unique resource. They complement other library holdings and therefore should be administratively integrated with other collections. As Bernard Fry suggests,

> Library administrators need to consider government publications collections as an information resource on an equal basis with books and serials, to the extent that they are integrated in information services, whether shelved as separate collections as in many major research libraries. The relationship between the documents collection and other library collections should be that of a single resource in meeting user needs. To restate: the key to a good government documents collection is integration into the mainstream of library information service.[5]

Thus this book considers documents reference service in light of general reference service. Our hope, therefore, is that IMPROVING THE QUALITY OF REFERENCE SERVICE FOR GOVERNMENT PUBLICATIONS will be of interest to library administrators, documents and general reference librarians, library school educators and students, government officials who administer depository library programs, and others interested in the application of unobtrusive testing to reference services.

The study reported here provides data which should be of value to the Government Printing Office in keeping the library community aware that "the purpose of depository libraries is to make U.S. government publications easily accessible to the general public and to insure their continued availability in the future." Further, depository libraries are supposed to provide reference service and, whenever necessary, "referral to a source or place where answers can be found."[6] The results of this study should also enable academic and other depository libraries to better structure their documents service programs in the best interests of their clientele as well as the general public. Comparative data among instititutions also provide insights into the functioning of the depository system in institutions of higher education that have various types of degree programs.

If the documents field is to build upon this study and attract the type of cross-institutional studies that are needed, government agencies and other funding sources must appreciate the value of research and be willing to support it. Because of the size, cost, potential benefit to information-seeking, and commitment made by libraries and government agencies, depository library programs require research and formal evaluation. Thus this study should be regarded as exploratory and providing a basis for further research related to documents reference services.

Indeed, the findings and recommendations in this book present a number of challenges to library administrators and librarians—especially government documents librarians, reference librarians, officials of the Government Printing Office, and other government agencies that provide depository library programs. The specifics of these challenges are suggested throughout the volume, but the critical challenge for all participants is to increase public access to government publications, improve the quality of government publications reference services, and integrate government information resources into the mainstream of library reference services. Only when they are accomplished will government publications be exploited to their full value as a significant and important complement to other library holdings.

CHARLES R. MCCLURE
School of Library Science
University of Oklahoma

PETER HERNON
Graduate School of Library and
 Information Science
Simmons College

Acknowledgments

We wish to acknowledge our gratitude to the students who assisted in the collection of the data. The participating students from Simmons College are Karyn Franzek, David Gordon, Christine Mandel, Laurence Prusak, Margot Rendall, and M. Pauline LeBlanc Wood. Those who participated from the University of Oklahoma include Vicky Baker, Deborah Anna Baroff, Elba F. Brooks, Laurence O. Keys, Michele S. King, Teresa Knott, Lisa M. Landrum, Mona L. Lemmings, Michele Moore Lovelace, Kathryn Joachim Nevaquaya, Malinda Shirley-Sattler, and Joan Schipper.

We also thank Ms. Judy Diehm for typing the various tables and figures, and the University of Oklahoma which partially supported data analysis. Finally, we acknowledge the support of our families (Elinor, Alison, and Linsay Hernon, and Vicky and Wendy McClure). Undoubtedly they were subjected to more discourses about unobtrusive testing, government publications, and reference services than they would have preferred.

1

Public Access to Government Information

Public access to information resources of the federal government has been hotly debated in recent years. Due in part to the establishment of the National Commission on Libraries and Information Science (NCLIS), increased marketing and commercialization of federal information sources by private brokers, growing concern on the part of many observers that the depository library program may be in need of a major overhaul, and ongoing assessment of national information policy, further investigation and analysis of public access to government information clearly is required. Yet the issue of public access to government information is imbedded in a number of other factors that affect the production, dissemination, and availability of information by the federal government.

The concept of public access to government information, which is elusive at best, includes more than the establishment of a depository library program, the addition of new member libraries each year, the distribution of government publications to depository libraries, and provision for the identification and bibliographic control of those publications. Public access suggests the same degree of bibliographic control, physical availability, professional service, and status that other forms of information resources receive within a library. Further, it suggests awareness or knowledge of those federal information resources that librarians can exploit to link users with appropriate government publications/information.

Even the term "government publication" has definitional difficulties. For purposes of this study, the term is defined, within the context of Title 44 of the *United States Code,* as informational matter which is published as an individual document at government expense or as required by law.[1] Since there is no centralized agency for control over the vast myriad publications produced by the federal government, virtually any federal agency can originate and disseminate this informational matter.

As part of a study completed for NCLIS, Bernard Fry concluded, on the basis of existing user surveys, that government publications in depository libraries were not utilized to their full potential.[2] Such a conclusion is of major concern in light of the federal government's financial commitment to producing and distributing documents. In fiscal year 1982, the budget of the Government Printing Office (GPO) totaled $809,176,000, including the expenses financed by the sale of publications and reimbursements from government agencies; the budget for the Superintendent of Documents for the same year was $86,889,000; and the budget of the Depository Library Program alone totaled $21,559,000.[3] Further, it has been estimated that printing and distribution costs for publications sent to depository libraries average $11,000 per depository.[4] Under this program, partial depositories can select from a list of GPO "item numbers"—i.e., from categories of publications (not all government publications currently issued, however)—those most appropriate for their particular needs and interests. Depository libraries then receive these publications free of charge, but incur costs for organization, storage, and servicing, as well as the purchase of additional reference sources, for improving access to these publications.[5] Given the commitment of the federal government to the depository library program, the GPO and the Joint Committee on Printing (JCP), the congressional oversight committee, should be concerned about the effectiveness with which libraries provide access to the information contained in depository publications.

The historical background of the GPO and the depository library program, which has been discussed elsewhere, need not be reviewed here.[6] However, it should be stressed that the program has been library initiated; it is a cooperative program, one in which the federal government has not "forced" libraries to participate. Yet a number of individuals believe that the depository library program should "insure that they (depositories) are complying with the law and maintaining reasonable standards of service."[7] The articulation of "reasonable standards of service" delineates the scope of public access to government publications at the local depository level.

Current Status

A brief review of selected, recent writings and research related to public access to government publications in depository libraries supports Fry's conclusion of underutilization (see table 1). These studies suggest that the federal government exercises limited bibliographic control techniques over its publishing programs,[8] that government-related indexes have fewer access points than indexes to more traditional information resources,[9] and that there is minimal production of in-house findings aids and automated retrieval systems for government publications.[10]

TABLE 1. Summary of Selected, Recent Research and Writings (1978–Mid–1982) Related to Access of Government Publications in Depository Collections

Authors	Date	Findings
Cook[a]	1981	Minimal staffing, reduced budget, and less resources for documents departments compared to other areas of the library
Fry[b]	1978	Underutilization and non-recognition of the value of government publications
Heisser, Palmatier, and McClure[c]	1981	Ineffectiveness of the Depository Library Inspection Program and compliance with "minimum standards" by depository libraries
Hernon[d]	1979	Non-use of government publications by social scientists and small minority of documents account for vast majority of all use
Hernon[e]	1982	Depository collections of microformatted government documents either go unused or a small percentage of the collection receives the most use
Hernon and McClure[f]	1982	Depository library staff answered 37% of test questions—reference service not of a high quality
Hernon and Purcell[g]	1982	Depositories are only one of the providers of government information and oftentimes they are a secondary source. Further, depositories often select more publications than are needed.

TABLE 1. (Continued)

Authors	Date	Findings
Hernon and Shepard[h]	1982	The <u>Social Science Citation Index</u> contains a minimal number of citations to government publications
Hoduski[i]	1982	Document libraries must publicize and promote documents as well as take political action to effect changes in the depository system or in the local library
McClure[j]	1977	Non-integration of microformatted government documents into the collection as a whole
McClure[k]	1978	Exclusion of many government periodicals from traditional periodical indexes
McClure[l]	1981	Non-integration of government documents into library administrative, reference, and collection development processes
McClure[m]	1981 & 1982	Inability of documents librarians to exploit new technologies such as on-line data base searching, OCLC, and in-house automated systems
McClure[n]	1982	Structural limitations, lack of measurable goals and objectives and meaningful performance measures, and limited evaluation of the effectiveness for the Depository System

McClure and Harman[o]	1982	Limited inclusion of references to government publications in doctoral dissertations
NCLIS[p]	1982	Confusion between the role of the public and private sectors as to responsibilities for acquisition, dissemination, and bibliographic control over government publications
Richardson, et al[q]	1980	Minimal bibliographic access points and in-house findings aids for documents

Sources

a. Kevin L. Cook, A Study of Varying Levels of Support Given to Government Documents Collections in Academic Libraries. Master's thesis, University of Oklahoma, 1981.

b. Bernard M. Fry, Government Publications: Their Role in the National Program for Libraries and Information Services (Washington, D.C.: Government Printing Office, 1978).

c. David C. Heisser, Roxanne Palmatier, and Charles R. McClure, "GPO Inspection Program," Government Publications Review 7A (1980): 450-52.

d. Peter Hernon, Use of Government Publications by Social Scientists (Norwood, NJ: Ablex Publishing Corp., 1979).

e. _____, Microforms and Government Information (Westport, CT: Microform Review, 1981).

TABLE 1. (Sources continued)

f. Peter Hernon and Charles R. McClure, "Testing the Quality of Reference Services Provided by Academic Depositories: A Pilot Study," in Communicating Public Access to Government Information, edited by Peter Hernon (Westport, CT: Meckler Publishing, 1982).

g. Peter Hernon and Gary R. Purcell, Developing Collections of U.S. Government Publications (Greenwich, CT: JAI Press, 1982).

h. Peter Hernon and Clayton A. Shepard, "Government Documents in Social Science Literature," in Collection Development and Public Access of Government Documents, edited by Peter Hernon (Westport, CT: Meckler Publishing, 1982).

i. Bernadine Hoduski, "Political Activism for Documents Librarians," in Communicating Public Access to Government Information, edited by Peter Hernon (Westport, CT: Meckler Publishing, 1983).

j   Charles R. McClure, "Administrative Integration of Microformatted Government Documents," Microform Review 6 (September 1977): 259-271.

k. ―――, "Indexing U.S. Government Periodicals: Analysis and Comments," Government Publications Review 5 (1978): 409-421.

l. ―――, "Administrative Basics for Microformatted Government Documents Librarians," in Microforms and Government Information, edited by Peter Hernon (Westport, CT: Microform Review, 1981), pp. 125-145.

m. _____, "Online Government Documents Data Base Searching and the Use of Microfiche Documents Online by Academic and Public Depository Librarians," Microform Review 10 (Fall, 1981): 245-259; and "Technology in Government Documents Collections," Government Publications Review 9 (1982): 255-276.

n. _____, "Structural Analysis of the Depository System: A Preliminary Assessment," in Collection Development and Public Access of Government Documents, edited by Peter Hernon (Westport, CT: Meckler Publishing, 1982) pp. 35-36.

o. Charles R. McClure and Keith Harman, "Government Documents as Bibliographic References and Sources in Dissertations," Government Publications Review 9 (1982): 61-72.

p. National Commission on Libraries and Information Science, Public Sector/Private Sector Interaction in Providing Information Services (Washington, D.C.: Government Printing Office, 1982).

q. John V. Richardson, Jr., Dennis C.W. Frisch, and Catherine M. Hall, "Bibliographic Organization of U.S. Federal Depository Collections," Government Publications Review 7A (1980): 463-480.

The literature documents an inability to integrate government publications into the library collection as a whole, physically and bibliographically, under the direction of professional staff, and with a higher status accorded to government publication and greater financial support.[11] When a library *does* automate its circulation, acquisitions, serials control, or other processes, it frequently excludes its collection of government publications.[12] Integration of government publications is difficult because documents collections typically are physically separated from other library collections and are seen by some library administrators to be of little value in contributing to overall library reference and service goals.[13]

Other studies have noted the wide range of use and non-use of government publications in libraries by social scientists, concluding that collection development for government publications is narrowly defined and that a small portion of the government publications collection accounts for the vast majority of use.[14] Further, many academic libraries are selecting more source material than their clientele regularly require and appear to be developing "self-contained collections" that presumably will require little outside referral.[15] These findings are supported by other studies that suggest, for instance, only minimal use of government information is made during the process of conducting doctoral research.[16] Further, the shift of the Government Printing Office to distribute the majority of documents to depository libraries in microfiche is not likely to encourage increased access to such information. Indeed, even further underutilization and inaccessibility are likely to result from the emphasis on micropublication.[17]

Inadequate staffing of government documents departments, and perhaps inadequate training of government documents librarians, also limits access to government information.[18] One study has shown that many government documents librarians have minimal training in new technologies such as online data base searching. Further, these librarians have not utilized computerized information systems (including OCLC) in order to increase access to government information.[19] It has been suggested that the lack of institutional resources, equipment, and clerical help forces documents librarians into activities which leave little time to work directly and effectively with patrons.[20]

In a broader context, controversies between the public and private sector concerning what types of government information are to be produced, how they are to be disseminated, the degree of bibliographic control to be provided, and the information services to be supported by the government are prevalent.[21] Another factor that has been studied is the structural weaknesses of the GPO depository library system and the effect of those weaknesses on public access to government information.[22] And, most recently, Congress has debated the appropriateness of establishing a national clearinghouse as a means for increasing the effective production and dissemination of government information.[23]

Yet, despite the above-listed considerations, the current controversies, and the various difficulties encountered by many libraries in providing access to government information, a recent report from NCLIS has concluded that

> the federal government should actively use existing mechanisms, such as the libraries of the country, as primary channels for making governmentally distributable information available to the public.[24]

Thus it is likely that libraries, and especially libraries which are members of the depository library program, will continue to be perceived as having a significant role in the dissemination of and access to government information in the foreseeable future. But specifics about that role—e.g., purpose, activities, required resources, and services that the libraries will provide—are yet to be resolved.

Background for This Study

Currently, the 1,365 depository libraries include academic, public, law school, government, state, and special libraries; however, almost two-thirds of the depository libraries are located in academic institutions.[25] Because of the heavy concentration of depository libraries in academic institutions and the importance of academic libraries as a primary channel for making governmentally distributable information available to the public ("the public" is narrowly defined in the context of higher education), the authors decided to investigate the quality of government publications reference service in a sample of academic depository libraries. Two primary benefits would result from such a study: the effectiveness with which academic depository libraries provide access to government information could be assessed, and recommendations and strategies could be made to improve the effectiveness of these and other depository libraries as providers of government information.

Although the study focuses on one part of library operations (the part that organizes and makes available government publications), an assessment of reference service for government publications serves as an indicator of the quality of reference services for the library as a whole. Fry has pointed out that no modern library can give adequate reference service without access to government publications, because these publications are up to date and reliable, cover an infinite range of topics, and are written for a broad range of audiences.[26] Effective reference use of government publications requires knowledge of these sources, administrative support, a "positive staff attitude" concerning the importance of government publications, and written collection development and reference policy statements that clearly include government publications.[27]

The utility of separating government publications from the rest of the library collection has been a predominant factor when discussions have focused on the effectiveness or impacts of depository collections on public access. But the separate versus integrated argument must be considered in assessing the degree to which documents are underutilized, as well as the "appropriate" role for government information resources in the library. The historical argument about the benefits and limitations of separate versus integrated collections of government documents will not be repeated here.[28] The authors of this book believe that government publications should be an integrated part of the resources of the library as a whole and *not* simply "other" publications set off to a side. The adage "Out of sight and out of mind" may have special application to Fry's assessment of the underutilization of government documents, as well as the confusing and often contradictory "roles" which academic depository libraries attempt to fill.

Institutions that agree to accept depository status take on a number of responsibilities that are detailed in *Instructions to Depository Libraries*[29] and *Guidelines for the Depository Library System*[30] (see appendix D). The latter clearly stresses the importance of exploiting government information resources in the context of general library reference services. Recent guidelines published by the American Library Association regarding reference services also stress the importance that the reference librarian be able to exploit *all* types of information resources, in various formats, for the benefit of the information seeker.[31] Such pronouncements by both the Government Printing Office and the American Library Association apparently express a view of what "ought to be" rather than what "is." In the final analysis, government publications are often not used to their full potential and are not integrated into the main library collections, either physically, bibliographically, or in terms of service. Rarely is there clear articulation of the role of government publications in fulfilling the library's mission related to providing information to its patrons.[32]

A key component to public access of government information in academic depository libraries, clearly, is the effectiveness with which depository staff members provide accurate answers to reference questions. Other factors (previously described) that relate to access may interact in unique ways, depending on the situation at a given library; they may either encourage or discourage access to government information. But the ability of depository staff members to answer reference questions, when they are unaware that they are being tested, is one of the best methods to view the extent and type of access that patrons will have when they search for government information in a depository library.

While the reference process is complicated and defies easy definitions, for purposes of this study it consisted of activities that occur between the time a proxy approached a documents staff member with a question and the time when either the question was resolved or the interaction between the librarian and the proxy was discontinued. Such a definition clearly emphasizes the perspective of the user. In-depth analysis of aspects of the reference process, such as question negotiation, search strategies, and subject analysis, are concepts that *librarians* apply to describe the reference process. This book, on the other hand, is written from the perspective of the user who attempts to obtain access to government information through academic depository libraries. Such a perspective is likely to provide excellent insights into the quality of reference services provided to patrons, the extent to which academic depository libraries encourage or inhibit access to government information, strategies by which depository libraries can increase their ability effectively to disseminate government information through the depository library program, techniques for further analysis and research of the reference process, and methods by which library school educators can identify effective reference services.

Unobtrusive Evaluation of Reference Service

General reference services in academic, public, and special libraries have been investigated by hidden or unobtrusive testing and collection of empirical data relating to the quality of responses to questions asked by people posing as clientele of that library. Published and unpublished reports that examine the quality of reference services provided by staff members responsible for depository collections, however, appear to be nonexistent. Due to the vast amount of government publications distributed through the depository program each year, as well as the cost of the depository program to both the government and individual libraries, assessment of the quality of reference services provided by depository libraries is needed.

Unobtrusive testing of reference service is the process of asking reference questions (for which answers have been determined) of library staff members who are not aware that they are being evaluated. Individuals who ask the questions, usually thought of as "proxies", and "replacements," for actual patrons typically have been trained beforehand regarding the asking of these questions. Lancaster, who has written an excellent overview of the evaluation of reference,[33] identifies the advantages of unobtrusive testing as including: observation of staff members under operating conditions assumed to be normal, measurement of the success with which staff members answer various types of questions, and ability to conjecture why certain types of questions were answered incorrectly.[34] Such an approach is especially appropriate when the ultimate objective is providing a high-level quality of performance.

The first major studies involving unobtrusive testing of reference service can be traced to the dissertations by Terence Crowley and Thomas Childers. Both studies, which were published in one volume in 1971,[35] focused on public libraries in New Jersey and involved testing by both telephone and in person. They showed substantial differences between the claims made by reference librarians and the results gathered from such testing. Librarians were much less effective in answering factual reference questions (e.g., those relating to changing political figures and current affairs) than was previously thought. In fact, they could answer only approximately half the questions correctly, and seemed to be unaware that they were disseminating outdated and incorrect information. Although the studies contained some government-related questions (e.g., "Would you give me the name of the Secretary of Commerce?" and "How did Senator Case vote on the 1957 Civil Rights Bill?"), testing was limited to general reference staff members.

In an academic library setting, Marcia Jean Myers discovered that even when academic libraries owned an appropriate source, staff members might not consult it or know how to use it. They might even misinterpret the information in a source. In addition, staff members infrequently volunteered the source of their response. Further, Myers concluded that "about 50 percent of the test questions were answered correctly . . . and that telephone reference service is in need of improvement."[36]

In a related study at another academic library setting, G. B. King and L. R. Berry had proxies telephone questions to several divisions within the library to determine the accuracy of responses, "attitude" of the librarian, and the amount of negotiation between the librarian and proxies. Results from the study showed that 60 percent of the questions were answered correctly, the negotiation process was inadequate in many instances, and the librarians rarely cited sources for their factual answers.[37] More recently, in an unobtrusive study of college library reference service, Jassim Muhammed Jirjees found that 56.6 percent of the questions were answered correctly and that the performance of reference librarians on the questions had high (but not significant) correlations with their previous reference experience, the number of FTE (full-time equivalent) professionals providing reference/information services, and number of hours spent at the reference desk.[38]

Thomas Childers also did unobtrusive testing, of fifty-seven libraries of the Suffolk Cooperative Library System. As with the other studies, he included some questions pertaining to governments and their publishing programs (e.g., "Where can I get a Federal publication called *Final Report: President's Task Force on Communication Policy* published in 1967?"). In addition to studying the accuracy of responses, this investigation was the first to find out "about the library staff's readiness to 'negotiate' a question."[39] The libraries, in several instances, "were scored not on the correctness of the answer they gave, but on their success in arriving at the ultimate step [the actual reference question]."[40] Childers also followed up on the referral process and "tested the response by any resource agency mentioned by a library."[41]

In another study, Ronald Powell examined the relationship between reference collection size and the ability of librarians from fifty-one public libraries in Illinois to answer predetermined questions correctly. Participants worked on twenty-five test questions and completed a questionnaire concerning their reference collection and educational background. This study, which provides a counterpart to the unobtrusive investigations, showed that 58.2 percent of the test questions were answered correctly and that further exploration of the ability of reference staffs to answer predetermined questions has importance for diagnosing reference service failures.[42]

Most recently, in a 1981 study, Terry Weech and Herbert Goldhor compared obtrusive versus unobtrusive evaluation of reference services in public libraries. Reference questions were administered by student proxies to a sample of five public libraries unobtrusively, while at the same time other librarians on the staff were tested obtrusively—they were aware that their answers were being evaluated. Overall, the two researchers found that library staff members tend to answer a greater proportion of reference questions completely and correctly when they are aware that they are being evaluated. In general, the percentage of correct answers was quite high, approximately 85 percent for the obtrusive and 70 percent for the unobtrusive evaluation.[43] Reasons for the relatively high accuracy rate are not clear but may be related to the nature of the questions asked, the limited sample of only five public libraries, the use of students not formally trained in library/information science, and the fact that the questions were not identified as representative of the type of questions these public libraries normally receive.

Despite the relatively high performance of reference librarians in the Weech and Goldhor study, a review of selected studies of unobtrusive reference evaluation suggests that the average for correct answers is approximately 50 percent. Table 2 summarizes some of the major studies and the percentages of correct answers.

The results from the unobtrusive study of reference service reported in this volume show a 37 percent overall rate of accuracy in answering test questions. This study included questions that were asked both by telephone

TABLE 2. Percentage of Correct Answers in Selected Unobtrusive Evaluation of Reference Service

Year	Author	Library Type	Percent Correct
1968	Crowley[a]	Public	54
1971	Childers[a]	Public	55
1973	King and Berry[b]	Academic	60
1974	House[c]	Public	40
1975	Peat, Marwick, Mitchell & Co.[d]	Public	40
1978	Childers[e]	Public	47
1980	Myers[f]	Academic	50
1981	Jirjees[g]	Academic	56
1981	Weech and Goldhor[h]	Public	70
1982	McClure and Hernon[i]	Academic	37

Sources

a. Thomas Childers and Terence Crowley, Information Service in Public Libraries: Two Studies (Metuchen, NJ: Scarecrow Press, 1971).

b. G.B. King and L. R. Berry, Evaluation of the University of Minnesota Libraries Reference Department Telephone Information Service, Pilot Study (Minneapolis: University of Minnesota Library School, 1973). ED 077 517.

c. David E. House, "Reference Efficiency of Reference Deficiency." *Library Association Record*, 76 (November 1974): 222-23.

d. Peat, Marwick, Mitchell and Co., *California Public Library Systems: A Comprehensive Review with Guidelines For the Next Decade* (Los Angeles, CA: Peat, Marwick, Mitchell and Co., 1975). ED 105 906.

e. Thomas A. Childers, "The Test of Reference," *Library Journal*, 105 (April 15, 1980): 924-28.

f. Marcia J. Myers, "The Accuracy of Telephone Reference Services in the Southeast: A Case For Quantitative Standards," in *Library Effectiveness: A State of the Art* (Chicago: American Library Association, 1980), pp. 220-231.

g. Jassim Muhammed Jirjees, "The Accuracy of Selected Northeastern College Library Reference/Information Telephone Services in Responding to Factual Inquiries," Ph.D. dissertation, Rutgers University, 1981.

h. Terry L. Weech and Herbert Goldhor, "Obtrusive versus Unobtrusive Evaluation of Reference Service in Five Illinois Public Libraries," *Library Quarterly*, 52 (October 1982): 305-324.

i. Charles R. McClure and Peter Hernon, *Improving the Quality of Reference Service for Government Publications* (Chicago: American Library Association, 1983).

and in person, but the sample was limited to academic library staff members at selected U.S. government depository libraries. In comparison, this average is below the accuracy rate for the unobtrusive studies of "general" reference services.

The studies that have been discussed in this section suggest that unobtrusive testing can be applied to reference librarianship and that such research provides insights into the quality of service extended to questions that require factual and bibliographic information. Most of such research has been done in a public library environment. However, the success of those studies suggests that such research methods could be used in the government publications field as a valid means of assessing the quality of reference service in academic depository libraries.

Purpose of This Study

This book examines the quality of reference service provided at selected academic depository libraries in order that librarians can (1) better exploit government information resources for the benefit of their patrons, (2) better identify and understand reference activities that require the use of government publications, (3) analyze aspects of the reference process related to obtaining government information resources, and (4) develop strategies and recommendations by which libraries and the depository library program can integrate government information resources into the mainstream of library reference service. Thus the book attempts to provide a basis by which the quality of government publications reference service can be assessed and then improved.

Because previous research has not examined the quality of reference service for depository collections by means of unobtrusive testing, this study should be seen as *exploratory*. Thus formal hypotheses were not developed; rather, research questions were stated as a means to guide the study:

> What factors can be identified that contribute to successful and unsuccessful answering of the questions by the depository library staff in terms of reasons for incorrect answers, telephone versus on-site delivery of questions, difficulty of questions asked, and duration of the reference process?
>
> What factors can be identified that encourage or discourage the referral of the reference question to another person on the library staff or information provider and how can the effectiveness of the referral process related to government publications be described?
>
> Will the quality of government publication reference services differ

significantly according to highest degree (baccalaureate, master's, or doctoral) offered at the institution of which the library is a part? Will the quality of government publication reference services differ significantly according to the geographical region of the libraries, the percentage of item numbers selected by the depository, the number of library volumes, the total library budget, the total number of library professional staff, or the number of government document FTE professionals or paraprofessionals?

The study of these research questions was limited to reference services provided in academic depository libraries in two geographical areas.

To recap, the documents community does not know the probability of success when library clientele request information that clearly can be obtained from government publications or the referral process. Furthermore, factors that impact on the likelihood of obtaining accurate answers to government publication reference questions are currently not known. Knowledge of the quality of reference services and factors affecting this quality can assist government documents librarians in developing strategies to improve existing services, gain further insights into the effectiveness of the depository library program operated by the GPO, and better integrate government publications reference services with reference services in the overall library.

Methodology

Population and Sampling Frame

Academic depository libraries that were eligible for investigation were from the northeast and southwest United States, as listed in the most recent *Government Depository Libraries.*[44] Academic depository libraries from these two areas were stratified by the highest degrees offered at the institution. Institutional control (public versus private) was not a significant factor in stratification due to the distribution of institutions within the two areas. Random sampling from each stratum (baccalaureate, master's granting, and doctoral) produced ten institutions in the Northeast and seven in the Southwest at which the unobtrusive testing would be done.

The total number of institutions identified for participation in the study was based on the following considerations. Because students enrolled in the government publications courses at Simmons College and the University of Oklahoma would conduct the administration of the questions, the number of available students limited the sample size. Another factor was the expected number of data elements within various data matrices. At twenty questions per site, a total of 340 questions for seventeen institutions was seen as producing adequate cell sizes for data analysis. Cost was another consideration. The number of institutions participating in the study was held to seventeen to minimize the budget of the study, which had no outside funding. Finally, data collection had to be completed within the semester.

Specific definitions of "Northeast" and "Southwest" cannot be provided since such information could lead to identification of actual depository libraries in the study. Given the small number of academic depositories within the sampling strata identified above, it is possible that use of other institutional data, in combination with data presented in this study, might lead to the identification of individual institutions. To preserve the anonymity of institutions, additional detail on the sampling process must remain confidential. Nonetheless, aggregate data can be provided to suggest the general characteristics of academic depository libraries in the study.

Table 3 indicates characteristics of the institutions in terms of highest degree offered, library volumes, library budget, FTE library professionals, FTE documents professionals, FTE documents paraprofessionals, percentage of item numbers selected by the depository, and the method by which the documents collection is physically organized in the library. (Additional discussion of these institutional variables can be found in chapter 3.) Data in table 3 came from *American Library Directory, 1980–1981*[45] or were obtained directly, but unobtrusively, from participating institutions. Thus the definitions that the *American Library Directory* uses for "volumes," "budget," "professional staff," and "paraprofessional" have been incorporated in this study. The percentage of items selected by the depositories is based on data provided or available at the participating institutions.

Organization of the documents collection was defined as follows: "separated" meant that the vast majority of government publications were physically organized as a collection, distinct from the rest of the library; "partially integrated" meant that some types of government publications, such as periodicals, were physically organized with other types of library materials; and "integrated" meant that the vast majority of government documents were physically interfiled with other library materials.

Table 3 suggests that in general, at an institutional level, libraries in the Northeast had a greater total of volumes, professional staff, and budget than those in the Southwest. However, the numbers of FTE professional documents librarians, paraprofessional documents staff, percentages of items selected, and organization of the documents collection for both regions were quite similar. The institutional variables for Northeast depositories, as represented in table 3, are skewed somewhat because of the participation of two libraries with significantly increased resources. (This factor should

TABLE 3. Characteristics of Study Participants

	Academic Depository Libraries In NE N = 10	Academic Depositories Libraries In SW N = 7	Average All N = 17
1. Highest Degree Offered			
Doctoral	50%	42%	47%
Master	20%	29%	24%
Bachelor	30%	29%	29%
2. Average Library Volumes	1,525,100	476,850	1,093,000
3. Average Library Budget	$3,324,700	$844,280	$2,303,000
4. Average FTE Library Professionals	48	14	34
5. Average FTE Documents Professionals	1	1	1
6. Average FTE Documents Paraprofessionals	2	1.3	1.6
7. Percent Item Categories Selected	46	52	49%
8. Organization of Documents Collection			
Separated	90%	86%	88%
Partially Integrated	10%	0	6%
Integrated	0	14%	6%

be kept in mind when one compares the institutional variables between Northeast and Southwest.) Nonetheless, the libraries that participated in the study appear to be a representative sample of academic libraries in each region.

Test Questions

Quality of government document reference services is equated with the number of correct answers given to a predetermined list of reference questions which can be answered primarily by use of government publication information sources. The test questions were developed according to the following criteria:

> The questions are reflective of the types asked by the public in search of government information.
> The questions are answerable, to a large degree, from more than one source.
> The questions are answerable with factual information or bibliographic references.
> The questions reflect a wide range of document types and time frames.
> The questions are answerable from individual depository collections or are dependent on the referral process.
> The questions are answerable from resources dealing with the U.S. government. These resources should be at the disposal of depository libraries.

In addition to these criteria for all test questions, other criteria were developed from questions that would be administered over the telephone:

> Questions would be reflective of the types asked by the public over the telephone.
> Questions would not call for an extensive amount of negotiation or interviewing in order to obtain a correct answer.
> Questions would be developed that library staff members would be less inclined to ask the proxy to come into the library in-person for an answer.

Based on these nine criteria, questions were developed from the collection of the GPO bookstore in Boston, Massachusetts, as well as from questions received by the City of Boston Consumer Council, the U.S. Bureau of the Census Regional Office, Boston, and documents librarians from the two geographic areas known to the researchers (but not part of the seventeen institutions selected for investigation). In addition, the preliminary list included questions of interest to the researchers and some from studies that tested the quality of general reference service.

The initial pool of test questions and their answers were submitted to documents librarians at four academic depositories (two from each area) of the study population, but not at the seventeen institutions where the investigation would take place. During the months of August and September 1981, these librarians critiqued the test questions and offered suggestions about rewording, as well as questions to add or drop. On the basis of their comments, the list was revised and finalized. It was decided that half of the study questions would be administered over the telephone and that the other half would be presented in person, with proxies posing as clientele of that institution or the general public, trying to resolve a particular information need. Appendix A contains the test questions that were used in this study and appendix B is a list of additional test questions that were pretested but not utilized for this study.

Administration of Test Questions

From October to December 1981, proxies administered the test questions at the seventeen libraries. These proxies consisted of students enrolled in the documents courses at Simmons College and the University of Oklahoma during the 1981 fall term. To ensure collection of valid data, the investigators discussed the project with interested students, conducted training sessions, coordinated and monitored the data collection process, and encouraged students to maintain an interest in the project after completion of the school term. Once the questions had been administered and responses obtained, the proxies completed the "Reference Question Tabulation Sheet," which is reprinted in appendix C. The investigators discussed the answers with the students to ensure accuracy, consistency, and completeness in data collection. The investigators also double-checked all responses to ensure consistency and completeness in the reporting of responses.

In administering the questions and tabulating the results, student proxies were reminded to follow these guidelines as much as possible:

Ask the question sincerely and accurately, appear to be conducting research or writing a paper in which the information is necessary.
Do not have the "Reference Question Tabulation Sheet" or the list of questions out in the open during administration. Remember the question and complete the tabulation sheet after administration.
Attempt to ask the questions during times of the day in which one could expect to find a professional librarian in the documents area or in the library.

Further, students were instructed to use the bottom and the back of the tabulation sheet to add descriptions, comments, notes, or questions regarding each question administration. These notes and comments were considered by the investigators before data coding and analysis to ensure that consistent tabulation practices were followed.

Many documents departments are understaffed and lack professional staff members to cover the documents reference desk during all hours that the library is open. Thus students attempted to vary the hours of their visits, but were encouraged to try to approach professional staff members. In those cases in which students were told to return when a documents librarian was on duty, the question was administered at a later time. Even though the testing process may have involved other than professional staff members, it indicates the type of service that library clientele can expect in their search for government information.

Students were reminded that unobtrusive testing requires the collection of data from participants without their knowing the real purpose of the questions. Students were asked not to discuss the project or reveal the study sites while the research was in progress. If participating libraries and their staffs realized that they were being studied, both their behavior and the findings would have been affected. Students also were asked not to discuss the project with students in other classes or with friends, since the information could conceivably have gotten back to the participating libraries and invalidated the findings. Furthermore, students agreed not to disseminate information about a library's scores. All the data are confidential and under no circumstances will be linked to an individual library.

Limitations

As was discovered during the pretest phase, some documents librarians are uncomfortable with unobtrusive testing. They question the purpose for which such data could be used, as well as raise ethical considerations about testing people who are unaware of the real nature of the reference inquiry. It should be remembered, however, that such testing has been used in the general reference field, as well as outside librarianship, for a number of years.[46] Unobtrusive testing is a legitimate means of data collection and it provides insights that cannot easily be obtained otherwise.

Unobtrusive testing, however, has certain limitations. Although the investigators carefully developed procedures for administration of the questions, it is possible that the proxies failed to provide accurate renditions of the test questions or otherwise aroused the suspicion of a depository library staff. Further, unobtrusive testing fails to consider local, unique situations within a library which may adversely affect the ability of staff to answer questions. Nonetheless, the investigators believe that the study design and proxy training minimized these difficulties.

Another limitation that may make documents librarians feel uncomfortable is the selection of test questions. These questions, which were developed according to specific criteria, were subjected to a rigorous pretest and gained the approval of professional depository librarians *before* their use. Some of the questions selected for the study had actually been asked at the pretest sites. Depository librarians went through lists of reference questions that are frequently asked them and shared with the investigators some of those questions which they believed were appropriate for inclusion in this study.

Another limitation that must be considered is the assumption that the investigated academic depositories maintain a "basic reference collection" of publications published by both the government and commercial firms. The investigators believe that if a library agrees to serve as a depository, it, in effect, agrees to maintain a "basic reference collection" necessary to provide at least minimal access to the collection. Still, as a precaution, selected questions often could be answered from two or more sources. Nonetheless, in some instances, "basic" document reference sources, necessary to answer the test questions, may not have been available in a depository under investigation.

Because of the unobtrusive nature of the study, it is likely that paraprofessional staff may have answered some of the test questions. Thus, throughout the study, "depository library staff" encompasses both professional and paraprofessional staff. Proxies were encouraged to ask questions of individuals at the documents reference desk who appeared to be professionals, rather than students or clerks. But such determinations cannot always be accurate. Although the investigators believe that the results emphasize the quality of reference service provided by professional librarians, paraprofessionals may have answered some questions.

The results from the study apply only to reference service for questions of a factual and bibliographic nature, covering the U.S. government and publications available through the GPO depository library program. Because of the nature of the study design, the investigators realize that the data can be generalized only to academic depository institutions within the two regions studied. Other depository libraries with institutional characteristics similar to those reported in this study, however, may be able to draw useful comparisons, insights, and implications, pertinent to improving the quality of their documents reference service.

In brief, the investigators believe that appropriate steps have been taken to minimize the impact of the above-mentioned limitations on the results. Indeed, the study shows the accuracy with which depository library staff answered reference questions that called for government publications. In this sense, the normal, operating conditions of the library provided the settings in which "real" reference service was provided to proxies who posed as actual library users.

Reliability and Validity of the Data

Whenever an instrument is developed to measure a specific variable— such as the quality of reference service—an attempt should be made to assess the reliability and validity of the data collected by that instrument. *Reliability* suggests stability and consistency of measurement—accuracy. One criterion for assessing reliability is the representativeness of the questions about the phenomenon that is being measured: the more representative the questions about the instrument, the higher the instrument's reliability.[47] On this criterion, the instrument should have high reliability, since the questions were based on specific criteria and pretested by practicing documents librarians. The final set of questions was accepted by both the researchers and the documents librarians as "representative" of typical questions encountered at the documents reference desk.

A second criterion of reliability is accurate and consistent coding,[48] and the following actions were taken to increase reliability of data according to this criterion. First, written procedures and standardized coding forms were used by all proxies for administering the questions and coding the librarians' responses. Second, all proxies went through a training session to assure their understanding of the procedures and definitions on the coding form, as well as to answer any questions regarding data coding. Also, the investigators reviewed all responses and comments provided by the proxies (often in the presence of proxies, in order to elicit additional information) about individual situations in an effort to maintain consistency of coding.

A third criterion for reliability is a coefficient of reliability. There are a number of reliability coefficients, but each coefficient (in general) expresses the ratio of true-score variance (perfect reliability, with no error) to observed-score variance.[49] Perfect reliability has a coefficient of 1.0, and a coefficient of 0 indicates no reliability. The Kuder-Richardson Formula 20, which assumes different degrees of difficulty on test items, was used to compute our reliability coefficient. This coefficient can be computed with knowledge of the mean and the variance of the scores, plus the number of items on the test.[50]

By considering administration of the twenty questions in each of the libraries as seventeen different test scores, a coefficient of reliability, based on the Kuder-Richardson formula, can be calculated. The coefficient of reliability was computed to be .72, indicating substantial reliability of the responses to individual questions when considered as a group.[51] Although the above factors suggest reliable instrumentation, they are only *indicators;* so they are reported to increase confidence in the reliability of the data.

The *validity* of data is the extent to which they accurately measure what they purport to measure: "One validates not the measuring instrument itself but the measuring instrument in relation to the purposes for which it is being tested."[52] Our purpose was to measure "quality of reference service," operationally defined as the percentage of correct answers to the predetermined list of twenty typical document reference questions. "Face validity," a conceptual criterion of validity, simply requires (1) a representative collection of test items and (2) "sensible" methods of test construction and administration. If the general literature on the methodology (unobtrusive testing) finds it to be appropriate and if users of the test and people knowledgeable about the topic agree that the method and instrumentation are sound and well administered—as in this study—the measure is said to have face validity.[53]

Another criterion of validity is the extent to which results can be generalized to a population as a whole. "Generalizability" is largely dependent on sampling procedure, the selection of study sites, and the characteristics of participants (in this case, institutions) in the study.[54] Although the study sample is limited to seventeen institutions, selection was based on a stratified random sample, based in turn on the highest degree offered at the academic institution. Furthermore, comparison of the characteristics of the academic depository libraries investigated in this study (see table 3) shows them to be similar to characteristics of the entire population of academic depository libraries.

For instance, this investigation found academic depositories selected, on average, 49 percent of possible items, while another study indicated that the average academic depository selected 45 percent of available items.[55] The typical depository collection in this sample had one FTE professional librarian and one FTE paraprofessional (including student assistants)—identical to what was found in another study of academic depository libraries.[56] Such similarities suggest that the sample of academic depository libraries in this study is representative of the population. Further, the general findings from this study tend to support findings from other studies related to unobtrusive testing of reference service.

The above discussion suggests *indicators* that the study obtained data that are both reliable and valid, within the limitations, definitions, and assumptions previously defined. As Herbert Blalock has pointed out, social science research is difficult (at best) due to the constant fear of omitting variables unknowingly, having measures confounded by other variables' affecting the study, and the measurement problems associated with human behavior. His advice is to clearly identify assumptions and limitations, and to distinguish generalizations from speculations.[57] Given Blalock's admonitions, the investigators attempted to utilize data analysis techniques appropriate to an exploratory study and to resist the temptation of utilizing sophisticated regression and factor analysis designs (to name a few), which the data do not support without significant and questionable assumptions. Although a more conservative approach to data analysis has been used, the investigators believe that the findings are likely to have more validity, given the limitations.

A final comment is in order about the data's reliability and validity in terms of the two geographical regions. In general, as table 3 suggests, the libraries in the Northeast were larger in total volumes, budget, and overall professional staff. However, the level of analysis (focusing on the documents department or area) displays similar characteristics for both regions. For this reason, as well as the indicators of reliability and validity discussed above, the investigators believe that neither the reliability nor the validity of the data is injured in terms of regional analysis. Thus it is appropriate—whenever possible, and in instances with adequate cases per cell—to provide results from each region individually as well as for the sample as a whole.

The Broader View

The quality of reference service for government documents has implications for the "performance" of a government documents collection, the reference services of a library as a whole, the utility of the depository library program, and national goals and objectives related to access and dissemination of government information vis-à-vis the general public. Regardless of one's professional position, institutional association, or preconceived assumptions on the role of depository libraries in the provision of government information, all have an interest in ascertaining the quality of reference service provided by depository libraries and in making improvements wherever and whenever they might be necessary.

As is evident, this book places documents reference service in the perspective of the literature on reference service in general. By so doing, it presents issues that will be of interest to anyone who is concerned with reference work. After all, with deletion of the words "government publication" the test questions could have been administered in reference settings in any type of information center. In the context of an academic depository library, however, all reference librarians have a stake in fulfilling the purposes of the depository library program as set forth in Title 44 of the *U.S. Code*.

The structure of the book is intended to facilitate ascertaining the quality of reference service provided by depository libraries and making improvements wherever they might be necessary. The quality of reference service, in terms of factors contributing to accurate and inaccurate answers by library staff members, will be presented first. Then an analysis of the relationship between institutional variables and the quality of government publications will be presented, followed by an analysis of the referral process. Next, strategies will be recommended by which the quality of reference service for government documents can be improved and better integrated into the library as a whole. The final chapter presents recommendations by which the overall depository library program and the quality of reference service for government publications can be improved.

The first step in improving a service, such as the reference process in academic depository libraries, is to investigate, describe, and understand the current situation and existing factors related to the effectiveness of that service. The further development of reference services for government publications and the role of the depository library program within a national information policy must be based on research and empirical evidence. It is within such a framework that the authors initiated this study and offer the following data and views to increase access to the resources made available through the depository library program.

Quality of Documents Reference Service

For this study, the quality of documents reference service has been defined as the percentage of correct answers to a predetermined set of reference questions. As such, the definition represents a performance measure, that is, an indicator of the effectiveness of the service resulting from library activities. Using performance measures to assess the quality of a service is a valuable method for evaluating the effectiveness of that service through the perspective of a user. Regardless of the various resources and constraints in a library, a performance measure suggests an overall quality of reference service that typical patrons might expect when they use the collection of an academic depository library. In this study, the performance measure might be called "correct answer fill rate,"[1] or the percentage of test questions answered correctly.

While the quality of reference service includes a number of factors, it is our view that the delivery of correct answers is an indicator of many factors related to the reference process. Specific factors, such as the interpersonal skills of both librarian and patron, the general knowledge, education, and experience of the librarian regarding government publishing programs and government publications, and knowledge of the collection, as well as bibliographic control, physical organization of the collection, and the availability of appropriate reference sources, are clearly related to quality reference services;[2] however, these factors are beyond the scope of this study.

This chapter emphasizes the quality of reference service, based on the accuracy with which library staff members answer predetermined reference questions. Primary factors related to accuracy of answers, such as reasons for incomplete answers, telephone versus in-person delivery of questions, difficulty of the questions, and duration of the interview and search process, are all examined. Subsequent chapters discuss the interviewing and search skills of library staff, the organization and bibliographic control of government documents, institutional variables, and other factors. Despite the myriad factors related to reference service, the *performance* or overall *quality* of a reference service must be based largely on one consideration: Do patrons obtain correct answers to their questions? This criterion, in our view, deserves primary attention.

Testing Process

The test questions were of two types: factual—that is, the name of an individual or a request for specific statistical or descriptive information—or bibliographic—that is, a request for a bibliographic citation, the availability of a publication in the library or through the GPO sales program, or obtaining a Superintendent of Documents classification number (appendix A gives the complete set of questions and appendix B provides additional pretested questions). Pretesting the questions helped to ensure that the questions were representative of those received by practicing documents librarians in the two geographical areas. However, testing did not attempt to examine all types of questions that *could* be asked at academic depository libraries.

To place study findings in proper context, a definition of a "correct" answer is necessary. For this study, responses from depository staff could be classified as "correct," "partially correct," or "incorrect." A correct answer matched the response predetermined by the investigators with the assistance of the librarians who aided with the pretest. The answer need not come from a predetermined reference source; it could come from whatever printed and referral sources were available to the documents staff at that particular library.

A partially correct answer involved answering only a portion of the question, *not* providing all the information requested by the question, or providing directional information to sources where an answer *might* be obtained. An incorrect answer included responses that were wrong or provided inaccurate data, or that might best be characterized as "don't know." Further, if the person at the documents reference desk asked the proxy to return when a professional was available, the proxy did so and did not count the original encounter as administration of the question.

In some instances, documents staff indicated that a question could not be answered because the necessary reference sources were not available in their collection. When the proxies (occasionally) checked on the accuracy of this response, they found that, indeed, the necessary sources were in the collection. When these situations occurred and the proxy had not been referred elsewhere, the response was labeled an incorrect answer.

If the proxies were told to come back or call back later, they followed up, as requested, to obtain a final disposition of the question. Proxies neither suggested types of sources or places where the answer might be obtained nor encouraged referrals, even when library staff members failed to answer the question. Finally, proxies were told not to argue with staff members or be persistent about obtaining an answer. If staff members indicated that the question was unanswerable, or (as in one case) suggested "nobody could find information like that in the mess of government publications," the proxies politely thanked them for their time and left. The response, however, was recorded as an incorrect answer.

Documents staff members occasionally told proxies that telephone reference services were not provided. In such instances, proxies were instructed to be persistent about obtaining an answer, stressing that they needed the information immediately for a research project. If this failed, they called back later in the hope that another staff member would accept the question. If the documents staff asked the proxy to call back later, the proxy called back. If, on the other hand, staff asked for a telephone number to return the call, this was supplied. In two cases, staff members began to question why closer depository collections were not consulted. In fact, they encouraged the proxy to consult other, closer depositories. In these cases the proxies held the question until they were in the community and could make a local call.

All proxies participated in a training session to encourage consistency in administration of the questions as well as coding (the coding form is reproduced in appendix C). Furthermore, the investigators occasionally observed the proxies when they administered questions, both by telephone and in person. Thus the investigators could assess the effectiveness of some of the question-administration process as well as observe the disposition of the questions by depository library staff members.

No control was attempted over whether the tested staff member was a professional or a paraprofessional. Further, the proxies could not inquire if the person who accepted the question had, in fact, a master's degree in library/information science. Consequently, every effort was made to ask the questions on weekdays and at times when one might reasonably expect a professional librarian to be available in the documents area. Table 4 ("Summary of Question Delivery Characteristics") indicates that most of the questions were asked on weekdays during regular working hours (8:00 a.m. to 5:00 p.m.). Proxies were instructed to ask questions when staff were available in the documents area and, if possible, to approach staff who "appeared" to be full-time professionals rather than student assistants or clerical staff.

Clearly, subjective assessment about which staff members were professionals would not always be correct. Every effort was made to ask the questions at times and to people who might reasonably be expected to be

TABLE 4. Summary of Question Delivery Characteristics

Day of Week Questions Asked (in percentages)

	NE	SW	All
Sunday	4	2	3
Monday	21	24	23
Tuesday	16	16	16
Wednesday	20	22	21
Thursday	11	18	14
Friday	24	16	20
Saturday	4	2	3

Time of Day Questions Asked (in percentages)

	NE	SW	All
Morning 8:00 AM-Noon	43	42	43
Afternoon Noon-6:00 PM	52	37	42
Evening 6:00 PM-11:00 PM	5	21	15

professional librarians. Nonetheless, such certainty cannot be assured, and undoubtedly paraprofessional staff members participated in answering questions; therefore, the study reflects reference services that library patrons can expect from documents staff members who service public service desks. The depository staff members tested treated all the questions as legitimate and did not dispute them. Further, the researchers are confident that the vast majority of staff members who responded to the questions were, in fact, professional librarians. Thus it is assumed that the quality of reference service received by the proxies is representative of the service that a typical user would receive.

Accuracy of Answers

Table 5 summarizes the percentage of correct answers for each question by geographic region. Overall, documents staff members correctly answered 37 percent of the questions; however, there was almost two and one-half times the likelihood of a question being answered correctly in the Northeast as in the Southwest. This difference is striking, given the similar institutional characteristics of the depositories in terms of item selection and staffing (see table 4).

Table 5 also identifies a wide variation in correct answers, depending on the nature of the questions. For example, all of the Northeast depositories answered question 7 (for information about a legislative history) correctly, but only 10 percent answered question 18 (for a government map) correctly. A similar pattern exists for responses from the Southwest depositories. Further, asterisks that precede questions in the table indicate that the questions were asked by telephone. Regardless of geographical region, a greater percentage of questions asked over the telephone was answered correctly than questions that were asked in person.

Table 6 summarizes the primary reasons for incorrect or partially correct answers. The most frequent reason (53%) was that librarians indicated they "did not know" the answer to the question and terminated the reference interview, often with no referral. Approximately 22 percent of the incorrect or partially correct answers were wrong data. An additional 9 percent were the result of librarians indicating that the necessary sources were not available in that library. Other reasons, including a citation rather than specific information (i.e., telling the proxy to look in the *Serial Set* as an answer to question 1), the unwillingness of depository staff to make a complete search, and staff identification of the correct source but inability to find the answer in that source, contributed to incorrect and partially correct answers. The reasons and frequency of those reasons are similar for the Northeast and the Southwest. Because fewer questions were asked in the Southwest than in the Northeast (200 versus 140), the relative percentage of inaccurate and partially correct answers is higher in the Southwest.

The "Summary of Correct Answers by Region" (table 5) suggests a much higher rate of accuracy for questions asked over the telephone than in person. To examine this relationship in greater detail, a chi-square test of association was computed between the variables "delivery method" (telephone or in person) and "correct answer" (correct, partially correct, or incorrect). Table 7, which summarizes the findings from that analysis, suggests that the relationship between the two variables is significant at less than the .01 level. Inspection of the table indicates that in both regions the proxies had almost twice the likelihood of obtaining a correct answer over the telephone than in person.

The impact of one type of communication channel (telephone) as opposed to another type of channel (in person) on the accuracy of the transmission and its effectiveness on the communication of the message has been discussed by a number of investigators.[3] Further, a recent unobtrusive test of reference service in a public library environment concluded that "a patron would have a higher probability of having a phone question answered completely and correctly than a question asked in person."[4]

A number of possible reasons can be put forward to explain this relationship. One might speculate that the library staff pays more attention to a question asked over the telephone, is less likely to be interrupted during the conversation, can work on the question as time permits, and perhaps works harder during a shorter period of time to resolve the question in order to return to other work activities. Another consideration—at least for this study—is that students delivered both the telephone and in-person questions. Because they may have "looked like students" or "acted like students," they may have been perceived as "less important" for the receipt of extensive reference services. Questions delivered over the telephone, on the other hand, do not allow for such assessments by library staff members. Indeed, other studies have suggested that the appearance, perceived importance, and attitude of the patron have a significant effect on the quality of reference service provided.[5]

Another consideration also should be raised. Brenda Dervin suggests that the channel selection (telephone, written, or in person) is less important than other factors related to message transmission, such as the content of the message, the interpersonal skills of the sender and receiver, the complexity of the message, and the objective of the transmission.[6] Further, she suggests that a better understanding of library activities, including reference services, can be obtained by studying the communication processes in specific situations and their relationships (such as the environment in which

TABLE 5. Summary of Correct Answers by Region

Question Number	Question
1	Army's Use of Camels in the 19th Century
2	Japanese Use of Balloons in WW II
3	FDA Study of Caffeine
*4	Head of Justice Dept. Civil Rights Division
*5	Availability of Overland Migrations
6	Availability of Clamshell Commerce
*7	Education Organization Act, Report
8	Purpose of Commission on Housing
*9	Availability of FTC Report about Television
10	Written Test Guide for Private Pilot
11	Article About Immigrants in U.S. Labor Force
*12	Percent Population Over 80 Years
*13	Illiteracy Rate 1950-1970
14	Post Office Revenues during 20th Century
*15	History Graduate Degrees in 1978
*16	Chair of Senate Committee on Small Business
17	R & D Funds Distributed by Agency
18	Map of Honduras
*19	Regulations about Indian Arts and Crafts Board
*20	Presidential Toast in Honor of Sadat

*indicates question delivery by phone

Percentage Answered Correctly NW	Percentage Answered Correctly SW	Percentage Answered Correctly ALL
30	14	24
10	0	6
40	0	24
50	14	35
40	29	35
30	14	24
100	43	77
40	14	29
40	57	47
10	14	12
60	29	47
50	14	35
70	29	53
80	0	47
70	29	53
80	86	82
50	0	29
10	14	12
50	0	29
70	14	47
49% Average	20% Average	37% Average

TABLE 6. Primary Reason for Incorrect or Partially Correct Answers

Reason	NE Frequency	SW Frequency	Total Frequency	Percentage
1. Staff members indicated they "didn't know"	45	66	111	53
2. Staff members provided wrong data	23	23	46	22
3. Staff members indicated that required sources were not available in that particular depository library	9	10	19	9
4. Staff members provided bibliographic citation rather than specific information required	10	0	10	5
5. Staff members not willing to do complete search	2	8	10	5
6. Staff members provided correct source but did not indicate where or how to find answer in source	5	0	5	2
7. Other	8	0	8	4
Total:	106	107	209	100%

TABLE 7. Summary of Correct Answers by Delivery Method*

	By Phone Question Delivery		In-Person Question Delivery	
	NE	*SW*	*NE*	*SW*
Correct answer	64%	29%	35%	10%
Partial answer	8	10	13	14
Incorrect answer	28	61	52	76
	100%	100%	100%	100%

*A chi-square test of association indicates that the relationship between method of delivery and correct answer (for both geographical regions) is significant at less than the .01 level.

reference services take place), rather than simply explore the transfer of information.[7]

Thus one must carefully consider other factors that may affect the relationship between provision of accurate answers and the telephone delivery method before final conclusions can be made about a direct, causal relationship between these two variables.[8] To explore this relationship further, each question was analyzed to determine if underlying factors could be identified that facilitated the answering of specific questions.

Analysis of Questions Answered

The previous discussion suggests that some questions had much greater likelihood of being answered correctly than others. To explore this finding, the questions were ranked, within each region, from "most frequently answered correctly" to "most frequently answered incorrectly." Table 8 lists the ranking of questions by percentage of correct answers. (When two or more questions had the same percentage of correct answers, they were ranked the same.)

Table 9, which depicts the response to each question, shows that questions 16 (chair of Senate Committee on Small Business) and 7 (Education Organization Act, report) were the most likely to receive a correct response.

TABLE 8. Ranking of Questions by Percentage of
Correct Answers

Northeast

Rank	Question No.	Brief Description
1	7	Education Organization Act, Report
2	14	Post Office Revenues During 20th Century
	16	Chair of the Senate Committee on Small Business
3	13	Illiteracy Rate 1950-1970
	15	History Graduate Degrees in 1978
	20	Presidential Toast in Honor of Sadat
4	11	Article About Immigrants in U.S. Labor Force
5	4	Head of Justice Dept. Civil Rights Division
	12	Percent Population Over 80 Years
	17	R & D Funds Distributed by Agency
	19	Regulations About Indian Arts & Crafts Board
6	3	FDA Study of Caffeine
	5	Availability of *Overland Migrations*
	8	Purpose of Commission on Housing
	9	Availability of FTC Report About Television
7	1	Army's Use of Camels in 19th Century
	6	Availability of *Clamshell Commerce*
8	2	Japanese Use of Balloons in WWII
	10	Written Test Guide for Private Pilot
	18	Map of Honduras

Southwest

Question No.	Brief Description
16	Chair of Senate Committee on Small Business
9	Availability of FTC Report about Television
7	Education Organization Act, Report
5	Availability of *Overland Migrations*
11	Article About Immigrants in U.S. Labor Force
13	Illiteracy Rate 1950–1970
15	History Graduate Degrees in 1978
1	Army's Use of Camels in 19th Century
4	Head of Justice Dept., Civil Rights Division
6	Availability of *Clamshell Commerce*
8	Purpose of Commission on Housing
10	Written Test Guide For Private Pilot
12	Percent Population Over 80 Years
18	Map of Honduras
20	Presidential Toast in Honor of Sadat
2	Japanese Use of Balloons in WWII
3	FDA Study of Caffeine
14	Post Office Revenues During 20th Century
17	R & D Funds Distributed by Agency
19	Regulations About Indian Arts & Crafts Board

TABLE 9. Form of Response by Individual Question

Question Number	
1	Army's Use of Camels in the 19th Century
2	Japanese Use of Balloons in WW II
3	FDA Study of Caffeine
*4	Head of Justice Dept., Civil Rights Division
*5	Availability of Overland Migrations
6	Availability of Clamshell Commerce
*7	Education Organization Act, Report
8	Purpose of Commission on Housing
*9	Availability of FTC Report about Television
10	Written Test Guide for Private Pilot
11	Article About Immigrants in U.S. Labor Force
*12	Percent Population Over 80 Years
*13	Illiteracy Rate 1950-1970
14	Post Office Revenues during 20th Century
*15	History Graduate Degrees in 1978
*16	Chair of Senate Committee on Small Business
17	R & D Funds Distributed by Agency
18	Map of Honduras
*19	Regulations about Indian Arts and Crafts Board
*20	Presidential Toast in Honor of Sadat

*indicates question delivery by phone

	Answer Was	
Correct	Partially Correct	Incorrect
4	1	12
1	6	10
4	1	12
6	1	10
6	3	8
4	4	9
13	2	2
5	0	12
8	2	7
2	2	13
8	1	8
6	2	9
9	1	7
8	2	7
9	0	8
14	0	3
5	2	10
2	4	11
5	3	9
8	1	8
Total: 127	38	175

Questions 2 (Japanese use of balloons in W.W. II), 10 (written test guide for private pilot), and 18 (map of Honduras), on the other hand, proved to be the most difficult. The category "partially correct" shows that respondents answered part of the question. By combining the categories "correct" and "partially correct," it can be seen that documents staff members could answer 165, or 48.5 percent, of the questions with some success. Over half the subjects tested could, therefore, provide immediate assistance for 9 (45%) of the questions (nos. 5, 7, 9, 11, 13, 14, 15, 16, and 20). (Seven of these questions were administered by telephone, which reinforces the point already made: tested personnel performed much better with telephone than with in-person questions.) If additional research grouped these nine questions by topic with similar questions, the objective would be to test performance by topical areas, such as bibliographic citations versus factual data, congressional versus executive branch information, administrative versus statutory law, and current versus retrospective information. From this exploratory study, it would appear that documents personnel perform best with requests for brief factual (statistical) data.

A composite of the questions that depository staff members in *both* regions found "easiest" and "most difficult" to answer was done as follows. Comparison was made between the top four ranks (easiest) for each region and the bottom ranks (difficult) to identify agreement on specific questions. To be identified as easiest or most difficult, *both* regions had to agree on the ranking of the question; otherwise, questions were not labeled either "easiest" or "most difficult." The purpose of this method was to identify representative questions that both regions found the easiest and most difficult to answer.

Figure 1 presents the results of this analysis. Four of the five questions most likely to be answered correctly were delivered over the telephone; questions 13 (percent of illiteracy in Oklahoma or Massachusetts), 15 (number of graduate degrees in history), and 16 (Who is chair of Senate Committee on Small Business?) can all be described as "quick answer" name or fact questions. However, question 7 (Education Organization Act) clearly is a legislative tracing–type of question, and no. 11 (immigrants in the labor force) is a source question; that is, it requires an article (any article) that deals with the topic. However, one underlying factor with each of these questions is inclusion *in the question* of a key, or primary, topic or search term that directly links the question to a number of sources. It is likely that the key search term in the question could be used to gain direct access to the required information from an appropriate reference source.

The questions identified as most difficult to answer were all delivered in person, and a number of factors may contribute to their perceived greater difficulty. First, in some of the questions there is no *direct* tie-in between a key term in the question and the source(s) where the answer might be found. In questions such as 1 (camels in the army during the 19th century), question 2 (Japanese use of balloons in W.W. II), question 8 (purpose of Commission on Housing), and question 10 (test guide for becoming a private pilot), depository staff members have to *translate* the question into an appropriate index term as well as decide on an appropriate source to examine.

Greater difficulty was associated with historical questions, such as question 2 (Japanese use of balloons in W.W. II) and question 1 (camels in the army during the 19th century). None of the easiest questions required historical, retrospective searching. Thus documents librarians may be less knowledgeable about retrospective indexes, such as the Congressional Information Service *U.S. Serial Set* index, and make less effective use of them, than of indexes and reference sources to more current materials.

Another interesting factor regarding the most difficult questions is that for 2 (Japanese use of balloons) and 6 (Clamshell Commerce), the question asks for a Superintendent of Documents (SUDOC) number, whether the publication is still in print, and its cost. Such ordering information is easily available from *Publications Reference File (PRF)*, yet librarians found these questions among the most difficult to answer. This result suggests that knowledge and use of *PRF* is limited, and supports recent research that identifies a surprising number of depositories that did not select this index as part for their collection.[9] Question 18 (map of Honduras) also proved difficult for many library staff members to answer. Maps and microforms are nontraditional formats of government publications and librarians may lack familiarity in access to such sources.

Another point of interest is the apparent difficulty of questions on regulations and regulatory agencies. Table 8 indicates that questions 19 (regulations about Indian Arts and Crafts Board), 3 (FDA study of caffeine), and 10 (written test guide for private pilot) proved to be of difficulty for the tested library personnel. Given the increased importance in recent years of rules and regulations promulgated by executive departments and independent regulatory agencies, inability to use the *Code of Federal Regulations (CFR)* and individual agency regulatory publications effectively is of some concern.

Finally, the questions identified as easiest to answer typically have multiple access points and multiple reference sources that might be used to provide a correct answer. The more difficult questions typically have fewer access points, require a specific reference source or index to obtain the answer, and require ability to reformat or translate the questions into the indexing or "thesaurus" system of appropriate government publications indexes.

Easiest

*7. Did the Department of Education Organization Act of 1979 (HR 2444 and S210) go through conference? If so, when did the House and the Senate pass the conference report?

11. I have heard that in the coming years immigrants may comprise 45 percent of the growth in the U.S. labor force. Can you help me find an article on this topic?

*13. What is the percent of illiteracy for Massachusetts (or Oklahoma) from 1950 to 1970. I just need ten year intervals for my term paper.

*15. I am considering graduate studies in history and would like to know the number of master's and doctoral degrees awarded for 1978.

*16. Who chairs the Senate Committee on Small Business, and who is on the Committee?

Most Difficult

1. For a term paper in history, I am studying the army's use of camels in the 19th Century. It is my understanding that there is a government document, from the 1850s, on the topic. Please help me find it.

2. I understand that during World War II the Japanese sent balloons over the ocean to drop on the U.S. By chance, is there a document on the subject? If yes, is it still in print and what is the cost?

6. In the mid 1970s, the Department of Commerce issued Clamshell Commerce, a publication on the origins of the seafood industry in the United States. Does the library have a copy? If not, what is the Sudoc number and how can I get a copy?

8. In June 1981, President Reagan set up a President's Commission on Housing. Is the commission supposed to review all existing federal housing policies and programs? Where can I find out exactly what the commission is supposed to do?

10. I am planning to get a license for flying as a private pilot. Is there a written test guide?

18. I need a map showing population density in various parts of Honduras. Since the atlases that I checked do not show sufficient detail, I was wondering it there was anything in government maps.

---

*indicates question delivery by telephone

Figure 1. Easiest and Most Difficult Questions to Answer Correctly

Marcia Bates suggests that increased competency in this area might be obtained by utilizing "term tactics," which are "tactics to aid in the selection and revision of specific terms within the search formulation."[10] She describes eleven types of tactics and notes that reference skills require much greater sophistication of the librarian, ability to associate similar key terms, and knowledge of "typical" key terms that might be used in each instance for government publications (for additional discussion of "term tactics," see chapter 5). Apparently, documents staff members must devise more "term tactics" for questions that are more difficult and require sophisticated search strategies.

Returning to the significant relationship between correct answers and delivery by telephone shown in table 7, we note that individual analysis of questions helps to explain the relationship. These same questions had an average length of 24 words, while the most difficult questions (in person) had an average length of 36 words. As pointed out previously, telephone questions sought a "quick fact or name" while in-person questions required broader ranges of information for a correct answer. Further, the (easiest) telephone questions typically had imbedded in them key index terms which were not in the in-person (most difficult) questions. Finally, the most difficult questions stressed nontraditional document formats and certain topical areas with which, apparently, documents staff were unfamiliar. Thus a number of factors may affect the apparent relationship between telephone delivery of questions and obtaining correct answers.

At the more "basic" levels of question difficulty (quick fact or name), library staff members provided moderate accuracy to questions (62%) while at "advanced levels" of difficulty the accuracy of the answers was poor (18%). In short, answering the questions defined as most difficult required greater knowledge about government document reference sources, greater ability to develop "term tactics" for search strategies, and (as table 10 will show) increased amounts of time by documents staff to provide a correct answer.

Duration of Reference Interview and Search

Data were collected on the time taken by library staff members to provide an answer to each question. For purposes of this section, the interview and search process (I&S) can be defined as all activities from the time the question was asked until a resolution to the question was provided and the I&S was terminated. The resolution could have been either a correct or an incorrect answer (those responses that were partially correct, incomplete, "don't know," wrong data, or other responses are listed in table 6). However, the study did not obtain data on the duration of each of the various aspects of I&S: the reference interview, question negotiation, and the search process.

Table 10 lists the average duration of I&S by question and region, as well as whether the question was answered correctly or incorrectly. Regardless of the question, the time spent on I&S by library staff members in each region is similar. When one compares the I&S time in terms of the resulting answers being correct or incorrect, however, there is a significant difference between the two regions. As listed at the bottom of table 10, the average duration for I&S in the Northeast was 7 minutes for a correct answer and 5 minutes for an incorrect answer. This relationship is reversed, however, in the Southwest, where 4 minutes, on average, were spent for a correct answer, as opposed to 6 minutes for an incorrect answer. In short, staff members in the Northeast spent more I&S time to obtain a correct answer than an incorrect one; those in the Southwest spent more time to obtain an incorrect answer than a correct one!

Another point of interest is to determine the average time necessary to obtain a correct answer for the questions identified as easiest versus those identified as most difficult (see figure 1). On average, 4 minutes were necessary for a correct answer to questions identified as easiest while 7 minutes of I&S were necessary to obtain a correct answer for questions identified as most difficult. This finding adds credibility to the proposition that those listed as easiest were, in fact, easier to answer than those listed in figure 1 as most difficult. For questions listed in figure 1 as most difficult, one might speculate that the more time the I&S process required, the less likelihood the question would be answered correctly.

Data about the duration of I&S for the various questions can be analyzed by additional factors, such as telephone versus in-person delivery of the question, and whether the question was answered correctly or incorrectly. However, duration of telephone I&S includes call-backs and other factors at the time of question delivery, which may not provide a completely accurate comparison between telephone versus in-person delivery of questions. Given these limitations, figure 2 plots *correct* answers by I&S duration and geographical region for both telephone and in-person delivery of questions, while figure 3 plots *incorrect* answers by I&S duration and geographical region for both methods of question delivery.

The correct answers from in-person delivery (figure 2, part A) indicate two different trends between Northeast and Southwest library staff members. The Northeast personnel increased their percentage of correct answers up to 6 minutes of I&S, then fell off sharply. Southwest staff members obtained the greatest percentage of correct answers with minimal I&S (1 to 2 minutes), and their success rate decreased the longer that I&S continued.

The correct answers from delivery of questions by telephone (figure 2,

TABLE 10. Average Duration of Interview and Search Process by Question and Region

Question	Average Time In Minutes NE	SW
1. Army's Use of Camels in the 19th Century		
Correct Answer	7	1**
Incorrect Answer	6	4
2. Japanese Use of Balloons in WW II		
Correct Answer	5**	-
Incorrect Answer	6	23
3. FDA Study of Caffeine		
Correct Answer	7	-
Incorrect Answer	9	10
*4. Head of Justice Dept., Civil Rights Division		
Correct Answer	3	3**
Incorrect Answer	3	2
*5. Availability of Overland Migrations		
Correct Answer	4	11
Incorrect Answer	5	1**
6. Availability of Clamshell Commerce		
Correct Answer	4	1**
Incorrect Answer	8	17
*7. Education Organization Act, Report		
Correct Answer	4	3
Incorrect Answer	-	1
8. Purpose of Commission on Housing		
Correct Answer	9	5**
Incorrect Answer	4	9
*9. Availability of FTC Report about Television		
Correct Answer	5	9
Incorrect Answer	4	2
10. Written Test Guide for Private Pilot		
Correct Answer	30**	5**
Incorrect Answer	6	7
11. Article About Immigrants in U.S. Labor Force		
Correct Answer	3	5
Incorrect Answer	5	4

Question	Average Time In Minutes NE	SW
*12. Percent Population Over 80 Years		
Correct Answer	6	2**
Incorrect Answer	3	8
*13. Illiteracy Rate 1950-1970		
Correct Answer	5	5
Incorrect Answer	6	2
14. Post Office Revenues during 20th Century		
Correct Answer	6	-
Incorrect Answer	5	3
*15. History Graduate Degrees in 1978		
Correct Answer	4	4
Incorrect Answer	4	2
*16. Chair of Senate Committee on Small Business		
Correct Answer	3	6
Incorrect Answer	5	1**
17. R & D Funds Distributed by Agency		
Correct Answer	9	-
Incorrect Answer	3	4
18. Map of Honduras		
Correct Answer	5**	5**
Incorrect Answer	5	6
*19. Regulations about Indian Arts and Crafts Board		
Correct Answer	7	-
Incorrect Answer	4	2
*20. Presidential Toast in Honor of Sadat		
Correct Answer	7	2
Incorrect Answer	6	2
All Questions	(NE)	(SW)
Correct	7	4
Incorrect	5	6

*Indicates delivery method by telephone

**One case only

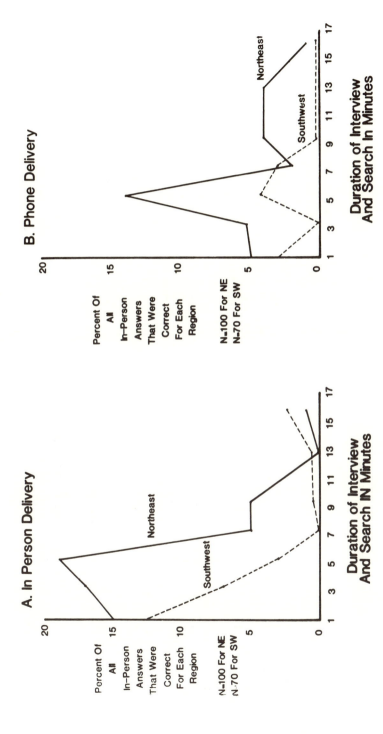

Figure 2. Correct Answers by Interview/Search Duration and Region

50

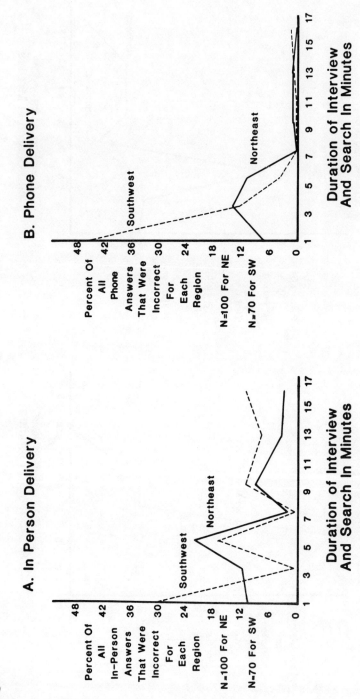

Figure 3. Incorrect Answers by Interview/Search Duration and Region

part B) suggest a similar pattern of I&S between Northeast and Southwest staff members. After an initial decrease in percentage of correct answers for Southwest depository staff, both groups increased their performance, until 5 to 6 minutes of I&S. After that, the overall percentage of correct answers decreased rapidly the longer the duration of I&S.

Figure 2 helps explain, in part, the difference between the Northeast library staff answering 49 percent of the questions correctly and the Southwest staff answering only 20 percent correctly. The Northeast library staff members appear to have a rational and perhaps more methodological approach to I&S than their counterparts in the Southwest. They build to a greater percentage of correct answers (both in person and over the telephone) after 5 to 6 minutes of I&S, whereas Southwest staff members do not build on I&S techniques. Apparently, either they provide the correct answer immediately for in-person questions or they are unable to find the answer with increased I&S. For telephone delivery of questions, they provide limited I&S.

Figure 3, "Incorrect Answers by Duration and Region," presents the "flip side" of figure 2 by examining I&S for *incorrect* answers. Again, for both in-person and telephone delivery of the question, the Southwest staff members provided the greater percentage of incorrect answers immediately upon contact with the proxy—1 to 2 minutes. Northeast staff members, on the other hand, spent additional I&S time for questions delivered both in person and by telephone, up to 4 or 5 minutes, before the maximum percentage of incorrect answers was provided. While it might be said that the Southwest personnel are more *efficient* than their Northeast counterparts (spend less time on questions, whether answered correctly or incorrectly), the Northeast staff members are much more *effective* (answer a higher percentage of questions correctly).

Another point of interest in figures 2 and 3 is the similar amounts of I&S time that document staff members are willing to spend on questions, whether they are answered correctly or incorrectly. Southwest library staff, however, answer the vast majority of questions—correctly and incorrectly—in the first 1 to 2 minutes. Personnel from Northeast libraries, however, consistently answer the greatest percentage of questions within 5 to 6 minutes. These findings suggest that there might be an "internal clock" in documents staff that affects the amount of time they are willing to spend on I&S. However, the minimal time spent on I&S by Southwest staff members, in comparison to their counterparts, may suggest a partial explanation for their much reduced rate of accuracy.

The findings in this section regarding duration of the I&S process for library staff members participating in this study must be seen in the context of numerous additional variables that the study did not investigate. Additional factors include the competency of the staff members and their knowledge of the reference interview, question negotiation,[11] and search strategies;[12] their workload at the time the questions were asked, activities at the reference desk, and the number of patrons waiting for service;[13] the sophistication of the user in presenting the question and providing follow-up information; the theory of reference practiced and adherence to a specific policy regarding the time to be spent on questions at each participating library;[14] and staffing patterns, use of nonprofessionals to provide reference services,[15] and the location of government publications within the library. Nonetheless, the I&S process appears to be an important factor in overall accuracy in answering questions. Depository staff members in the Southwest, who consistently "rushed to judgment" in the first 1 to 2 minutes, did not perform as well as those in the Northeast, who spent additional time on the I&S process.

First-Contact Answers

Another aspect of the overall quality of reference service might be termed "first-contact answers." For purposes of this study, a first-contact answer can be defined as a specific answer to the proxy, whether it was correct or incorrect. Referrals that received an answer (any answer) resulting from the first contact are considered first-contact answers. If a proxy was asked to return at a later time or call back after the search process had been completed, or not given a specific response (other than "don't know"), the answer was *not* considered a first-contact answer.

Data were collected on this variable because the investigators wanted to determine the degree to which proxies were unable to obtain *any* specific answer to questions asked. Such data might indicate the frustration encountered by patrons who attempt to obtain answers to their questions. Table 11, "Percentage of First-Contact Answers for Each Question," suggests that the percentage of first-contact answers for all twenty questions is quite similar; it ranges between 59 and 88 percent. Overall, 72 percent of the questions received a first-contact answer. However, the converse can be stated as, on average, 28 percent of the time proxies did not receive *any* answer to their questions.

In other words, 111 of the 340 questions (33%) received the response "don't know." In some instances when depository staff members indicated that they "did not know," proxies were referred to another member of the staff or another information provider (see chapter 4 for more discussion on this point). In 24 percent of the instances, however, where the response was "don't know," no referral was provided. This finding is somewhat surpris-

TABLE 11. Percentage of First-Contact Answers for Each Question

Number	Question	Percentage of First-Contact Answers
1	Army's use of camels in nineteenth century	71
2	Japanese use of balloons in W.W. II	65
3	FDA study of caffeine	71
*4	Head of Justice Dept. Civil Rights Division	77
*5	Availability of *Overland Migrations*	77
6	Availability of *Clamshell Commerce*	71
*7	Education Organization Act, report	77
8	Purpose of Commission of Housing	71
*9	Availability of FTC report about television	82
10	Written test guide for private pilot	71
11	Article about immigrants in U.S. labor force	77
*12	Percent population over 80 years	71
*13	Illiteracy rate, 1950–1970	65
14	Post Office revenues during twentieth century	82
*15	History graduate degrees in 1978	71
*16	Chair of Senate Committee on Small Business	88
17	R&D funds distributed by agency	71
18	Map of Honduras	71
*19	Regulations about Indian Arts and Crafts Board	59
*20	Presidential toast in honor of Sadat	59
	Average	72

*Delivery by phone.

ing since the depository library system has "built-in" structures for referral to regional and other selective depository libraries.[16]

It is interesting to look at these three findings together: 33 percent of all answers were "don't know"; 28 percent of the questions resulted in no first-contact answer; and of the "don't know" answers, 24 percent did not benefit from referral. Each of these findings points to the conclusion that a sizable number of proxies (if typical patrons) received inadequate service. The questions of numerous patrons would not have received an answer, and in a number of instances when referral should have occurred, it did not. Perhaps of equal importance: some patrons are frustrated in their attempts to utilize government publications, and in such instances, research has shown, they are hesitant to return to a staff member after they have received either a "don't know" or a vague response to their questions.[17]

Summary

The findings in this chapter do not present an optimistic view of the quality of reference service in the academic depository libraries tested in the study. The primary criterion for quality of reference, for this study, was accuracy of answers to pretested questions, but the results indicate that, overall, only 37 percent of the questions were answered correctly. Further, inasmuch as the questions were categorized "easiest to answer" and "most difficult to answer," the findings are even less encouraging. Basic, ready-reference questions received 62 percent accuracy, but questions at a more advanced level, requiring reference interview skills, knowledge of government documents, and ability to identify appropriate search terms, received only an 18 percent accuracy rate.

Although a significant relationship was identified between delivery of a question over the telephone and obtaining a correct answer, a direct causal relationship cannot be confirmed. Closer analysis of telephone-delivered questions versus in-person questions suggests that the telephone questions were shorter, had imbedded index or search terms, stressed quick facts or names, and required less knowledge of government document reference sources. One might conclude that if patrons have a quick-reference question, they should attempt to obtain an answer over the telephone and should follow up in person only if necessary. Telephone delivery may help produce a correct answer, but the interaction of other variables with telephone versus in-person delivery deserves additional research.

Data on the duration of the interview and search process identified a number of interesting findings. Both the Northeast and Southwest library staff members apparently have a predetermined criterion for how long I&S should be provided, regardless of obtaining a correct or incorrect answer.

Of special interest is the finding that library staff in the Northeast spent more I&S time to obtain a correct answer than an incorrect one (about 2 minutes more). Southwest library staff members, on the other hand, spent more I&S time to obtain an incorrect answer than a correct one. Throughout the unobtrusive test, Southwest depository personnel "rushed to judgment" in the first 1 to 2 minutes to give either a correct or incorrect answer. This difference in I&S technique may help explain the finding that the Northeast group had a 49 percent accuracy rate while their Southwest counterparts had only a 20 percent accuracy rate in answering questions.

In a related area, the study investigated the frequency with which proxies received a first-contact answer—that is, a specific-content answer to the question posed, whether the answer was correct or incorrect. Some 28 percent of all 340 questions did not result in a first-contact answer. Furthermore, 33 percent of all 340 questions were answered with "don't know"; and of those "don't know" answers, 24 percent were *not* referred to another information provider or individual. These findings suggest the likelihood of high user frustration when users attempt to obtain specific answers from academic depository staff. Further, such findings raise questions as to the viability of the depository library program and the ability of documents staff to provide adequate access to even basic government information.

A most surprising finding is that depository personnel had problems with certain types of test questions. First, staff members might associate a particular question with the *Monthly Catalog* but not with *Publications Reference File*. In fact, their library might not even select this microfiche index. Second, they experienced problems in identifying recent changes in the administration (e.g., question 4, head of Justice Dept., Civil Rights Division); here personnel from Northeastern libraries performed better than their counterparts in the Southwest. Third, they either do not have access to or do not know how to use retrospective indexes that provide access to nineteenth-century documents. Fourth, they may not be fully aware of the diversity of information in the *Federal Register* (questions 3, 8, 19), the *Code of Federal Regulations* (question 19), *Statistical Abstracts of the United States* and *Historical Statistics of the United States* (questions 13, 14, 15), and *Weekly Compilation of Presidential Documents* (question 20). Finally, the request for a government map (question 18) proved difficult to answer, which should be kept in mind by other researchers in testing the performance of documents staff members.

Almost all of the twenty questions administered to depository staff members could have been answered correctly from a variety of sources, printed and institutional (e.g., Federal Information Centers and GPO bookstores). Some of the questions had several parts, all of which might not have received an answer. For example, question 12, which requested information on the elderly, called for data from the 1970 Census as well as the publication date for the equivalent 1980 data. Tested personnel may have answered the question for the earlier data but been unwilling to suggest referral for the second part of the question. Alternatively, question 5, which requested a document on the Oregon Trail, required a bibliographic citation as well as information about the current availability of the publication. Location of the citation, but not information about current availability, would have resulted in the proxy checking the category "partially correct." Inability to find even the citation would have led to a check in the category of "incorrect" response. It is important to emphasize that these two categories together encompassed a variety of options:

> Supplied wrong data.
> Did not know.
> Claimed they did not have the sources to answer the question.
> Provided incomplete data.
> Checked the right source but could not find the answer.
> Found part of the answer but were unwilling to pursue the question further.
> Found the citation but would not say if the publication was still in print and what it costs.
> Found the correct series but were unsure whether it was the right one.
> Provided 1970 data but did not address the request for 1980 Census data.

Of all these options, proxies were most likely to check the following three:

> Did not know (111, or 52.1%).
> Received wrong data (46, or 21.6%).
> Claimed they did not have the source necessary to answer the question (19, or 8.9%).

Together, these reasons accounted for more than three-fourths of the situations (82.6%). It is important to note that for the response "did not know," 37.8 percent were administered by telephone, which shows that, even by telephone, the proxies received less than full service. More about the "did not know" response will be presented in chapter 4, which discusses provision of referral service, but analysis of the responses on the basis of institutional and library variables (e.g., the number of library staff members or the percentage of item numbers selected), as well as whether the response was a first- or subsequent contact answer, does not alter the findings. Due to the small number of responses per cell when analysis extends to geographic region, the impact, if any, of geographic location cannot be determined.

Throughout the study, data consistently indicated better performance by Northeast academic depository personnel than by those in the Southwest. The reasons for this difference are likely to be multifaceted; however, the data indicate that interview and search skills of the Southwest staff require improvement—at least as represented in the amount of time they were willing to spend on the question and the quality of their final response. Although these factors are likely to have considerable impact on the performance of Southwest depository staff, one might speculate that there are additional factors as well. For example, the individual competency and training of Southwest library staff might be less than that of their counterparts in the Northeast, the collections in the Northwest might be better, and depository personnel in the Southwest might have less knowledge of various government reference sources. Additional discussion of the impact of various institutional factors on the quality of reference will be discussed in the next chapter. Nonetheless, additional research, perhaps conducted obtrusively, would be necessary to address these issues properly.

Further, it should be noted that the overall performance of depository staff members in answering these questions raises a number of additional concerns at a broader level of analysis. First, the usefulness of maintaining a large depository library program of 1,365 libraries should be reexamined. Second, the training and competency of government documents librarians deserves careful attention. Third, the procedures by which quality is controlled throughout the depository program (namely, the GPO inspection process) must be reassessed. Finally, given the rate of failure for answering many of these questions, provision of adequate access to government information by the depository library program must be reevaluated. The question can be asked: Why should the federal government continue to support the depository program, as currently constituted, and why should the academic institution support depository membership, given the high costs and low performance?

The failure rate (answering 63% of all questions incorrectly) is relative, but it compares poorly with other unobtrusive reference tests in library environments. In many instances, document librarians may not be aware of the magnitude of the problem and would not accept such a failure rate for service at *their* library. However, professional documents librarians must become aware of "what is happening" as opposed to "what ought to be happening" in reference services for government publications. Clearly, new strategies must be developed and implemented in the academic depository library if the quality of reference services for government documents is to be improved and citizen access to government information increased.

3

Institutional Variables and Quality of Reference Service

Unobtrusive testing took place at seventeen academic institutions with depository status in the Southwest and Northeast of the United States, and the research design took into account the highest degree offered (baccalaureate, master's, and doctoral)—and to a certain extent the control (private or public) of the academic institutions within the study population. Because the institutions were selected on the basis of a stratified random sampling technique, study findings are generalizable to the academic depository institutions within the two regions studied. It should be repeated, however, that the authors have disguised the institutions so that readers will not be able to identify them, but general institutional characteristics can be reported so that the findings can be placed in proper perspective.

For the purpose of this study, institutional variables that were examined for a possible relationship to the quality of reference service included highest degree offering of the institution, number of library volumes, library budget, FTE library professionals, FTE documents professionals, FTE documents paraprofessionals, percentage of item numbers selected, and collection organization. These variables were selected for investigation because they were seen as factors that might impact upon the overall quality of reference services.

The central question to be addressed in this chapter is to what degree do the above-mentioned institutional variables affect the quality of government documents reference services, remembering that "quality" is measured in terms of correct answers to a set of predetermined questions. To address this question, the remainder of the chapter will examine the relationship between the institutional variables and the accuracy of answering the questions; but first there will be a brief review of the literature on the impact of institutional variables upon general reference services. The chapter, which will also present a model of the impact of institutional variables on the quality of government documents reference service, will conclude with an examination of the implications of the quality of documents reference services in four areas: planning, topics for further research, institutional variables, and staff performance.

Importance of Variables as Reflected in the Literature

On the basis of the findings, it would seem that the size of a library and its collection is not related to the question-answering ability of its documents staff members. Further, documents staff members are unaware (and perhaps in certain instances do not care) that they are disseminating outdated, incorrect, and incomplete information. Studies from the general reference field substantiate the second but not always the first finding.

Terence Crowley discovered that public libraries with high expenditures and per capita support did not answer significantly more current affairs–related questions than did public libraries with lower expenditures and support.[1] In a separate study of public library service in New Jersey, Thomas Childers found that, to the contrary, certain institutional variables (budgetary considerations, number of professional staff members, and number of hours the library is open) were all significant factors. Seven independent variables (total income, paid professionals, hours open, equal valuation, service population, total staff, and books added plus books discarded) accounted for approximately 57 percent of the variation in the dependent variables as measured on "scale a," which scored all incorrect answers as zero. Childers, however, believed "it would be reasonable to hypothesize that the accuracy of a library's response to questions is directly related to the size of its reference collection."[2] Further, "the quality of reference service is directly related to a combination of the number of professionals and the size of the collection."[3]

Marcia Myers, who investigated the effectiveness of reference services in academic libraries in the southeastern United States, discovered that "even when the library owned the appropriate source, staff members either did not consult, did not know how to use, or misinterpreted the information given in the source."[4] Significant differences in performance emerged for the type of institution (college versus university) but not for institutional control (public or private) by itself. Fewer differences were evident when both institutional control and type of institution were considered together. In this case, the number of correct responses was significantly different between private and public colleges that have undergraduate programs. Nonetheless, "differences in effectiveness among types of institutions can be attributed to the size of the library rather than its classification per se."[5] The best, overall library variables for explaining performance became total expenditures, as well as the number of volumes held and number of hours open per week. Further, the hours of service and the number of volumes in the collection are associated more with the accuracy of responses to factual questions than are variables concerned with staffing. Given these findings, Myers encouraged academic libraries to develop quantitative standards (including minimal levels) for reference/information services.[6]

In a similar study, unobtrusive testing of reference service with question delivery by telephone showed no significant association between any of the institutional or "resource variables" and the library's performance on the various test questions. Variables that had a high correlation to performance (although not statistically significant) included the reference experience of the librarian, the number of FTE professionals who provide reference services, the number of hours spent at the reference desk, and the number of hours the library is open.[7]

Using obtrusive rather than unobtrusive measurement, Ronald Powell explored the ability of librarians in fifty-one Illinois public libraries to answer twenty-five test questions correctly. He found a significant relationship between the size of the reference collection and the percentage of questions answered correctly. Still, he cautioned that

> there was less to be gained by increasing the size of a reference collection indefinitely, because beyond a certain point the rate of increase in reference staff performance on the percent of questions answered correctly began to decline. This diminishing return was especially noticeable once a reference collection size of approximately 3,500 volumes was reached.[8]

In effect, "once a reference collection exceeds a certain size, it may begin to be less efficient, and hence the associated rate of increase in performance starts to decline."[9]

All of the studies discussed in this section used "artificial" questions, but they were intended to represent real information needs of library users. Further, the questions were of the type that might have reasonably been asked of the reference staff of a library. These studies reinforce the importance of understanding the effect of reference service upon library users. However, they focus on one aspect of the topic: the accuracy of the answers given by library staff members—those typically associated with general reference departments in academic and public libraries. Undoubtedly the staff members themselves, their ability to conduct a reference interview, and to implement sound search strategies also impact upon reference service, but such factors comprise a secondary consideration of the studies discussed. As Myers correctly cautions,

It has not been established that patrons really care about the accuracy of the response; they may be more concerned with the librarian's attitude. It should be pointed out that patrons do continue to use our less than perfect reference/information services. Perhaps they know the librarian performs better than they would in both accuracy and search time.[10]

Research into the information-seeking patterns of the general public has also found that accuracy is but one criterion that is viewed as important in the resolution of an information need. Depending on the information seeker and his or her specific need, other criteria, such as understandability of the answer, up-to-dateness of the response, and the cost in time and money in gathering the necessary information, may be equally important. The information-seeking public may be willing to settle for some tradeoffs for speedy resolution of an information need.[11]

Overview of Institutional Characteristics

Because ten of the institutions are located in the Northeast and seven are situated in the Southwest, 200 questions were administered in the former and 140 in the latter. The unequal numbers do not influence statistical analyses as long as tables minimize cell sizes or cells where there was no response. In addition, since only seventeen institutions were investigated, the total number of cells was kept to a minimum. Given the distribution of data resulting from analyzing the responses of staff members at these institutions, every effort was made to utilize small matrices and to maintain cell sizes of at least five (this number is generally accepted as adequate for chi-square and other statistical tests).

Volumes Held

Volume counts for the baccalaureate institutions did not exceed 500,000. The number of volumes held by master's level institutions was similar to, or higher than, that for baccalaureate institutions; none of the master's institutions, however, held 1 million volumes. The volume count for doctoral institutions reflected the most variation; it ranged from fewer than 1 million to well over 1 million.

Library Budgets

The baccalaureate and master's institutions had the most similarities. Two baccalaureate institutions and one master's institution had library budgets of less than $200,000, while the remaining five baccalaureate and master's institutions had library budgets ranging between $200,000 and $1 million. All of the doctoral institutions had budgets exceeding $1 million.

Item Number Selection

Table 12 examines the percentage of item numbers selected by the seventeen depository libraries. Twelve, or 70.6 percent, of them take 50 percent or less of the more than 5,200 available item numbers. In fact, five, or 29.4 percent, take less than 25 percent. This finding provides one indication that a substantial number of depository libraries (even those at master's institutions) select less than the 25 percent recommended by *Guidelines for the Depository Library System.*[12] Given the fact that so much source material is available each year for depository distribution and that so many libraries do not adhere to the recommended percentage, this percentage must be reexamined and a more realistic recommendation put forth.

The doctoral institutions that were tested, especially those that held more than 1 million volumes, were most likely to select more than 50 percent of the available item numbers. Library budget and highest degree offered do not, by themselves, explain the percentage of item numbers selected. Three of the eight doctoral institutions with library budgets exceeding $1 million currently select less than 50 percent of the available item numbers.

TABLE 12. Percentage of Item Numbers Selected by Academic Institutions Tested

	The Number of Institutions Selecting				
Highest Degree Offered	Less than 25%	26-50%	51-75%	More than 75%	Total
Baccalaureate	4	1	0	0	5
Master's	1	3	0	0	4
Doctorate	0	3	1	4	8
Total	5	7	1	4	17

Staffing

The baccalaureate institutions had between three and six professional library staff members, while the number of professionals at the master's institutions ranged from seven to fifteen. The number of librarians at the eight doctoral institutions reflected substantial variation: from twenty-one to more than two hundred.

Examination of the number of documents librarians (FTE) by highest degree offered indicates that, for the baccalaureate institutions, the range was zero to 1, while for master's level institutions it was between 0.5 and 1; the range at the doctoral institutions was between 1 and 3. The two institutions with three documents librarians had volume counts exceeding 1 million and library budgets of more than $1 million; they also selected more than 75 percent of the available item numbers. For the remaining fifteen institutions, library budget and volume count were not a good predictor of the number of documents librarians. Institutions that had one FTE documents librarian ranged from those with libraries containing fewer than 100,000 volumes to those with over 1 million volumes.

Differences also emerged between institutions that employed one documents librarian and the percentage of item selections; the range was less than 25 percent to more than 75 percent, with an average range of 26–50 percent. The libraries with fewer than one FTE documents librarian had volume counts under 500,000 and budgets well under $1 million. In fact, the institutions with 0.2 or fewer FTE documents librarians had library budgets of less than $200,000 and volume counts ranging from fewer than 100,000 to close to 500,000. Interestingly, two libraries with similar characteristics (volume counts under 100,000 and budgets of less than $200,000) had one FTE documents librarian.

The number of FTE paraprofessional staff members (including student hours, in which 40 hours of student help equal one FTE) shows substantial variation on an institutional basis. These differences cannot be explained solely by highest-degree offering. Suffice it to say, the number varied from 0.5 to 4.0, with nearly two-thirds of the institutions (64.8%) having 1.5 or fewer FTE paraprofessionals; this percentage includes three of the doctoral institutions, all the master's institutions, and all but one of the baccalaureate institutions. The one baccalaureate institution had 3.5 paraprofessionals.

No statistically significant relationship emerges between volume counts and the institutions that employ fewer than two paraprofessionals in the documents area. With the exception of the one baccalaureate institution, libraries with two or more FTE paraprofessional staff members had volume counts in excess of 1 million; the one baccalaureate school had fewer than 100,000 volumes, while the master's schools had more than 500,000 volumes. Similar patterns emerge when the number of FTE paraprofessionals is compared to the various library budgets and the percentage of item numbers selected. Again, this one baccalaureate institution stands out. It has a library budget of less than $200,000, employs 3.5 paraprofessionals for documents work, has one FTE documents librarian and fewer than 100,000 volumes, and takes less than 25 percent of the available item numbers. Clearly, this depository collection is regarded as a key resource of the library; depository publications receive collection and service priority.

Collection Organization

Only one of the libraries (in a baccalaureate institution) totally integrates its government publications into the general collection. The rest of the libraries maintain separate documents collections that house all or a large part of the government publications. It may be that certain reference titles and periodicals are held in other parts of the building, or that subject titles of interest to special collections are sent to branches within the library system. A limitation to the study is that the characteristics of individual reference collections were not examined. The authors did not attempt to identify the extent to which the tested libraries held all the resources necessary to answer each question.

Overview of Institutional Variables

The institutional variables make for interesting analysis; however, their significance must be interpreted with caution for two reasons. First, the study design called for sampling based upon highest degree offered and did not involve random sampling with the highest degree stratified by variables such as the percentage of items selected, library budget and volumes, and number of staff members (either the total or the number assigned exclusively to documents work). Second, although every effort was made to ask the questions at a time when professional staff members might be available, testing was performed on the person at the public service desk who accepted the question.

The level of analysis is on the questions, rather than on the institutional characteristics. The institutional analysis is therefore limited because of the reduced sample size, which occurs when there is shifting from a question to an institutional level. Further, data were not gathered on the individuals who responded to the test questions (e.g., whether they were professional staff members, whether they had taken a documents course in library school, and number of years of documents and reference experience). Since this was not the case, this exploratory study can suggest areas for subsequent research. Nonetheless, the study indicates the type of reference service received by the student proxies to the 340 questions administered at the seventeen libraries over a two-month period.

Relationship of Variables to Quality of Service

Commonly held assumptions are that the higher the degree offering of the institution, the larger the percentage of item numbers selected; the greater the number of volumes held, the larger the budget; the greater the number of staff (professional and paraprofessional) and the likelihood that government publications are housed in separate collections serviced by experienced personnel, the greater the possibility that library users will receive more accurate and individualized reference service. It has even been claimed that "documents are practically useless under any system except as there is a trained person in charge."[13] Other writers opine that "when documents are integrated with the general collection, a less specialized reference librarian handles inquiries concerning them and cannot gain the detailed experience necessary for full effective service."[14]

With these views in mind, it becomes important to examine the number of correct responses on the basis of eight institutional variables: highest degree offered, number of library volumes held, size of library budget, percentage of item numbers selected, collection arrangement, and number of staff members (total librarians as well as FTE documents librarians and their staffs). A chi-square statistical test (unless otherwise noted) was used to identify significant relationships between each of the variables and correct answers. A score of .05 or less was used as the criterion to indicate a "significant" relationship.

Highest Degree Offered

Surprisingly, highest degree offered was not a statistically significant variable; regardless of geographic area, staff members from doctoral institutions were no more likely to answer questions correctly than were their peers at institutions with lower-degree programs. Personnel from doctoral institutions received a total of 160 questions (20 questions administered at the eight institutions), but only answered 58 (36.3%) correctly. However, staff members from doctoral institutions in the Northeast were twice as likely (45%) to answer questions correctly as their counterparts in Southwest libraries (21.7%). In fact, personnel from three Northeastern, doctoral institutions answered 35 of the 58 correctly answered questions (60.3%). On the other hand, staff members from two well-endowed, doctoral institutions in the Northeast could correctly answer only 4 and 6 (of 20) questions!

Regardless of highest degree offered, staff members from Northeastern libraries consistently scored higher. Interestingly for the Northeast, personnel from baccalaureate and master's-granting institutions answered a higher percentage of questions correctly than did staff members from the doctoral institutions. For the Southwest, personnel from master's-granting institutions outperformed their counterparts at the other institutions. Staff members from baccalaureate institutions in the Southwest had the lowest overall performance rating. Nonetheless, the large percentage of incorrectly answered questions should be kept in mind in analyzing the correct responses. This fact underscores the overall ineffectiveness of library staff members in coping with a list of typical reference questions.

Library Volumes

The number of volumes held did not constitute a statistically significant variable. An increased volume count does not augment the likelihood that there will be a correct answer to a reference request. Evidence for this conclusion can be seen from the fact that 57, or 44.9 percent, of the correctly answered questions came from staff members in libraries that receive 500,000 or fewer volumes. The five libraries that held between 501,000 and 1 million volumes produced 42 correct responses, while the four libraries that held more than 1 million volumes produced only 28 of the correct responses. Viewed from another perspective, staff members from the four libraries correctly answered only 35 percent of the questions posed to them.

Library Budget

Similar to the previously mentioned variables, library budget also does not produce statistically significant differences. Libraries with budgets of $1 million or less account for more than half of the correct responses (69, or 54.3%). Staff members from the eight remaining libraries correctly answered 58, or 45.7 percent, of the questions. It should be noted that libraries with budgets of less than $201,000 accounted for 30, or 23.6 percent, of the correct answers, while libraries with budgets of more than $2 million supplied 35, or 27.6 percent, of the correct answers.

Percentage of Item Numbers Selected

Table 13, which examines the accuracy of an answer in terms of the percentage of item numbers selected, indicates that the number of items selected does not significantly affect the percentage of correct answers. Regardless of the percentage, the majority of responses were incorrect. However, of the 127 questions that were answered correctly, three-fourths were done by depositories that selected 50 percent or less of the item

TABLE 13. Summary of Answers by Percentage
of Items Selected

	Depositories Selecting		
Answers	50% or Fewer Items	51% or More Items	Total
Correct	96(75.6%)	31(24.4%)	127(37.4%)
Incorrect	144(67.6%)	69(32.4%)	213(62.6%)
		Total:	340

numbers. As is evident, library staff members with access to large depository collections (ones taking more than 50% of the item numbers) did not perform better than their peers at institutions with smaller depository collections.

Collection Organization

Overwhelmingly, the tested libraries had separate documents collections with varying percentages of depository items. Nonetheless, libraries with separate collections had staff members who were unable to answer all the test questions. Staff members from one doctoral institution (with a separate documents collection) performed the best. They were able to answer correctly 70 percent of the questions presented to them; however, the significance of this finding decreases when the percentage is averaged with the performance of staff members from the other doctoral institutions. Still, the high performance at that one library might be attributed to the competencies, training, education, interest in reference service, and experiences of individual staff members.

Staffing

The total number of library professionals was not a statistically significant variable. Interestingly, institutions that employed no more than ten librarians accounted for 36.2 percent of the correct responses, while institutions that had thirty or more librarians supplied another 32.3 percent of the correct responses. It would seem, therefore, that the size of the institution and its library does not significantly impact the quality of reference service.

Table 14 reflects the distribution of responses by the number of FTE documents librarians and indicates that there is no statistically significant difference. In evaluating the table, it should be remembered that the highest degree offering comprised the primary sampling unit; consequently the distribution among the three categories depicted in the table is unequal. It would appear that libraries that employed three FTE documents librarians potentially have the best performance, even though that percentage is only 50. Such a supposition, however, is questionable; data have been skewed by the fact that only two libraries fit the category. Staff members at one of these libraries answered 70 percent of the questions, while the personnel at the other library supplied correct answers in only 30 percent of the instances.

Table 15 reflects the distribution of responses by the number of paraprofessional staff members. It does not show a progression in the number of correct responses from libraries that employed fewer than one paraprofessional to those that had larger numbers. Nonetheless, the column for one to two paraprofessionals stands out. It is difficult to understand why overall performance at these seven libraries was potentially higher than at the other institutions. The explanation probably rests within the institutions themselves and the characteristics of the individuals tested. Still, by focusing on the column rather than the row data, it can be seen that the 51.2 percent shrinks to 46.4 percent; in other words, only 65 of the 140 questions were answered correctly.

Regardless of the highest degree offering and the other institutional variables, the proxies were more likely to receive a correct answer by telephone than in person. The relationship between correct answers and delivery by telephone was statistically significant, but part of the explanation of this finding may relate to the nature of the questions selected for telephone probing (see chapter 1). These questions were selected with the expectation that documents staff members would be more likely to accept them and not require the questioner to appear at the library in person.

When the correct answer index, the percentage of correct responses arrayed on an ordinal scale, is correlated to the eight institutional variables, no statistical significance of .05 or less can be discovered by use of either the Kendall tau or the Spearman rho tests.[15] This finding provides further support to the finding that the examined institutional variables do not explain performance levels. The same analysis also confirms findings of previous studies which have found a statistically significant relationship between certain institutional variables. Table 16 reports those institutional variables found to have statistical significance in this study. In brief, when the institutional variables are compared to the responses of the subjects tested, no statistical significance emerged. Staff performance, therefore, is

TABLE 14. Summary of Answers by Number of Documents Librarians

Answer	Number			
	Less than 1 FTE	1FTE	3FTE	Total
Correct	25(19.7%)	82(64.6%)	20(15.7%)	127(37.4%)
Incorrect	55(25.8%)	138(64.8%)	20(9.4%)	213(62.6%)
			Total:	340

TABLE 15. Summary of Answers by Number of Paraprofessionals

Answer	Number				
	Less than 1	1-2	2-3	More than 3	Total
Correct	13(10.2%)	65(51.2%)	15(11.8%)	34(26.8%)	127(37.4%)
Incorrect	67(31.5%)	75(35.2%)	25(11.7%)	46(21.6%)	213(62.6%)
Total:	80(23.5%)	140(41.2%)	40(11.8%)	80(23.5%)	340

TABLE 16. Significant Relationships among Institutional Variables

	Library Volumes	Library Budget	Percentage Item Numbers Selected	Library Professionals	Documents Librarians	Paraprofessionals
Library Volumes	—	.001	.001	.001	.01	.009
Library Budget		—	.001	.001	.009	.009
Percentage of Item Numbers Selected			—	.001	.008	.025
Library Professionals				—	.005	.032
Documents Librarians					—	.023
Para-Professionals						—

A. Kendall Tau

TABLE 16. (Continued)

	Library Volumes	Library Budget	Percentage Item Numbers Selected	Library Professionals	Documents Librarians	Paraprofessionals
Library Volumes	—	.001	.001	.001	.009	.025
Library Budget	Library Budget	—	.001	.001	.01	.041
		Percentage of Item Numbers Selected	—	.001	.006	.029
			Library Professionals	—	.005	.05
				Documents Librarians	—	.02
					Para-Professionals	—

B. Spearman Rho

not related to the institutional variables examined; however, significant relationships can be found among various institutional variables themselves.

As a final check on the nonsignificance of the institutional variables (the number of volumes held, the budget, percentage of item numbers selected, and the number of library and documents staff members) related to correct answers, an analysis of variance was performed.[16] These institutional variables, as well as a first-contact answer, method of question delivery, length of reference interview, and day of the week and time of the day that the question was asked, were all considered. Together, these variables accounted for 43 percent of the variance related to correct answers; the first-contact answer alone accounted for 23 percent of the variance, and all the other variables accounted for less than 5 percent each. In other words, another factor(s) was potentially more important than those that were investigated in this study. Even the highest degree offering or the other institutional variables by themselves do not adequately account for the quality of service provided. Such findings add evidence to the proposition that the major factor may be the competency and attitude of individual staff members. This topic, however, merits additional probing through unobtrusive investigations or combined unobtrusive and obtrusive studies, where staff members are partially aware that they are being tested. Such studies would permit investigation of various personal and professional traits.

Impact of Variables on Answering Questions

This section examines individual questions on the basis of the eight institutional variables. In addition, the analysis will identify any response patterns that emerge on the basis of the following five factors:

> Delivery method (telephone vs. in person)
> Whether a request was for current or historical information
> Whether a question was easy or difficult (see figure 1 for a list of pertinent questions)
> Whether the question involved other than a paper format (e.g., microfiche or map)
> Whether the question asked for a bibliographic citation or factual data

Highest Degree Offered

Personnel from doctoral institutions performed the best on three questions: 7 (report for Education Organization Act), 13 (the illiteracy rate, 1950–70), and 16 (composition of Senate Committee on Small Business). For the remaining questions, no more than half of the doctoral institutions could supply the correct answer. In three instances, staff members were unable to give any correct response (questions 2, Japanese use of balloons in W.W. II; 10, written test guide for private pilots; and 18, map of Honduras).

A comparison of the performance of staff members at doctoral institutions with those at both master's and baccalaureate institutions produced recognizable patterns for eight questions. Of the six correct responses to question 4 (head of Justice Department's Civil Rights Division), four, or 66.7 percent, came from doctoral institutions. However, personnel from the combined lower degree programs performed better than their peers at doctoral institutions on questions 2 (Japanese use of balloons in W.W. II), 10 (written test guide for private pilots, 11 (article about immigrants in U.S. labor force), 12 (percentage of population over 80 years), 16 (composition of Senate Committee on Small Business), 18 (map of Honduras), and 20 (presidential toast in honor of Sadat). In fact, for questions 2 and 10, staff members from baccalaureate institutions had the best performance.

The patterns detailed in chapter 2 were reaffirmed. For example, the request for historical information (question 1, army's use of camels in the nineteenth century) presented a problem for staff members. Clearly, the higher degree offering does not enable users to assume that they will receive a higher quality of reference service. Further, it is difficult to anticipate the type of questions that might generate the best performance.

Library Volumes

As already noted, the number of library volumes was not a statistically significant variable. Staff members from libraries with volume counts of more than 1 million did not perform, on average, better than their counterparts at libraries that held fewer volumes. In fact, the only correct response to question 2 (Japanese use of balloons in W.W. II) came from a library that had no more than 100,000 volumes. The best performance on questions 10 (written test guide for private pilots), 11 (article about immigrants in U.S. labor force), and 18 (map of Honduras) came from libraries with volume counts that did not exceed 500,000. All of these questions were administered in person and called for bibliographic citations. In addition, three of the questions (2, 10, 18) could be classified as difficult, while questions 2 and 18 necessitated use of the *Publications Reference File* or a search for a map.

Library Budget

Although the amount of the library budget was not statistically significant, there were variations in performance on certain questions. Basically, these variations indicate that an increased budget does not increase the likelihood that a correct response will be given. The correct answers to questions 2 (Japanese use of balloons in W.W. II) and 10 (written test guide for private pilots) came from smaller institutions, with budgets not exceeding $200,000. For question 18 (map of Honduras), the two correct responses were provided by staff members from institutions with budgets under $1 million, while for question 17 (R&D funds distributed by agency), all but one correct response came from libraries with budgets under $1 million. Four of the correct answers (66.7%) to question 12 (percentage of population over 80 years) came from a similar type of institution. Question 4 (head of the Justice Department's Civil Rights Division) presented the only main exception to this pattern; it was more likely answered correctly by libraries with budgets exceeding $1 million.

Percentage of Item Numbers Selected

Table 17 depicts the distribution of correct responses to each question based on the percentage of item numbers selected. Since twelve of the libraries selected less than 50 percent of the available item numbers and five a higher percentage, data are skewed. Libraries that take 50 percent or less of the item numbers performed the best with two of the easier questions (7 and 16), while the other libraries had their best performance with questions 7, 9, and 16 (two of these could be classified as easy). Questions 7 and 16 were administered by telephone, while question 9 was not. Because each question could receive a potential total of seventeen correct responses, it is interesting to observe that only four questions received nine or more correct responses.

Collection Organization

There were no discernible patterns among institutions that answered questions correctly on the basis of collection organization. Obviously, the location of government publications largely or entirely in separate documents collections does not ensure high-quality reference service. Libraries with separate documents collections performed the best with questions 7 (report on Education Organization Act) and 16 (composition of Senate Committee on Small Business), and had the most difficulty with questions 2 (Japanese use of balloons in W.W. II), 10 (written test guide for private pilots), and 18 (map of Honduras).

Staffing

Having a large number of professional staff members does not result in better reference service. Libraries that employed no more than twenty professionals performed better than their counterparts at institutions with more staff members on the more difficult questions (2, Japanese use of balloons in W.W. II; 10, written test guide for private pilots; and 18, map of Honduras), as well as on questions 12 (percentage of population over 80 years), 16 (composition of Senate Committee on Small Business), and 17 (R&D funds distributed by agency). Only with question 4 (head of Justice Department's Civil Rights Division) did libraries with more than twenty librarians have an appreciably higher performance rate.

Table 18, which depicts the correct answers to each question according to the number of FTE documents librarians at the institutions, clearly indicates that the majority of institutions employed one FTE documents librarian. However, in many cases, having a full-time documents librarian was not an advantage. For fifteen questions, such institutions could generate no more than five correct answers. Only on question 7 (report on Education Organization Act) could ten of the eleven libraries that employed one FTE documents librarian provide the correct answer.

Two institutions had three documents librarians. Presumably, they have greater flexibility in scheduling professionals at the reference desk; yet, together, these libraries could answer only half of the questions correctly. Only questions 8, 13, 15, and 16 yielded the highest value possible: two correct responses. Furthermore, libraries with fewer than one FTE documents librarian answered a similar percentage of overall questions correctly.

A greater number of FTE paraprofessional staff members does not ensure higher-quality reference service. Question 2 (Japanese use of balloons in W.W. II) provides the only exception; the library that supplied the correct answer had more than three documents paraprofessionals. However, since there was only one correct response to this question, the significance of this finding can be discounted.

Examination of individual questions on the basis of the eight institutional variables indicates that the most important factor was whether the question could be classified as easy or difficult (see figure 1). Of the four most frequently discussed questions in this section, three (2, Japanese use of balloons in W.W. II; 10, written test guide for private pilots; and 18, map of Honduras) were difficult to answer, while the final one (16, composition of Senate Committee on Small Business) was much easier. Following in terms of frequency of mention were questions 4 (head of Justice Department's Civil Rights Division), 7 (report on Education Organization Act), and 12 (percentage of population over 80 years), all of which were administered by telephone. In conclusion, the staff members showed substantial variation in their ability to answer a set of reference questions correctly. The range of correct responses was from 1 for question 2 (Japanese use of balloons in W.W. II) to 14 for question 16 (composition of Senate Committee on Small Business).

TABLE 17. Summary of Correct Answers to Individual Questions by Percentage of Items Selected

Question Number	Depositories Selecting 50% or Fewer Items	51% or More Items	Total
1 (Army's Use of Camels in 19th Century)	3	1	4
2 (Japanese Use of Balloons in WW II)	1	0	1
3 (FDA Study of Caffeine)	3	1	4
*4 (Head of Justice Dept., Civil Rights Div.)	5	1	6
*5 (Availability of Overland Migration)	3	3	6
6 (Availability of Clamshell Commerce)	3	1	4
*7 (Education Organization Act Report)	9	4	13
8 (Purpose of Commission on Housing)	3	2	5
*9 (Availability of FTC Report about Television)	4	4	8
10 (Written Test Guide for Private Pilots)	2	0	2

11	(Article about Immigrants in U.S. Labor Force)	7	1	8
*12	(Percent Population over 80 Years)	6	0	6
*13	(Illiteracy Rate 1950–1970)	7	2	9
14	(Post Office Revenues during 20th Century)	7	1	8
*15	(History Graduate Degrees in 1978)	7	2	9
*16	(Composition of Senate Committee on Small Business)	10	4	14
17	(R & D Funds Distributed by Agency)	4	1	5
18	(Map of Honduras)	2	0	2
*19	(Regulations about Indian Arts and Crafts Board)	4	1	5
*20	(Presidential Toast in Honor of Sadat)	6	2	8
	Total:	96	31	127

*indicates that the question was administered by telephone

77

TABLE 18. Summary of Correct Answers to Individual Questions by Number of FTE Documents Librarians

Question Number	Less than 1	Number		Total
		1	3	
1 (Army's Use of Camels in 19th Century)	0	3	1	4
2 (Japanese Use of Balloons in WW II)	0	1	0	1
3 (FDA Study of Caffeine)	1	2	1	4
*4 (Head of Justice Dept., Civil Rights Div.)	0	5	1	6
*5 (Availability of Overland Migration)	0	5	1	6
6 (Availability of Clamshell Commerce)	1	2	1	4
*7 (Education Organization Act Report)	2	10	1	13
8 (Purpose of Commission on Housing)	1	2	2	5
*9 (Availability of FTC Report about Television)	1	6	1	8

Item				
10 (Written Test Guide for Private Pilots)	2	0	0	2
11 (Article about Immigrants in U.S. Labor Force)	3	4	1	8
*12 (Percent Population over 80 Years)	0	6	0	6
*13 (Illiteracy Rate 1950–1970)	2	5	2	9
14 (Post Office Revenues during 20th Century)	2	5	1	8
*15 (History Graduate Degrees in 1978)	2	5	2	9
*16 (Composition of Senate Committee on Small Business)	3	9	2	14
17 (R & D Funds Distributed by Agency)	1	3	1	5
18 (Map of Honduras)	2	0	0	2
*19 (Regulations about Indian Arts and Craft Board)	1	3	1	5
*20 (Presidential Toast in Honor of Sadat)	1	6	1	8
Total:	25(19.7%)	82(64.4%)	20(15.7%)	127

*indicates that the question was administered by telephone

Implications

Planning

The quality of reference work, in terms of the accuracy of answering questions, is subject to evaluation. The major studies discussed in this chapter were concerned with identifying factors that might affect the quality of library reference services. On the basis of these studies, individual libraries should be able to identify their own strengths and weaknesses, and to take corrective action, where necessary, to improve performance. For example, they can implement procedures for staff selection and training, improve the quality of reference collections (quality is not totally a function of collection size), and acquire new reference sources as needed. It may be that collection and service weaknesses can be traced to specific subject areas, types of questions, or staff members.

As demonstrated in figure 4, libraries must use their resources (human, collection, and financial) to meet stated goals (long-term aspirations) and objectives (short-term statements which are measurable, time limited, and facilitate the accomplishment of goals) of both the institution itself and the depository library program. To achieve their objectives, libraries must identify activities for which responsibilities and resources can be assigned and mutually agreed upon target dates established. One important activity, then, becomes the performance of public service staff members and determination of the impact of their assistance upon library clientele.

The three circles in figure 4 can overlap, to a greater or lesser extent. The point is that institutional goals and objectives must be compatible with the points specified by the Government Printing Office through *Guidelines for the Depository Library Program* (see appendix D) and other documentation. Chapter 6, which will examine these factors in more detail, emphasizes that the depository library program must operate under clearly defined goals and objectives, if it is to engage in the type of planning necessary to make the program a more effective and efficient conveyer of government information.

Collections and other library resources must meet the information needs of client groups, present and potential. Depository libraries, however, are expected to develop collections designed to meet the information needs of their primary clientele as well as the elusive concept "general public." Yet, when needs assessments are undertaken, they are perhaps more likely to center on the primary clientele.

The ultimate purpose of collection development in terms of service is to make information resources accessible to the library's community. The evaluation process, therefore, must be both collection and user or needs oriented. As William Robinson notes,

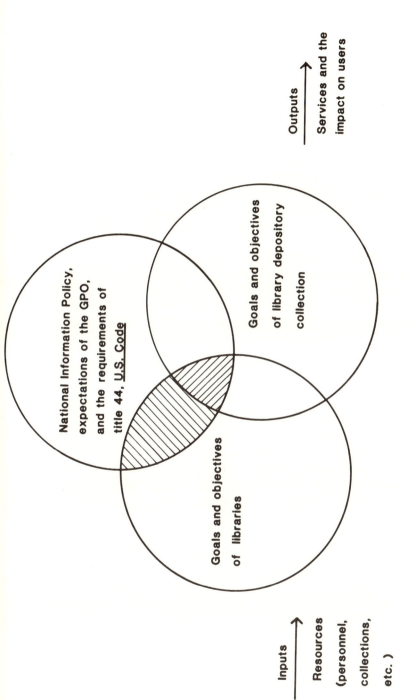

Figure 4. Conceptualization of Effectiveness for Government Document Depository Collections

Because collection value or utility is so often a function of the quality and amount of physical and intellectual access, collection evaluation cannot stand alone. It should be part of a larger document program evaluation examining the quality and degree of access provided to the information contained in government documents.[17]

In this regard, undertaking a needs assessment can be useful, especially if it begins with the community rather than with just present users. One purpose of a needs assessment is to change potential users into present users and to ascertain if non-use is related to the collection and services provided by library staff members.[18]

It can be argued that the development of standards might help libraries, to a degree, in "standardizing" levels of resource input. However, standards do not adequately assist libraries in measuring and monitoring the impact of their services upon user groups.[19] Thus the establishment of performance measures (e.g., accuracy of answering reference questions) would be a more productive strategy. The authors, therefore, do not fully agree with Myers, who (as noted earlier in this chapter) recommends that attention focus on the development of standards for reference services. It might be equally productive to develop performance measures and to work toward a determination of the effectiveness and efficiency of services (including reference services) provided by depository libraries.

Further Research

To assist the formulation of performance measures, which are necessary for planning and evaluation purposes, further research in the documents field might build upon the findings of this study and explore the variables studied here, as well as additional ones, by means of both obtrusive and unobtrusive methods. The intent would be to compare the percentage of test questions answered correctly to

The number of reference questions received by staff members on an average work day or week

Staff salaries

Familiarity with the reference collection

The academic degrees held by participants

The number of hours the documents department is open for public service

The manner in which documents are organized

The training of paraprofessionals

Whether professional staff members have taken a documents course in library school

The average number of hours spent answering reference questions each week

Professional activities (number of conferences and workshops attended, reading professional literature, etc.)

Time spent working with government publications and particular collections

Expenditures for reference materials, both of a documents and non-documents nature

Adequacy rating of documents reference collection in terms of comprehensiveness, currentness, scope, depth, and other criteria.

Future studies of the quality of reference service for government publications might explore additional library variables. Can it be assumed, for example, that study results would be significantly different if only professional staff members had been studied? One study compared the ability of librarians with and without a master's degree in library science to answer correctly a predetermined list of reference questions, and there was no statistically significant difference between the two groups. Staff members of medium-size public libraries in Illinois who held the master's degree could answer the questions more efficiently but not more accurately.[20]

Since this study explored some variables unique to depository collections, it is not surprising that the findings do not agree totally with those from studies in the general reference area. However, the testing of more depository libraries might diminish these differences and show greater similarities. The inclusion of more depository libraries would increase the potential number of cases per cell and permit construction of larger tables, as well as the use of factor-and-regression analysis for more sophisticated statistical analysis. In this way, the impact of institutional variables on quality of reference service could be more fully tested. Until such studies are performed, the importance of institutional variables on receiving correct responses to reference questions appears to be limited. Further, individual characteristics of test subjects also may be important. If this is so, some libraries apparently are better able than others to recruit high-quality personnel and to provide them with sufficient training and motivation.

Future research might investigate the reference aids selected by depository libraries and determine if the staff would benefit from acquisition of additional reference titles. Instead of merely adding new titles to the collection, staff members should initiate a needs assessment. In doing so, they might discover that certain subscriptions or items could be discontinued and that better use of their funds could be made. This becomes an important consideration as many libraries are now faced with hard choices involving zero growth for documents collections as well as for conventional library materials. Greater emphasis should be placed on weeding and selective acquisition of government publications in order to avoid congestion in processing, servicing, and storage space. Selectivity necessitates continuing review and revision of item numbers selected. Similarly, this study points to the need for better staff awareness of reference sources already in their collections. Apparently, staff members do not fully realize the potential value of a title for a specific information need.

Given the diversity in size of institutional libraries and the number of depository items received, it is surprising that more of the master's and doctoral institutions did not have additional staff members assigned to documents activities. Even depository collections in well-endowed doctoral institutions, which received more than 75 percent of the available item numbers, relied heavily upon paraprofessional support. The number of FTE librarians assigned to documents work is exceedingly small. This finding suggests that a study of staffing patterns for depository collections would be most important.

A study might also examine the range of activities performed by both professional and nonprofessional staff members, and make comparisons to general reference departments.[21] After all, public service librarians, regardless of the department in which they work, serve a common end: resolution of information needs. More extensive cooperation among staff members should be encouraged so that administrative integration extends over all library resources. Chapter 5 will elaborate upon ways that librarians can diagnose their own competencies and institutional situations and take corrective action as necessary.

Institutional Variables

Analysis of the data suggests that the number of correct responses cannot be explained on the basis of highest degree offered at an institution. Further, no significant relationships appear to exist on the basis of the number of staff members, size of budget, percentage of item numbers selected, or number of volumes held. As was noted in the previous chapter, the method of question delivery (telephone vs. in person) is significantly related to the quality of reference service provided at the academic depository libraries examined.

These findings call into question long-held assumptions about document collections and services. Previous research has also challenged basic assumptions about depository collections. For example, one study showed that there is no statistically significant difference between frequency of documents use and such variables as organization of the collection, classification scheme, percentage of depository items received, percentage of government publications entered in the public catalog, and number of staff members serving government publications.[22] In frequency of use by social scientists, the most important criteria might be the institutional mission, the commitment of individual faculty members to research, and the perceived value of government information to their information needs.[23] In such instances, all library variables, therefore, become secondary considerations.

Staff Performance

Readers might suggest that the number of test questions answered correctly was influenced by the number of other library clientele that the documents personnel were assisting at the same time, as well as the assorted work-related activities the staff members had to complete. The assumption is that, with more time, a larger percentage of questions would have been answered correctly. However, such reasoning ignores the fact that almost one-third of staff members responded that they did not know the answer and terminated the reference interview, or that half of the questions were administered by telephone and that the documents personnel could return the calls at their convenience. Concerning in-person questions, documents staff members could refer the proxies to a particular reference source (e.g., the *Monthly Catalog*) and provide additional assistance when traffic at the public service desk was minimal.

Each year an increasing amount of source material (hardcopy/paper and microfiche) becomes available for depository distribution, and even depository collections that receive 25 percent or less of the available item numbers are developing extensive holdings of government publications. Further, a vast range of bibliographic aids is available to assist library staff members and document users in their search for needed publications (see chapter 5 for a listing of such aids). Against this background, it is obvious that many document staff members have inadequate familiarity with the resources in their collections, even ones that the *Guidelines* describe as essential to any depository collection. For example, the *Federal Register* and the *Code of Federal Regulations* contain a wealth of information—more than many documents personnel apparently realized. If staff members cannot use even these basic sources effectively, how can they provide effective service for the diverse source material in separate documents collections and in the depository system as a whole? Here is another reason for reexamination of the recommended minimal level of selection (25%). A more realistic percentage must be formulated to provide a basis upon which collections can be evaluated.

The idiosyncratic nature of staff members provides a better explanation for the quality of reference service than do the institutional variables.[24]

Since the most important criterion related to answering questions correctly is the competency of individual documents staff members, their interest in public service and their personal ability to negotiate a variety of reference questions and to engage in problem solving can be improved. Thus there is a distinct possibility that documents departments, as well as government agencies that administer depository programs, can effectively attack the low rate of job performance demonstrated in this study. Well-devised and -executed continuing education programs and training sessions, as well as opportunities to take formal courses, should improve the overall quality of service.

Whatever strategies are undertaken require formal, ongoing evaluation so that performance can be monitored, modifications made, and new stimuli added. Government agencies that administer depository programs must take greater interest in performance measures. They should expect that public access to the sources they provide (free of charge) is accomplished through high-quality reference service, whereby library clientele receive personalized and accurate assistance. The depository library program should become an interlocking network for the delivery of needed source material and for referral to more complete collections. Referral should be regarded as access not only to printed sources but to human ones as well. Finally, emphasis must be given to increasing the competencies of individual library staff members, rather than increasing collection size and modifying other institutional variables.

4

Referral Services

When libraries provide information and referral services, they are "facilitating the link between a person with a need and the service, activity, information, or advice outside the library which can meet the need."[1] Referral also encompasses sending a patron to another library staff member or department. It can therefore occur within and outside a particular library setting. Studies in the general reference field have discovered that, contrary to expectations, reference librarians infrequently provide referral service and that the general citizenry is unaccustomed to such service. Since they neither look for it nor expect to receive it, the provision of referral service is not an essential criterion by which members of the general public label an information provider as most helpful.[2] Nonetheless, given the complexities of government activities and publishing programs, referral *can* serve a useful purpose. Referral can lead library staff members and library clientele to a wide range of information sources, not all of which are available in printed form. Further, as shown in figure 5, referral can result in access to timely and easily understandable information, and can demonstrate that libraries provide an essential link in the flow of information. Libraries may not contain comprehensive collections, but their staff members can assist the public in finding various sources for prompt resolution of a question.

Depending upon the knowledge of individual staff members, the type and availability of local resources, and the extent of local cooperation, numerous opportunities for referral could conceivably exist. On the one hand, referral could be "internal"—to another area of the library or member of the library staff, or to another part of the immediate institution. On the other hand, it could be "external"—to other information providers, such as other depositories (selective or regional), GPO bookstores, Federal Information Centers, or specific government agencies. The depository library program, in theory, encourages referral so that depository libraries will attempt to meet the information needs of their own clientele while also extending backup assistance to other depository libraries. This assistance might be in the form of interlibrary loans or answers to specific questions. Variation,

To *Library*	To *Library Clientele*
Meets clienteles' information needs	Meets information needs
Extends cooperation to other information providers	Understands the complexities of meeting specific information needs
Increases access to more documents types and formats	Gains awareness of amount and type of information available on the topic
Provides access to current, timely, and easily understandable information	Gains access to current, timely, and easily understandable information
Demonstrates role of the library as a mediator of information environment	Sees the library as a mediator of information needs
Enables library to meet its mission, goals, and objectives	Views library staff as professional and committed
Reaffirms role and value of interpersonal communication	Develops a personal relationship with library staff members
Demonstrates that referral is an integral part of reference service	

Figure 5. Benefits from Effective Referral Service

however, occurs in how depository libraries interpret their responsibility to fulfill these obligations.[3] A central question becomes: How frequently do documents staff members engage in referral, either of an "internal" or "external" nature? With this question in mind, this chapter examines the literature relating to the general references field and places the referral activity of the tested documents staff members in this wider context.

Literature on Referral Service

The literature of librarianship most frequently examines referral activity within the context of information and referral services (I&R), usually operated out of public libraries. An important aspect of I&R is to reach more segments of the general population and to assist them in meeting a wider variety of their information needs. I&R centers within the libraries supplement information in printed reference sources and provide current information on the community, perhaps through the maintenance of community information files. Some of these files are available online and permit members of the community to consult the information contained therein without having to visit the library (see chapter 5 for a more extended discussion of I&R).

The literature also examines referral activity in the context of cooperative reference service and networking.[4] In certain cases, statewide or local networks are in place, so that when individual libraries cannot answer a reference question, they can transmit it up a hierarchical network; each level builds upon and supports the efforts of the others. Project CHIN (Cooperative Health Information Network) is a cooperative program between Mt. Auburn Hospital and six public libraries in Massachusetts whereby the libraries receive assistance in developing health-related collections and services. In this regard, the libraries can refer to each other's collections or to the resources of the hospital. The Nassau Library System, Long Island, New York, provides an example of cooperation among member libraries whereby these public libraries can refer patrons to professional career counselors or a job center.

Referral, as is evident, can be more than sending someone to the card catalog, a particular reference source, or member of the library staff. Referral can and does take place in a wider context than a particular library or, in the case of academic libraries, the immediate resources of the institution. An expanded concept of referral service views it as actively helping clientele "make contact with an outside resource by making an appointment, calling an agency, etc."[5]

Much of the literature describes, but does not evaluate, referral programs and services. Some research studies, however, have discovered that general reference staffs infrequently engage in referral activity either within or outside the institution, even in instances in which it might help clientele resolve their information needs.[6] For example, in one study conducted by telephone,

> only 27.6% of the 282 respondents who failed to find the acceptable answer made referrals. The most frequent referrals (50.3%) were

either substitute answers or suggestions to come into the library, call other offices on campus, or check other types of materials in that library or another library. Twenty-four referrals were specifically made to other libraries; public libraries were the most popular. . . . Fourteen referrals or 7.9% of all referrals were made to external agencies such as the post office or a travel agency.[7]

Apparently, certain questions are more likely than others to generate referral activity. Noting this, Thomas Childers has called for research into the referral process. Such research could therefore address questions such as At what point in the search for an answer does a respondent decide to refer a question to another agency?[8] and Why do library staff members make referral suggestions but not follow through on the appropriateness of the referral site? In one instance, when reference staff members referred to an out-of-library resource, the appropriateness of that resource was tested. Two-thirds of the responses could be classified as correct or mostly correct; the remaining responses turned out to be wrong or mostly wrong.[9]

Finally, one study examined the information-seeking strategies of 2,400 New England residents and discovered that approximately three-fourths of the referrals had been made by interpersonal information providers, predominantly friends and colleagues.[10] Institutional providers of any kind seldom engaged in referral practices. Those who were interviewed most typically did not consult either a least or most helpful provider as a result of referral (only 20% of all the situations involved referral). Overwhelmingly, respondents explained that the least helpful providers had not suggested additional resources to consult. Since respondents expressed some satisfaction with the least helpful provider, it might be inferred that the public as a whole either does not expect referral or is unaccustomed to it.

Such findings suggest that libraries that are committed to referral practices must explain the value of it to their staffs, library clientele, and other information providers. The subject of referral, as Childers pointed out, indeed merits further investigation, if it is to be regarded as an integral part of reference service. If more libraries provide referral and if more clientele come to expect it, libraries can develop a capability that is not adequately provided by other information providers. They can therefore become more effective and efficient mediators of the information environment.

In summary, the literature on referral service is, to a large extent, descriptive. Methodologies and criteria by which to evaluate referral services and the impact of these services on total library services have not been fully examined. Even the unobtrusive studies reported in chapter 1 have not adequately analyzed the implications of limited referral activity on the quality of reference service. Referral service, which must be tied effectively to staff performance and the library's philosophy of service, merits coverage in reference policy manuals.

Findings

Overview

Three of the 127 correctly answered questions involved referral activity on the part of library staff members. Consequently, for the remaining 124 correctly answered questions referral was not regarded as necessary. By including the three correctly answered questions, referral service was suggested in only 59 instances (17.3% of all the 340 questions administered). One library staff member made referral with an incorrect answer, while in the other instances referral was extended with a:

> "I don't know but you might try . . ." response (33 of the 59, or 55.9% of the questions referred)
>
> "We don't have the sources necessary to answer the question, but you might try . . ." response (14 of the 9%, or 23.7% of the questions referred)
>
> partial answer (8 of the 59, or 13.6% of the questions referred).

Basically, this rank-order prevailed, regardless of geographical area or question. Viewed from another perspective, five of the referrals (8.5%) were general; library staff members encouraged the proxy to try another depository library, but would not specify which one. In the remaining instances, referrals were specific—to a particular depository library (a regional or another selective depository: fifteen, or 25.4 percent, of all referred questions), an individual in the same library (15, or 25.4%, of the referred questions), a government agency, including a GPO bookstore (22, or 37.3%, of the referred questions), or a nearby airport (2, or 3.4%, of the referrals). In several instances, library personnel suggested more than one referral source. It is important to note, though, that the libraries were in states that had regional depositories. Yet, few referrals were directed to these more complete collections. This chapter will examine these general and specific referrals, as well as the referral process, in more detail.

Specific comments by staff members about referral practices during the course of administering the test questions can be categorized as follows. The first type of comment related to the difficulty of referral. In this instance, library staff members indicated that there was no reason to refer the question outside the documents area because "no one else on the staff knew enough about documents" to be of assistance on that particular question.

A second typical response left the proxies with the responsibility for determining where a correct referral could be obtained; in other words, the proxies were told that "the answer can probably be found if only you could talk to someone who knew a lot about documents." A third typical response referred the question out of the documents area because "documents are difficult to access and locate." Instances in which such types of comments are made create the impression that documents are not easily accessible for the average person, that documents personnel are unable to locate needed information (if documents personnel cannot provide access to documents, who can?), and that the patron—not the library staff—has the responsibility for obtaining an answer and, as well, identifying and pursuing alternative courses of action.

To explore the referral process related to government documents reference services, a number of assumptions were identified and tested. Unless otherwise noted, a chi-square test of association was used to test the assumptions and a criterion of .05 or less was used to identify significant relationships. Based on this and other appropriate statistical tests, the following frequently mentioned assumptions can be examined.

Assumptions Tested

Willingness to engage in referral activity was contrasted to whether the proxies received a definite answer to the reference question as first posed (the answer could be either correct or incorrect). It might be assumed that whenever staff members could not provide a first-contact answer, they would be more willing to make a referral. Such an assumption, however, can be rejected. Tested library personnel infrequently provided referral service, either from a first-contact answer or from a follow-up request. Variation occurs when the data are analyzed on the basis of geographical region. Staff members from northeastern libraries were more likely than personnel from the Southwest to provide referral from first-contact answers. Still, library staff members view the assistance they provide in isolation from the expertise of their co-workers and other referral options. If they cannot answer the question or if they are unwilling to do so, they do not suggest other ways for addressing the information need. In effect, it is up to the patron to identify other avenues for information gathering. The other assumptions in this section support this conclusion.

It should be noted that for 245 of the 340 questions administered (72.1%), the proxies received a first-contact answer. This pattern did not vary according to which question was asked. As expected, library staff members gave some response to patron queries. This response, however, might not be the correct answer or an attempt to lead patrons to proper sources, within or outside the library, for answering the question. The "I don't know" response, or even a partially correct response, infrequently contained a referral component.

Another assumption is that in virtually all instances where the library staff member responded to a reference question by stating "I don't know," a referral would be forthcoming. However, as previously indicated, this assumption is not supported from the findings of the study. In 24 percent of the instances where library staff members responded that they did not know, there was no referral activity to another person on the staff or information provider (e.g., another depository library or a government agency). Thus, in a number of instances, staff members told the proxies, in effect, that they did not know the answer, had no ideas of where else to try to obtain the answer, did not offer additional assistance, and terminated the reference interview.

One might also assume that the longer the duration of the reference interview and search process, the chance for referral increases. This assumption can also be rejected. There were only 59 instances of referral, and 44, or 74.6 percent, of them came within the first five minutes of the search process. Extending the search process another five minutes added only another 6 referrals (10.2%). Analysis on the basis of geographical region does not alter this finding.

Another assumption to be examined is that the highest degree offered by the institution and the number of professional librarians at an institution would be significant factors in influencing referral. However, the assumption can be challenged because nearly two-thirds of the referrals (38, or 64.4%) came from institutions without doctoral programs. Further, nearly half of these referrals (28, or 47.5%) were made by staff members of baccalaureate institutions, predominately those with three professionals on the staff. Perhaps realizing the limitations of their collections and in-house service potential, staff members from such institutions are somewhat more willing to engage in referral.

Approximately three-fourths of the referrals (44 of the 59, or 74.6%) came from staff members associated with depository collections that selected less than 50 percent of the available item numbers. However, particularly in the Southwest, these referrals were to other members of the same library staff. Outside referrals on behalf of the personnel of depositories that select less than 50 percent of the item numbers occurred in 33 instances (55.9% of all referrals). Again, library personnel from the Northeast made the majority of these outside referrals. When staff members from the Southwest referred a question, it was primarily to a regional library.

The number of documents staff members also does not influence willingness to engage in referral. Some 64.4 percent (38) of the referrals came from libraries that employed either one or three FTE documents librarians. Still, the overwhelming majority of questions asked of these same libraries (222 of the 340, 65.3%) did not result in referral of any kind. An increase in the chance of referral is also not related to a larger number of FTE paraprofessionals; the majority of referrals came from institutions that employed 1.5 or fewer paraprofessionals (37 of the 59, or 62.7%).

Another assumption tested is that personnel who are assigned to manage *separate* documents collections actively and regularly engage in referral activity when they are unable to answer a reference question. A presumed advantage of separate documents collections is that specially trained personnel are available to assist in meeting information needs. This assumption concerning separate collections can be rejected. Staff members in separate collections infrequently suggested referral; only 15.3 percent of the questions administered at depositories with separate collections resulted in referral.

The final assumption to be examined is that documents personnel refer questions to other members of the library staff when they cannot answer a particular question. The data clearly show that little referral (even during morning and afternoon weekday hours) occurs within the libraries tested. During normal work hours, there is a much greater chance that professional staff members are available in the library for such referral activity.

The lack of referral to other members of the library staff raises some issues of concern. Apparently, documents personnel do not believe that other members of the staff can cope with government-related questions. Perhaps the tested personnel made a subjective judgment about the importance of the proxies' status and information needs, and did not believe that referral was necessary. If this was so, documents personnel may have prematurely terminated the reference interviews. In other cases, documents personnel might not have realized that a test question could have been answered from general reference sources held in the main reference area. A more active dialogue between documents staff members and general reference personnel would be beneficial. In this way, both could become aware of a greater range of library resources and meet a wider variety of information needs.

If necessary, all aspects of the library collection should be brought to bear on a particular information need. Libraries that receive government publications have a responsibility and obligation to make effective use of these rich information resources. These libraries cannot afford to operate one collection development policy for government publications and another for other library resources. Exploiting available information resources, including government publications, to their full potential requires a policy of administrative integration of government publications. Many libraries must realize that they cannot attempt to develop and maintain comprehensive collections of government publications (see chapter 5). They need to develop collections of the more heavily used source material while at the same time expanding their referral capability. Referral must be considered a legitimate and necessary aspect of reference service.

Analysis of Questions

Overview. Additional insights into the referral process are evident from examination of the individual questions (complete listing of questions is provided in appendix A). Three questions did not receive the benefit of any referral suggestions. These questions called for information concerning the creation and function of the President's Commission on Housing (question 8), an article on the number of immigrants in the U.S. labor force (question 11), and the composition of the Senate Committee on Small Business (question 16). Yet the question on the President's Commission on Housing was answered correctly by only 29.4 percent of the staff members tested, while the request for the article received a correct response in 47.1 percent of the cases. The membership of the Senate committee was answered correctly in 82.4 percent of the cases. The remaining seventeen questions received varying degrees of referral.

Questions Referred. Nine questions received a maximum of three referrals (questions 3, 7, 9, 12, 13, 14, 15, 17, and 20). Table 19 depicts the eight questions which received between three and ten referrals. The mean number of referrals for these particular questions was 5.6; viewed another way, these questions accounted for three-fourths (45, or 76.3% of the 59 referrals). Question 10, which called for the written test guide, was frequently referred to a local airport or the Federal Aviation Administration. The other questions were referred to another member of the library staff, another depository library, or a GPO bookstore.

The most-difficult-to-answer questions (figure 1) received nearly half of the referrals (29, or 49.1%, of the 59 referrals). They called for bibliographic citations to historical works (questions 1, 2, and 5) as well as to current publications (questions 6 and 10). Question 19 requested source material contained in the *Federal Register* or the *Code of Federal Regulations;* question 8 (purpose of the Commission on Housing) required use of the same sources, but for some unexplained reason this question did not generate referral activity.

The questions calling for bibliographic citations could have been answered from a basic index for the nineteenth century, the *Monthly Catalog,* or the *Publications Reference File.* It may be that many of the tested depository libraries house these and other basic titles (including the *Federal Register* and *Code of Federal Regulations*), but that staff members do not

TABLE 19. Questions Most Likely to Be Referred

Question	Number of Referrals
10 (Written Test Guide for Private Pilots)	10
2 (Japanese use of Balloons in WW II)	7
*5 (Availability of Overland Migrations)	7
*19 (Regulations about Indian Arts and Crafts Board)	6
6 (Availability of Clamshell Commerce)	5
1 (Army's Use of Camels in 19th Century)	4
18 (Map of Honduras)	3
*4 (Head of Justice Dept., Civil Rights Division)	3
Total:	45

*indicates that the question was administered by telephone

know how to use them. These findings suggest that future studies might also investigate the holdings of the tested libraries.

Question Delivery. Referral for individual questions can also be compared to the method of question delivery (telephone vs. in person). It is interesting to note that seven of the telephone questions involved two or fewer referrals; the other three questions involved either three or six referrals. Question 4 (head of Justice Department's Civil Rights Division) resulted in three referrals, all to government agencies. Questions 5 and 19, which are depicted in table 19, together received thirteen referrals. The in-person questions appeared to be harder for the tested staff members and were more likely to be referred. Only half of these questions received two or fewer referrals. As shown in table 19, questions 1, 2, 6, and 10 received a fair share of referrals (more than four); question 18 (for the map of Honduras) received three referrals.

Questions Not Referred. Since the discussion has focused on those eight questions that received the most referrals, it might be helpful to compare the remaining twelve questions. Overwhelmingly, they were administered by telephone (questions 7, 9, 12, 13, 15, 16, and 20); these seven questions received a total of nine referrals, most often (88.9% of the time) to a specific information provider. Five questions (3, 8, 11, 14, and 17), asked in person received infrequent referrals. These questions, which received only five referrals, called for an article, statistical data, and information in the *Federal Register.* Three of the questions requested publications on a particular topic, while the other two asked for factual information. Only one of these questions called for retrospective information—summary statistics for the revenues and expenditures of the Post Office Department for all available years during the twentieth century.

The willingness to engage in referral services did not show statistical significance on the basis of the eight institutional variables described in the previous chapter: highest degree offered, library volumes and budgets, percentage of item numbers selected, collection organization, and total librarians, documents librarians, and paraprofessionals on the staff. As already suggested, it may be that the nature of the test questions and a person's perceived ability to answer a question are more important considerations. Nonetheless, geographical region produced some variations concerning the referral location.

Staff members from Northeastern libraries accounted for all the referrals to a GPO bookstore, which is understandable, given the location of one of these bookstores in Boston (see table 20). Further, staff members from Northeastern libraries made the majority of referrals to government agencies, which again is explained by the fact that many agencies have regional

TABLE 20. Referral Site on Basis of Geographic Area

Question	Government Agency		Librarian in Same Library		Librarian Different Library	
	NE	SW	NE	SW	NE	
1 (Army's Use of Camels in 19th Century)	0	0	0	1	0	
2 (Japanese Use of Balloons in WW II)	0	0	0	4	0	
3 (FDA Study of Caffeine)	1	0	0	0	0	
*4 (Head of Justice Dept., Civil Rights Division)	1	0	0	1	0	
*5 (Availability of Overland Migration)	0	0	1	2	0	
6 (Availability of Clamshell Commerce)	0	0	0	1	0	
*7 (Education Organization Act, Report)	0	0	0	0	0	
8 (Purpose of Commission on Housing)	0	0	0	0	0	

GPO Bookstore		Other Selective Depository		Regional Depository		Airport		Total
NE	SW	NE	SW	NE	SW	NE	SW	
0	0	2	0	0	1	0	0	4
1	0	2	0	0	0	0	0	7
0	0	0	0	0	1	0	0	2
0	0	0	0	0	1	0	0	3
3	0	0	0	0	1	0	0	7
1	0	0	0	2	1	0	0	5
0	0	0	0	0	1	0	0	1
0	0	0	0	0	0	0	0	0

TABLE 20. (Continued)

Question	Government Agency		Librarian in Same Library		Librarian in Different Library	
	NE	SW	NE	SW	NE	SW
*9 (Availability of FTC Report about Television)	0	0	0	0	0	0
10 (Written Test Guide for Private Pilots)	6	1	0	0	0	0
11 (Article about Immigrants in U.S. Labor Force)	0	0	0	0	0	0
*12 (Percent Population over 80 Years)	1	0	0	0	0	0
*13 (Illiteracy Rate 1950–1970)	0	0	0	1	0	1
14 (Post Office Revenues during 20th Century)	0	0	0	0	0	0

GPO Bookstore		Other Selective Depository		Regional Depository		Airport		Total
NE	SW	NE	SW	NE	SW	NE	SW	
1	0	0	0	1	0	0	0	2
0	0	0	0	1	0	1	1	10
0	0	0	0	0	0	0	0	0
0	0	0	0	0	0	0	0	1
0	0	0	0	0	0	0	0	2
0	0	0	0	1	0	0	0	1

Table 20. (Continued)

Question		Government Agency		Librarian in Same Library		Librarian in Different Library	
		NE	SW	NE	SW	NE	SW
*15	(History Graduate Degrees in 1978)	1	0	0	1	0	0
*16	(Composition of Senate Committee on Small Business)	0	0	0	0	0	0
17	(R & D Funds Distributed by Agency)	0	0	0	1	0	0
18	(Map of Honduras)	2	0	0	0	0	0
*19	(Regulations about Indian Arts and Crafts Board)	2	0	0	1	0	0
*20	(Presidential Toast in Honor of Sadat)	0	0	1	0	0	0
	Total:	14	1	1	14	0	1

*indicates the questions administered by telephone

GPO Bookstore		Other Selective Depository		Regional Depository		Airport		Total
NE	SW	NE	SW	NE	SW	NE	SW	
0	0	0	0	0	0	0	0	2
0	0	0	0	0	0	0	0	0
0	0	0	0	0	1	0	0	2
1	0	0	0	0	0	0	0	3
0	0	0	0	0	3	0	0	6
0	0	0	0	0	0	0	0	1
7	0	4	0	5	10	1	1	59

offices in Boston. Personnel from Southwestern libraries made most of the referrals to other members of the same staff. Further, if there was referral to another library, it was most likely to a regional depository. Staff members from Northeastern libraries were almost as likely to make referrals to another selective depository as to a regional depository. The reason for this might be that there are more depositories in the Northeast and that it is easier to exhaust local resources before consulting staff members from the regional depository.

Improving Referral Services

Similar to the findings of research in the general reference field, documents personnel, like their counterparts in general reference departments, infrequently engage in referral. They tend to view their collections as self-contained; if they perceive that they lack the immediate resources to address an information need, they seldom call upon co-workers or other information providers—even regional depositories to which, in theory, they report. Instead, documents staff members tell patrons that they do not know the answer, or speculate that the question might be unanswerable. In effect, they leave the information seeker to decide whether the question merits further searching and which information provider might be the most helpful. This finding is especially troublesome in that many people lack a clear understanding of government structure and the methods for obtaining government information.

Interestingly, none of the subjects suggested consultation with staff members from a Federal Information Center, whose function is, in part, to assist the public in negotiating the maze of federal bureaucracy. Further, there were infrequent referrals to GPO bookstores. In the case of Northeastern personnel, both information providers would have formed the basis for appropriate referral. The GPO bookstore in Boston, for example, receives an updated version of *Publications Reference File* on a weekly basis and is willing to check a maximum of three titles per call. It will also accept written requests to check the availability of additional titles in the sales program.[11]

On the basis of the findings presented in this and preceding chapters, it would seem that academic depository libraries must re-examine what they regard as acceptable levels of reference performance. The GPO and its advisory group, the Depository Library Council, must do the same. Depository libraries must develop written reference policy statements that provide clear guidelines covering referral activity.[12] The policy statements should, for example, specify the actions that paraprofessionals, working evenings and weekends, should take if they encounter reference questions that cannot be answered. They might be instructed, for example, to obtain the name and telephone number of the person so that a professional staff member could provide follow-up services.

The level of service most typically offered by staff members could be characterized as "conservative" or "moderate"; library personnel attempted to answer the question but did not spend much time with it.[13] In some cases, staff members merely pointed out which reference source might be useful, and would actively assist the user only when further assistance was requested. Referral service definitely was not viewed as necessary or as an integral part of reference service. Undoubtedly, staff members cannot answer all the reference questions they receive, but in such cases they should not leave the patron wondering where else to turn for resolution of an information need.

"Liberal" or "maximum" service consistently involves staff members in finding the answer or a source from which the answer can be obtained. Under the maximum approach, library personnel view reference service as more than assistance to the resources in a particular collection. They are willing and eager to assist patrons, even by drawing upon external resources. Special libraries most closely attempt to implement the "maximum" reference philosophy. This approach can be adapted to other library environments, but it requires changes in the way that reference service is conducted.

Maximum service entails leading the requester to the desired information, regardless of its location, and necessitates knowledgeable referral. Perhaps depository libraries offer varying levels of service, depending on the status of the requester. Perhaps—if the proxies had not been students, but faculty members of the tested institutions—the type and extent of service might have been better. Regardless, the study shows the type of referral service that the general public might encounter in their search for government publications/information is frequently inadequate.

A few examples of maximum service were discovered during the testing. For instance, a staff member from one depository library took a telephone request and called the proxy back later in the morning. This person mentioned that the library did not own the title requested, but that it was available from both the regional depository library and the GPO bookstore in Boston. The proxy was then given the Superintendent of Documents classification number, the stock number, and the price, as well as the telephone number and address of the regional library and the GPO bookstore.

This chapter has called into question basic assumptions held by documents librarians (see figure 6 for a summary of these assumptions) and has shown that personnel from baccalaureate institutions are the most likely to

Assumptions	*Status*
Documents staff engage in referral activity (either of "internal or external" nature) when they are unable to answer a reference question.	Not supported
Whenever staff members cannot provide a first-contact answer, they make a referral.	Not supported
The longer the reference interview and search process, the chance of referral increases.	Not supported
Highest degree offering of institution, number of professional librarians at institution, and percentage of item numbers selected are significant factors influencing referral.	Not supported
Number of documents staff members influences willingness to engage in referral.	Not supported
Personnel assigned to manage separate documents collection actively and regularly engage in referral activity when they cannot answer a reference question.	Not supported
Consultation with staff members servicing separate documents collections results in high-quality reference service.	Not supported
Documents personnel work with other members of library staff when they cannot answer a question.	Not supported

Figure 6. Summary of Frequently Stated Assumptions Related to Documents Referral

provide referral service. However, even in those instances, referral is not routinely offered. Perhaps some depository staff think referral is a sign of collection weakness or individual incompetency. One would think, however, that incomplete service or saying "I don't know" would have the same result. Staff members should be encouraged to regard referral service as a normal part of their responsibility. Knowledgeable referral may make library users more willing to consult staff members in the future. In order to provide effective access to government publications, library staff members should provide aggressive and personalized service to users of the documents collection. Without such service, inexperienced users of government information will continue to encounter difficulty in gaining direct access to desired source material.

One might suggest the hypothesis that as users of different libraries encounter variations in classification systems, arrangements of documents holdings, and services, they experience difficulty or confusion in use of the documents collections. Further, with separate collections, users have to rely on the depository library staff for assistance. The literature of government publications has characterized this as a strength of the system, in that clientele receive high-caliber assistance.[14] However, this study calls such an assumption into question. Further, research in the area of general reference service suggests that many library users are hesitant or unwilling to request assistance.[15] If these findings are fully applicable to the field of government publications, many users will not avail themselves of reference service. Instead, they will browse through documents collections and explore other information providers. As an alternative, they might seek out those on the staff who are the most informed and bypass other library personnel.

Social scientists make infrequent use of indexes and abstracts. Increased depository distribution in microfiche will lessen their capability to browse government publications and make that "random find."[16] In order to make information more accessible and to build upon the fact that many people prefer to gather information through interpersonal contacts, libraries might expand their role as mediators of the information environment and their ability to handle telephone reference questions. In some cases, they might reconsider the types of questions that they will accept over the telephone.

Libraries will also have to establish current awareness services and prepare staff members to provide high-quality reference service for government publications. Provision of such services would enable libraries and their clientele to negotiate problems related to the fact that they must first associate government publications with specific information needs and then investigate the various formats in which the information might appear. Even after they make the appropriate decision to use government publications, problems may arise in relation to retrieving needed source material. Referral service therefore may be essential to determine the type of sources required, and should be the subject of continuing education and staff training programs. Chapter 5 will elaborate on this point.

Documents staff members must not only focus on their ability to answer questions from their own collections, but improve the quality of their referral services. In this regard, they need a more complete awareness of local resources (library and other) as well as alternative methods for addressing the referral needs of their clientele. These methods must take into account the speed with which information is needed as well as the cost to the library in supplying the information. For example, it may not be feasible for the documents personnel to make long-distance telephone calls on behalf of their clientele. However, libraries might exploit methods by which staff members of a Federal Information Center, GPO bookstore, or area agency can make the calls on their behalf. Libraries can also develop their collections of agency telephone directories and refer requests for recent information on census data to state data centers or regional offices of the Bureau of the Census. For this study, these offices comprised an underutilized source of referral.

Personal and aggressive reference service cannot be equated with the size of the collection and the number of staff members assigned to service it. Instead, it is associated with an activist philosophy of service, a willingness to engage in referral activity, and knowledge of government organization and information providers that are willing to provide reference and referral service. Depository collections should not be regarded as self-contained; they are part of an interlocking network—one that unites depository to depository, and depository to other information providers. The availability of source material in a variety of formats (e.g., paper, microform, audiovisual, and machine readable) underscores the importance of viewing documents collections in a larger perspective and of not merely translating a question into a staff member's knowledge of the printed sources in the collection. Figure 7 is a general model of the breadth of potential documents referral processes. Better knowledge of one's collection and the type of information contained in sources such as the *Federal Register,* the *Code of Federal Regulations,* and the *Publications Reference File,* however, might reduce the need for some referral, especially for the questions asked in this investigation.

Chapter 5 discusses specific strategies and administrative techniques that can be implemented to increase the competency of documents and reference personnel to achieve better cooperation among them, as well as to enhance referral and interpersonal skills. At the same time, librarians must be aware of information-seeking patterns of various segments of the population and provide high-quality service to each. We must keep in mind what *we* would do if we encountered incomplete service. Our decision would undoubtedly be conditioned by the fact that we are librarians, and have our own expecta-

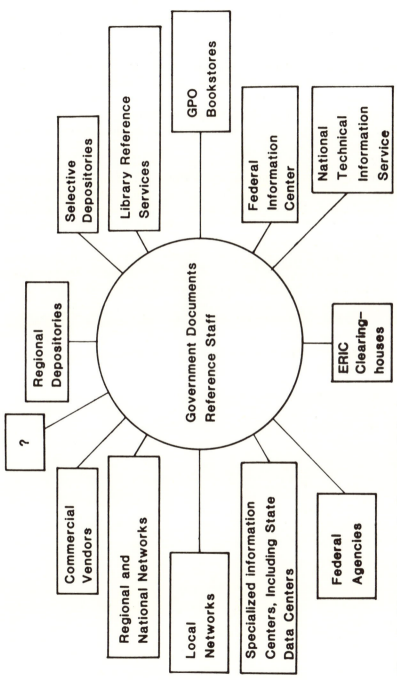

Figure 7. Selected Avenues for Documents Referral

tions. The general public, however, often does not have a similar understanding. Undergraduate students, for example, often view librarians as anyone who works in a library and as holding low-status positions.[17] Low-quality service, as identified in this study, may reinforce such perceptions.

Documents staff members must fully realize their role as *disseminators* and *mediators* of information and assume the responsibilities that such roles demand. If depository librarians cannot disseminate specific information, including knowledgeable referral, for what purpose do they provide reference service?

In the final analysis, reference and referral service is individualized service to every library user, helping that person find material that will answer his or her information need at that moment—pinpointedly, exhaustively, and expeditiously, both on request and in anticipation of additional knowledge and collation of useful information.[18] The tested documents staff members did not, as a whole, demonstrate this view of reference and referral service. When they thought of referral service—which was only occasionally—it was usually directed to only a few of the conceivable options. Curiously, documents librarians want other information providers to be aware of, as well as make referrals to, the various depository libraries. Yet documents librarians themselves infrequently provide "external" referral services. Such a paradoxical perspective inhibits the ability of the patron to gain access to government information and requires immediate clarification and improvement by documents librarians.

5

Improving Government Documents Reference Service

The overall quality of government documents reference service in the vast majority of academic libraries investigated can be significantly improved. At times the interpersonal skills and service attitudes of the staff members who answered the test questions were abrasive, inadequate, and self-defeating for the maintenance of quality reference service. These and other findings from the study underscore the likelihood that the individual library staff member *is the single most significant factor* affecting the quality of reference service for government documents. Concentrating on the skills and competencies of individual library staff members may well upgrade the quality of reference service provided by the depository libraries we tested.

Although the study has identified a number of areas related to reference service which require immediate attention, the quality of documents reference service can be improved significantly only if documents librarians and staff members, reference librarians, library administrators, and officials at the Government Printing Office want such change to occur. Improvement will result from the development of specific strategies to refine the individual reference skills of library staff, as well as the administrative environment in which the documents area operates.

Despite this emphasis on the individual documents staff member, other factors will impact on strategies to improve the quality of reference services. However, the responsibility for developing and implementing strategies to improve the quality of reference services will fall on the documents librarian. Therefore, this chapter will provide an overview of strategies that documents and nondocuments librarians can use to better exploit government publications and to integrate these resources into overall library services and operations.

Three broad areas must be stressed if the quality of government documents reference service is to be improved. First, if government documents are to be integrated into the library as a whole, there must be a conceptual understanding of the relationship between documents and other library resources. Second, documents and general reference librarians must improve their reference skills and competencies on general reference techniques as well as aspects related primarily to government documents. Third, administrative strategies can be employed to provide an environment that will encourage the exploitation of government publications and assist in the overall integration of these important resources. This chapter, which will discuss strategies in each of these areas, offers specific recommendations which, in the opinion of the authors, can significantly improve the quality of government document reference services.

Conceptual Factors

Before devising specific strategies that will improve individual skills or detail administrative approaches to improve the quality of reference services, a framework that sets forth goals and criteria for excellence should be developed. Once such goals and criteria have been agreed upon, specific strategies are more likely to be successful. Two general conceptual considerations provide a basis for developing strategies necessary for improvement of reference services. The first concept, integration, is summarized in figure 8.1[1] Overall, integration suggests a contingency approach for comparing government documents to existing services and conditions in the library. This contingency approach, then, allows for unique conditions in that particular library to impact on the *level* of excellence that the clientele can reasonably expect. In short, the treatment of government documents collections and services should be *at least* at the same level extended to other types of materials and services.

There are four major criteria to examine regarding integration. The first, bibliographic accessibility, asks if clientele have the same probability of *determining the existence* of a government publication as any other type of material in the library. This criterion is critical because many patrons are automatically referred away from documents because these resources are discriminated against in traditional indexes; they index few government publications. For example, when a reference librarian sends a patron to use *Reader's Guide* or *Business Periodicals Index,* that librarian has said, in effect: "You will not be using government publications."[2]

The problem of selective inclusion of government publications in general indexes is compounded by the fact that, in the vast majority of libraries that maintain separate government documents departments, the primary indexes to government publications (e.g., *Congressional Index Service, American Statistics Index, Index to U.S. Government Periodicals,* and *Monthly*

Catalog) are removed from the general reference area. Bibliographic accessibility can be improved simply by duplicate purchases of key government document reference tools or by placing such reference tools and indexes where *both* general reference and documents reference staff can easily access them.[3]

The second criterion of integration, physical availability, asks if the patron has the same probability of being able to locate a specific document on the shelf and check it out as any other type of material in the library. This factor implies that government documents are logically organized on open stacks, that a knowledgeable patron can identify a specific document, obtain it directly from the shelf, and, regardless of its format (hardcopy, map, poster, microform), check it out for external use. Four of the documents collections in this study had "closed stacks," in which patrons were not allowed to obtain directly (or browse) government publications; two collections in private institutions barred the proxies from entering the library until the authors obtained special permission for the proxies to use *only* the government documents part of that library; and in a number of the collections studied, publications could not be checked out or depository microfiche was unavailable for circulation. These factors, which are easily remedied if a library wishes, can significantly increase physical availability to government publications.

The issues of open versus closed stacks, circulation versus noncirculation of documents, and access or lack of access to collection browsing affect the physical availability of government documents. Currently, no research has investigated the impact of these factors on access and user services. Additional study is required to assist documents librarians in better organizing and administering documents collections for increased user access and physical availability.

The third criterion, professional service, suggests that the patron obtain the same level of professional service for government publications as for other types of materials and services in the library. As indicated earlier in this book, the accuracy rate of 37 percent is less than the rate found in the unobtrusive studies of general reference services. It might even be suggested that the *overall* adequacy of documents reference service is less than that of general reference personnel. The criterion of professional service, which is of key importance for improving overall reference services, will be discussed in greater detail in subsequent sections of this chapter.

The fourth criterion, status, relates to attitudes, perceptions, and power relationships in the library; but the impact of status on government documents collections and services is readily apparent. The documents librarian's vision and ability to articulate ways to obtain adequate resources are critical. One indicator of the status criterion is the degree to which the

Criteria	Indicators
1. Bibliographic assessibility	Does the patron have the same probability of determining the existence of a certain government publication as the existence of an information source of a more traditional format?
	Does the patron have equal access to indexes and reference tools related to government publications as to those related to other information sources in the library?
	Does the patron have the same probability of obtaining specific information with the government publication as with an information source of a more traditional format?
2. Physical availability	Does the patron have the same probability of locating and obtaining a specific government document (once its existence within the library is verified) as any other type of material in the library?
	Does the patron have the same opportunity to locate and obtain government publications regardless of format, i.e., microforms, maps, and A-V?
3. Professional service	Does the patron have the same awareness of the information sources available in government publications as for other information sources in a more traditional format?

Does the patron have the same opportunity to be referred to an appropriate government publication as to other information sources in the library?

Does the patron deal with librarians who are as competent, trained, and knowledgeable about government publications as librarians with other specific competencies, training, and knowledge related to their areas of responsibility?

4. Status   Do government documents receive similar resource support (staff, materials, equipment, etc.) as do other areas/departments in the library?

Do documents librarians participate in library administrative matters to the same extent as other librarians?

Do the director and librarians perceive government publications to be as valuable an information resource as other library information resources?

Figure 8. The Concept of Integration

documents area has access to and receives support for new technology. A recent study has shown that the documents areas frequently are excluded from participation and use in automated information systems[4] and that documents librarians have less competency than other librarians regarding use of automated information systems and on-line bibliographic data base searching.[5] Further, documents librarians believe they receive less material resource support than other areas of the library.[6] Perhaps most importantly, documents librarians must be involved in decision making and be able to influence library policy. Documents librarians must have *at least* equal status, equal resources, equal physical facilities, and equal impact on library policy, in comparison to other library staff, if they are to integrate government documents collections and services. The criterion of status requires at least one full-time, specially trained, professional documents librarian with administrative authority over the depository collection.

Space does not permit additional discussion of these criteria. However, the concept of integration is holistic, and suggests a combination or interaction of these criteria that sets an organizational climate that significantly influences the overall effectiveness of reference services for government documents. Self-assessment, centering on these criteria, will identify areas where attention is needed. Relevant environmental factors must be considered and understood as a *prerequisite* for improving the quality of reference services for government documents.

The second conceptual framework to be considered as a basis for improving the quality of reference services for government publications might be termed "constraint analysis." The first conceptual framework, integration, suggests criteria to compare the services and operations of the documents area to other areas and operations in the library. Constraint analysis, on the other hand, focuses on environmental situations that directly affect the documents department or area. Further, its purpose is to identify constraints that hinder the government documents' services and operations from performing *above* comparable levels of services and operations in other parts of the library.

A constraint, which may be defined as a factor or condition that currently affects a specific service or operation, limits or reduces the likelihood that the goals or criteria suggested in figure 8 can be accomplished. Figure 9 suggests potential constraints within the context of each of four criteria for integration. The figure seeks to determine the degree to which constraints are "actionable," that is, the degree to which the documents librarian can impact the limiting effect of the constraint. The potential constraints in figure 9 are selected; however, additional constraints within the various criteria will arise, given the individual setting for the documents collection in each library. The purpose of utilizing constraint analysis is to identify which specific areas that affect reference services for government documents have the best chance of being modified or eliminated, so that the librarian can concentrate on specific priorities rather than attempt to attack all issues simultaneously.

By determining the target for constraint removal and the degree to which the constraint is actionable, documents services can be assessed more rationally. This process encourages a rational approach to determine which constraints have to be identified, who or what is responsible for the constraint, the likelihood that the constraint can be minimized, and possible strategies to minimize the effect of the constraint. Such an approach encourages the setting of priorities for concentrating efforts on those areas where change is likely and reference services can best be improved.

Although it is realized that the number of personnel typically assigned to government documents activities is small and that (in many depositories) the staff has an overwhelming amount of work to perform, depository librarians must examine their duties and routines critically. Setting priorities, recognizing that some tasks are less important (not *un*important) than others, and developing plans to affect change in areas that are actionable are necessary. Analysis of constraints can assist in setting these priorities.

With these two considerations in mind, integration and constraint analysis, the environmental setting that impacts on the quality of reference services for government documents can be better understood. All of these factors provide an interdependent, holistic environment that affects the quality of documents reference services in the library. Within this context, the remaining portion of this chapter, which emphasizes the criterion "professional service," suggests specific strategies by which reference services for government documents can be improved.

Factors in the Reference Process

Of all the criteria listed in figure 8, professional service has the greatest potential for improvement because it is the area in which documents personnel have the greatest direct control. Constraints in this area typically center around the degree to which documents and reference staff members are willing to engage in personal change and self-development. Such constraints, which are self-imposed, have the best chance for modification. Specific strategies can be developed to improve the quality of government documents reference services by (1) improving skills and competencies directly related to the reference process, and (2) developing administrative strategies to modify the environmental setting in which the reference process takes place.

The following factors are directly related to improving the reference

INTEGRATION CRITERION	POTENTIAL CONSTRAINTS	TARGET FOR CONSTRAINT REMOVAL	DEGREE TO WHICH CONSTRAINT IS ACTIONABLE
BIBLIOGRAPHIC ACCESSIBILITY	Nonduplication of key government documents indexes and reference sources Exclusion of government documents from traditional indexes Exclusion of government documents from library catalogs and finding aids Other		
PHYSICAL AVAILABILITY	Closed stacks for government documents, thus no browsing No portable microfiche readers for lending Inability to circulate government documents Documents area hours of operation less than those of main library Other		
PROFESSIONAL SERVICE	Too many responsibilities to attend continuing education opportunities Inadequate staff size for documents reference service General reference librarians afraid of government documents Limited knowledge of specific document reference sources and indexes Other		
STATUS	Noninvolvement in library committees and decision making Need to obtain additional equipment or technology Librarians, administrators, patrons unaware of value of document sources No budget control by documents librarian for equipment or collection Other		

Figure 9. Potential Constraints Related to Improving Government Documents Reference Services

118

process, and many of the suggested techniques stem logically from the findings of this study. The techniques are worthy of additional discussion of specific strategies by which they can be implemented. However, the purpose of this chapter is to present an overview of techniques with suggestions for improving the quality of the reference process for government documents, rather than providing detailed emphasis on any specific technique. Further, depending on the specific situation of the library, the degree to which the criteria listed in figure 8 are being met, and the degree to which the constraints in figure 9 impact on the library and the government documents collection, some techniques will be more appropriate than others. In the final analysis, in-house evaluation and research will be necessary to determine which techniques can be most successful.

Knowledge of Government Documents Reference Sources

Surprisingly, a number of documents staff members demonstrated unfamiliarity with basic government document reference sources. In particular, the failure to utilize the *Publications Reference File (PRF),* which can be considered as the *Books in Print* for GPO sales publications, suggests a lack of knowledge of key reference sources.

Other examples reported by the proxies confirm this. They were referred to the *Monthly Catalog* and *Reader's Guide* for a question that clearly asked for a government periodical article; to the *Monthly Catalog* and *American Statistics Index* for access to retrospective information (nineteenth century) that typically is contained in the serial set; and to the *Statistical Abstracts* for *any* question whose answer called for obtaining statistics. Some staff members could not use the *PRF,* and in one case the documents department had *PRF* but no microfiche reader. In general, the vast majority of the 63 percent wrong answers resulted from the library staffs' having only very superficial knowledge of basic reference sources for government documents, being unable to recognize which sources are best for which reference questions, and failing to suggest alternative sources where answers might be located.

A primary area of attention for improving the quality of government document reference services is to increase the knowledge of documents and reference librarians about basic reference sources for government documents. One method for increasing knowledge levels of basic reference sources is to refer to the various guides that provide an excellent means to establish a "basic" collection of document reference sources and enhance the librarian's awareness of which sources are available. In recent years there has been a significant increase in the number of reference works published by both the federal government and private publishers, related to documents. A summary of selected recent guides and reviewing sources is listed in figure 10. Librarians who wish to increase the quality of government reference services *must* stay informed, and examine these basic sources, if they are to provide adequate reference services for documents collections.[7]

For more current information of "fast-breaking" reference publications, perusal of *Documents to the People* and regular columns in *RQ, Booklist,* and *Reference Services Review* would be beneficial. Further, when new reference sources arrive in the collection, they should be routed to and reviewed by both documents and general reference librarians. Finally, librarians must take advantage of local workshops sponsored by library schools, regional depositories, professional associations, and the Government Documents Round Table (GODORT) of the American Library Association. There is no excuse for being unaware of current sources or relying on outdated sources.

Knowledge of reference sources for government documents necessitates awareness of nontraditional reference formats such as microforms, maps, and audiovisuals. As this study clearly indicated, the quality of reference service for nontraditional materials is in special need of improvement. Further, to enhance the quality of reference service, documents reference staff must also be knowledgeable about on-line reference tools, which government document data bases are available, and how to search them.[8] Given the rapid growth of government numeric data bases, expertise with reference sources and finding aids to access these valuable information resources also is required. As Kathleen Heim has pointed out, enormous amounts of information are available through government numeric data bases, and must be made available.[9]

Finally, increasing knowledge of reference sources for government documents requires "hands-on" experience. Reference librarians may wish to use the actual test questions employed for this study (appendix A), as well as additional test questions pretested but not used (appendix B), as in-house reviews of basic reference sources. These questions offer a unique opportunity for documents and other reference librarians to assess their knowledge of basic reference sources. Although *all* key reference sources are not used for these questions, they represent a useful summary of some of the key *types* of reference sources that can be considered basic for improving the quality of reference services for government documents.

In addition to using these specific questions, librarians can produce their own "favorite questions" and exchange them with their colleagues. They can also keep track of interesting or typical reference questions and use them as practice questions for other members of the reference staff. In-house training sessions that incorporate "hands-on" use of reference sources for government documents and role playing will be more effective than simply getting together and talking about reference sources in general. Only when a user need can be linked directly to a specific reference source can the value of that particular reference source be appreciated.

Effective Reference Interviews

Although every reference question will not require an extensive interview to provide the correct answer, this study demonstrated that the reference interview and the ability of documents staff to utilize the reference interview, both in person and over the telephone, had important impact on the resolution of questions. Indeed, the interview techniques of the Southwest library staff apparently played a significant role in the low rate of effectiveness for their answers (see chapter 2). No attempt will be made to review all the writing and research related to the reference interview; examples of the relevant literature, however, include William Katz's excellent overview of the topic,[10] Mary Jo Lynch's study of interview techniques used by public librarians,[11] Nice de Figueiredo's methodology for error prevention in reference work,[12] Charles Steward and William Cash's[13] excellent nonlibrary-oriented text on interview techniques, Robert Taylor's classic examination of reference negotiation,[14] and Raymond Gordon's text on interviewing techniques.[15]

Before the reference interview can be improved, librarians must understand how they are currently conducting one. In short, self-description of existing interview techniques is a prerequisite to self-evaluation and change. Although colleagues should assist each other in this process, reference evaluation should *not* be linked to salary increases or promotions. It is suggested that a first step is to have a colleague unobtrusively observe the interview and write a specific *description* of what occurred during the interview process. No attempt should be made by the colleague to evaluate the interview at this time; instead, this person should simply describe what actually occurred. Some librarians have been able to utilize voice recordings, or have videotaped the interview, as a means of accomplishing this first step.[16]

After the librarian has a number of such examples, it is time for self-assessment. He or she should review the literature on strategies for conducting effective reference interviews and then compare those strategies to what actually occurred. Further, specific criteria and reference policy guidelines for that library should be available as a means of assessing the interview. Additional areas of skill building, such as nonverbal language, can be included as appropriate.[17] Finally, documents staff (meaning all staff that provide reference assistance) can then have group meetings to discuss the "cases" and suggest alternative strategies and techniques.

One problem that is frequently encountered with such group discussion

Guides

Business Services and Information: The Guide to Federal Government. New
  York: Management Information Exchange, 1978.

King, Richard. Business Serials Publications of the U.S. Government.
  Chicago: American Library Association, 1978.

Larson, Donna R. Guide to U.S. Government Directories. Phoenix: Oryx
  Press, 1981.

Leidy, W. Phillip. A Popular Guide to Government Publications. New York:
  Columbia University Press, 1976.

Morehead, Joe. Introduction to U.S. Government Publications, 2nd ed.
  Littleton, CO: Libraries Unlimited, 1978.

Nakata, Yuri. From Press to People: Collecting and Using U.S. Government
  Publications. Chicago, American Library Association, 1979.

Newsome, Walter L. Government Reference Books (1978-79, 1980-81).
  Littleton, CO: Libraries Unlimited, 1980, 1982.

Newsome, Walter L. New Guide to Popular Government Publications.
  Littleton, CO: Libraries Unlimited, 1978.

Palic, Vladmir M. Government Publications: A Guide to Bibliographic
  Tools, 4th ed. Washington, D.C.: Library of Congress, 1975.

Sachese, Gladys. U.S. Government Publications for Small and Medium Sized
  Public Libraries. Chicago: American Library Association, 1982.

Schorr, Alan Edward. Government Reference Books (1974-75, 1976-77). Littleton, CO: Libraries Unlimited, 1976, 1978.

Wynkoop, Sally. Government Reference Books (1968-69, 1970-71, 1972-73). Littleton, CO: Libraries Unlimited, 1970, 1972, and 1974.

Van Zant, Nancy Patton. Selected U.S. Government Series. Chicago: American Library Association, 1978.

Zink, Steven D. United States Government Publications Catalogs. New York: Special Libraries Association, 1982.

Reviewing Sources and Periodicals

Booklist (regular column)

Documents to the People (ALA, Government Documents Round Table)

Government Publications Review

Jurisdocs (Government Documents Special Interest Section, American Association of Law Libraries

Microform Review

Reference Services Review (regular column)

RQ (regular column)

Serials Librarian (regular column)

Wilson Library Bulletin (regular column)

Figure 10. Selected Recent Guides, Reviewing Sources, and Periodicals for U.S. Government Publications (as of Summer 1982)

techniques is the difficulty some staff members experience in allowing their skills to be openly criticized. This difficulty can be resolved by one of two basic strategies: (1) develop case studies or examples *based* on actual experiences, which then are not tied to any individual in the group, or (2) exchange descriptions, voice recordings, videotapes, etc., with other reference librarians in the area and preserve anonymity during the exchange process.

Throughout this process, it is important to include the personnel at the main reference desk—assuming there is a separate reference department for government documents. Although the interview process at the main desk may have different objectives than at the documents department, interview techniques to clarify patron information needs are similar, regardless of location. However, two scenarios can be established: reference interviewing, with one set of goals and criteria appropriate in the documents area, and another set that is more appropriate at the main reference desk.

Two additional areas should be considered for skill building during the reference interview. The first is ability to conduct an effective interview over the telephone, to obtain adequate information to answer the question, to have procedures for returning the patron's call at a later time, and to know how much time and effort to spend on telephone queries. A second area has to do with referral skills and building those skills into the interview as a normal activity. Reference staff must be constantly aware of the myriad sources of government information *outside* the depository collection and be able to refer patrons to such sources, if necessary. Clearly, developing or improving referral skills is a key component to improving the quality of reference services for government documents.

Although reference interviews are relatively "unprogrammable," a recent article identifies four dimensions of the reference interview over which the reference librarian has some control. A summary of these dimensions and topics within each dimension are reproduced in figure 11.[18] The "structure" dimension refers to the content and arrangement of the interview, and two different approaches to interviewing can affect the structure. A first approach is a systematic one, in which the interview is reasonably complete before the actual search begins; in a holistic search, the interview may be integrated into the search process. The structure of the interview will depend on which of these two approaches the librarian chooses to employ.

The second dimension, coherence, "refers to the perception of the structure and is dependent on systematic connection and integration of interview parts."[19] This dimension is closely related to users' understanding of the reference process, their ability to cooperate with the librarian during the interview, and the ability of the librarian and user to interact effectively during the interview. Coherence, which is the perception of the user, is especially critical during provision of reference services for government documents because many users may be "afraid of documents." Thus the librarian must establish a rational approach or method for the interview and obtain the confidence of the user.

The third dimension, pace, "refers to the speed and efficiency of the question/response interchange."[20] The librarian has considerable control over this variable and must attempt to match the pace of the interview to the attributes of the users, as well as their information needs.

Pace should not be confused with the fourth dimension, length, which is the total time devoted to the interview. Constraints on the availability of time can come from both the reference librarian and the patron. However, the reference librarian can modify the techniques in the previous dimensions to lengthen or shorten the interview.

Additional description and explanation about these dimensions can be found in the original publication by Marilyn White, which readers are encouraged to examine carefully. The dimensions and topics suggested by White (and summarized in figure 11) can be seen as diagnostic tools in assisting public service personnel to better identify what is happening in the interview, and then to modify interview strategies as appropriate. The key to interviewing is that there are no general principles or guidelines appropriate for all situations. These dimensions should be seen as holistic aspects of interviewing, which, with other variables, impact on the overall effectiveness of the reference interview. Contingency relationships among the reference interview, the librarian, the patron, the search strategy, referrals, and available reference sources must be optimized by the individual reference librarian for maximum interviewing success.

Search Strategy Techniques

The search process comprises the physical and mental techniques to obtain a specific source that resolves the information needs of the patron. For purposes of analysis, the reference interview and the search strategy are often examined separately. However, the two reference skills are typically used together during an actual reference encounter. Search techniques, which have been utilized for general reference, are useful for review and have been discussed by Katz,[21] as well as a number of other writers.[22] However, specific search strategies for reference work in government documents collections have not been investigated.

As evidenced from the written reports of the proxies who participated in this study, the search techniques utilized by documents staff frequently were ineffective. For example, there were instances in which the documents librarian, reference librarian, and the director of the library all looked for a specific reference source for twenty-five minutes but were unable to find it. When they could not find it (or a suitable alternative source), they gave

Dimensions	Topics
STRUCTURE	• the problem creating the original question • the subject of the request • the nature of the service to be provided, i.e., answer requirements • situational constraints likely to affect selection or use of information, such as a deadline • personal variables that constitute long-term constraints, such as attitude and intelligence • prior search history, i.e., what the user has already done to locate the information
COHERENCE	• outlining the framework early in the interview • making transitional statements to reveal relationships between or among questions or to place them within a broader framework • summarizing the information exchange • establishing the context of the interview and obtaining accurate feedback from the patron
PACE	• defining the type of question to be answered • determining the sequencing of questions • determining which information should serve as the basis for continued interaction

- determining the nature or method of providing and obtaining feedback
- influencing the extent of digression tolerated or necessary within the interview
- the funnel sequence, moving from braod open questions to closed, restrictive ones
- the reverse-funnel sequence moving from closed to open questions
- the tunnel sequence, using a series of the same type of questions, either open or closed

LENGTH

- time constraints imposed on the interview-search by the librarian
- time constraints imposed on the interview-search by the patron
- degree to which other topics from the various dimensions are emphasized or limited

* Adapted from: Marilyn Domas White, "The Dimensions of the Reference Interview," <u>RQ</u> 20 (Summer 1981): 373-381.

Figure 11. Dimensions of Reference Interview for Self and Group Diagnostics

up; they did not suggest referral as an option. In other cases, documents personnel would not leave the immediate confines of the reference desk but merely "point" to general search locations; or correctly identified the *PRF* as the necessary source, but then did not know how to use it; or stated: "I get so confused with government documents that I doubt if I could help you."

Clearly, improving search strategy techniques for various types of reference questions for government documents can significantly improve the quality of reference services. The authors suggest that, although general search strategy techniques may provide a useful overview for searching government documents, the unique features inherent in the structure of government publications, the availability of limited indexes and reference sources, and oftentimes confusing bibliographic entries and listings may modify the search strategies relevant to general reference work. To date, no research into the use of search strategies appropriate for government documents has been reported.

Such research would be helpful because general techniques for searching government documents should be developed within the various depository libraries and should take into account the unique situations in those collections. Document librarians should "log" or "monitor" their search strategies as a means of describing the process to other personnel in that library. Further, describing, *in writing*, the search process for specific types of questions will facilitate group discussion of those search strategies and perhaps assist in development of general models that describe search strategies appropriate for documents collections.

Because of a general lack of adequate reference sources, limited bibliographic access, and nonintegration of reference sources for government publications, search strategies for government documents must often be much more "free wheeling," innovative, and nonstructured than those in the general reference area. Indeed, library staff members, in providing documents reference services, must develop numerous contingency searching techniques which can be chosen, or revised, and implemented according to the specific information requested. Toward that end, work by Marcia J. Bates on "information search tactics"[23] and "idea tactics"[24] provides an excellent framework to encourage innovative, self-developed, contingency search strategies.

Figure 12 summarizes information search tactics which can assist librarians in developing search strategies and in improving reference services. Tactics can be utilized in a number of areas, including monitoring, file structure, search formulation, and term development. The study and use of this figure should be an excellent catalyst for the improvement of documents search strategies. After describing, in writing, the search process for a specific information need, that process can then be compared to the tactics listed in the figure. Which of these tactics were used? Which were not used? Why? One might even provide a self-analysis of the search strategy by listing the search steps taken, on the left side of a piece of paper, then listing the tactic that search step represents, on the right side of the paper. Such self-assessment techniques for government document search strategies are essential if document librarians are to improve the quality of reference services and if they wish to explain and teach the intricacies of searching government documents collections to nondocuments librarians.

In response to another search problem identified in this study, the concept of idea tactics (also developed by Bates) is suggested. Such tactics are appropriate if documents staff are easily stymied and prone to give up the search after appropriate materials are not found. Idea tactics are "tactics to generate new ideas or solutions to problems in information searching."[25] These suggestions can serve as useful catalysts for devising a new search strategy to resolve a particular information need. Again, the tactics listed in figure 13 can be of significant assistance for self-diagnostics and teaching search strategies for government documents.

Reference staff in documents areas must carefully consider the search strategies they are currently using. Self-assessment of those strategies can be done by referring to the general literature, but use of the tactics suggested in figures 12 and 13 should assist librarians who search government documents to develop innovative search strategies and to utilize contingency strategies. Perhaps one of the reasons why general reference librarians find documents reference work to be difficult is that traditional models or search techniques are not fully effective for government documents. Nonetheless, documents librarians must assess their own search strategies as a basis for self-improvement, as well as to provide in-house training and instruction to other public service staff in that library.

Professional Attitude and Interpersonal Skills

In its broadest sense, interpersonal skills are all the skills that affect the relationship between two or more people. These skills encompass verbal and nonverbal communication, courtesy, friendliness, effective listening, respect for the other as a person, and, in library/information science, an attitude of professionalism and service. Interpersonal skills can compensate for a lack of knowledge about specific sources, the reference interview, or search strategies. Lack of interpersonal skills can produce an unsatisfactory reference conclusion even when the correct answer is provided.

The proxies that administered the questions in this study commented on the interpersonal skills and attitudes of the documents personnel who attempted to answer their questions. One of their most revealing comments is quoted below:

MONITORING TACTICS: Tactics to keep the search on track and efficient.

CHECK   To review the original request and compare it to the current search topic to see that it is the same.

WEIGH   To make a cost-benefit assessment, at one or more points of the search, of current anticipated actions.

PATTERN   To make oneself aware of a search pattern, examine it, and redesign it if it is not maximally efficient or if it is out of date.

CORRECT   To watch for and correct spelling and factual errors in one's search topic.

RECORD   To keep track of trails one has followed and of desirable trails not followed up or not completed.

FILE STRUCTURE TACTICS: Techniques for threading one's way through the file structure of the information facility to desired file, source, or information within source.

"BIBBLE"   To look for a bibliography already prepared, before launching oneself into the effect of preparing one; more generally, to check to see if the search one plans has already been done in a usable form by someone else.

SELECT   To break complex search queries into subproblems and work on one problem at a time.

SURVEY   To review, at each decision point of the search, the available options before selecting.

CUT   When selecting among several ways to search a given query, to choose the option that eliminates the largest part of the search at once.

STRETCH   To use a source for other than its intended purposes.

SCAFFOLD   To design an auxiliary, indirect route through the information files and resources to reach the desired information.

CLEAVE   To employ binary searching in locating an item in an ordered file.

Source: Marcia J. Bates, "Information Search Tactics," Journal of the American Society for Information Science 30 (July 1979); p. 208. Reprinted by permission of John Wiley & Sons, Inc.

Figure 12.   Information Search Tactics

SEARCH FORMULATION TACTICS:
Tactics to aid in designing or redesigning the search formulation.

SPECIFY To search on terms that are as specific as the information desired.

EXHAUST To include most or all elements of the query in the initial search formulation; to add one or more of the query elements to an already-prepared search formulation.

REDUCE To minimize the number of elements of the query in the initial search formulation; to subtract one or more of the query elements from an already-prepared search formulation.

PARALLEL To make the search formulation broad (or broader) by including synonyms or otherwise conceptually parallel terms.

PINPOINT To make the search formulation precise by minimizing (or reducing) the number of parallel terms, retaining the more perfectly descriptive terms.

BLOCK To reject, in the search formulation, items containing or indexed by certain term(s), even if

it means losing some document sections of relevance.

TERMS TACTICS: Tactics to aid in the selection and revision of specific terms within the search formulation.

SUPER To move upward hierarchically to a broader (superordinate) term.

SUB To move downward hierarchically to a more specific (subordinate) term.

RELATE To move sideways hierarchically to a coordinate term.

NEIGHBOR To seek additional search terms by looking at neighboring terms, whether proximate alphabetically, by subject similarity, or otherwise.

TRACE To examine information already found in the search in order to find additional terms to be used in furthering the search.

VARY To alter or substitute one's search terms in any of several ways.

FIX To try alternative affixes, whether prefixes, suffixes, or infixes.

REARRANGE To reverse or rearrange the words in search terms in any or all reasonable orders.

Figure 12. (Continued)

CONTRARY To search for the terms logically opposite from that describing the desired information.

RESPELL To search under a different spelling.

RESPACE To try spacing variants.

Idea Tactics: Tactics to help generate new ideas or solutions to problems in information searching.

Think To stop and think about the search and try to come up with new ideas for solving search difficulties.

Brainstorm To generate many ideas and to suspend critical reactions until the ideas are well-formed and can be fully evaluated.

Meditate To develop and utilize the skill of quickly achieving a mind state in which rational and intuitive capacities work together in solving search problems.

Consult To ask a colleague for suggestions or information in dealing with a search.

Rescue To check for possibly productive paths still untried, in an otherwise unproductive approach.

Wander To move along one's resources, being receptive to alternative sources and new search ideas triggered by the materials that come into view.

Catch To catch oneself in an unproductive search, to notice that a change in approach might be more productive.

Break To break an habitual search pattern, that is, put it aside temporarily, in order to take a search task more suited to the particular problem in question.

Breach To breach the boundaries of one's region of search, to revise one's concept of the limits of the intellectual or physical territory in which one searches to respond to a query.

Figure 13. Idea Tactics

When I entered the documents room the documents librarians were working busily around a table piled with documents. I walked across the room to gain their attention. When I got to the table, I asked one of them my question. She informed me that the question was impossible to answer, that I would have to look through

Reframe To examine implicit frame-of-reference information coming along with the user's query, to deal with it explicitly with the user and to negotiate changes in the query to eliminate distortions. (See text for explanation of notation.)

Notice To watch for clues that revise one's notions of the nature of the question or of the answering information.

Jolt To think "laterally"—to snap out of conventional thought patterns and redefine a problem in a dramatically different way.

Change To change something, anything, in one's search behavior—to try a different term, a different subject field, etc.

Focus To look at the query more narrowly, in one or both of two senses: (1) to move from the whole query to a part of it or (2) to move from a broader to a narrower conceptualization of the query.

Dilate To look at the query more broadly, in one or both of two senses: (1) to move from a part of the query to the whole query or (2) to move from a narrower to a broader conceptualization of the query.

Skip To shift laterally in one's view of the query, in one or both of two senses: (1) to move from searching one part of a complex, multipart query to another angle, that angle being neither broader nor narrower, but simply different.

Stop To cease searching temporarily on a problem and do something else.

Source: Marcia J. Bates, "Idea Tactics," *Journal of the American Society for Information Science,* 30 (September 1979): 282. Reprinted by permission of John Wiley & Sons, Inc.

year after year of indexes, and that it would take hours. I felt that at this point she was brushing me off.

The lack of immediate recognition of the proxy, the lack of interest in assisting her, and the brusqueness with which the documents staff member responded may produce a *feeling* that discourages the proxy from not only wanting to pursue the question but also returning for resolution of subsequent information needs.

Other student summaries point out the attitude that some documents library staff projected to patrons concerning the difficulty of using documents:

> The librarian had an interesting attitude towards the indexes in her collection. She portrayed them as difficult and unfathomable. There was one that she knew of as "the PRthingy" *[PRF]* but would not use because she was unfamiliar with it.

Or:

> The most important thing to come out of this study is that the librarian's attitude is tremendously important in acquiring government documents. Proxies wanting to know if a document was still in print were told to write the GPO, but my favorite was the question having to do with balloons used in World War II fighting. I was told to go to the books in the history area of the library and browse!

Additional examples support the view that, at times, documents personnel who were tested projected an attitude that (1) tried to persuade the proxie that reference work in documents is extremely difficult and obtaining answers to certain questions is unlikely, (2) they did not have adequate time to work with the proxy and thus sent him or her to a vast number of indexes or sources to "browse"; and (3) they did not care if correct answers were provided or not. In some instances, "we found ourselves staring at the very reference source that would have answered the question, but the librarian never went to it; instead, the librarian said that the collection lacked the necessary resources to answer the question."

Although there are other accounts of documents library staff dealing with the questions in a friendly, courteous, and professionally effective manner, the number of instances similar to those reported above suggests that a real problem in the provision of effective reference service for government documents relates to the attitudes and interpersonal skills of documents staff members. The importance of attitude and interpersonal skills cannot be overemphasized. In class discussions about the project after its completion, many students indicated that, given the treatment they received in some instances, they would not return for additional service, regardless of the appropriateness of government documents for the question.

Reasons for negative attitudes and limited interpersonal skills are many. Perhaps the documents staff members were not professionally trained; perhaps they were insecure about their knowledge of reference sources for government documents; perhaps they were overworked and had too many other tasks to do at the time the question was administered; perhaps the proxies asked questions that *were* "too difficult for them to answer"; or perhaps . . . Endless possible reasons exist. The "bottom line," however, is that in a number of instances an abrasive, noncaring, insecure attitude detrimentally affected the outcome of the reference process and increased user (proxy) frustration. Such instances help explain why patrons "don't ask questions"[26] and why some collections might have low visibility in the community.

Strategies to deal with poor attitude toward government documents and limited interpersonal skills are dependent on the library situation, recognition that such skills and attitudes need to be improved, and identification of specific weaknesses by the individual documents staff member or by some other member of the library. A number of useful texts, articles, and self-improvement books exist on positive thinking, attitude adjustment, development of interpersonal skills, communication skills, and effective interpersonal relationships.[27] Further, attendance at workshops, seminars, and formal courses in human relations can provide assistance. But identification and recognition of the problem has to precede strategies to resolve it, and most individuals (including library staff) may not believe that *they* need to improve their attitude or interpersonal skills. Indeed, some of the commentaries submitted by the students regarding their treatment suggest that some documents librarians are in the process of "burnout" (to be discussed later) and may need more than additional training on positive attitudes and interpersonal skills.

Information and Referral Skills

A frequent comment made by a number of proxies after administering the questions had to do with the hesitancy of documents staff to provide specific information in answer to questions. There was a preference to send the proxies to a number of indexes or general reference sources. Further, the study has already pointed out the minimal number of referrals by documents staff, even where the response of the staff was "don't know."

The combination of these two factors—providing specific information to reference questions and ability to refer questions that can be best answered elsewhere—are important considerations for academic depository reference services. These factors are part of the larger issue of providing "minimum or maximum" reference services,[28] the issue of "information or instruction,"[29] and the use and encouragement of referral techniques in an academic library setting. As noted in chapter 4, greater emphasis on provision of specific information and less instruction, combined with more referral service, would greatly improve the quality of documents reference services.

Clearly, academic libraries have different missions than public libraries. Yet the model of information and referral service (I&R) developed in the public library has great potential for improved government documents reference services.[30] Given the uniqueness of government reference sources and the expertise that frequently is required to obtain necessary information, less emphasis on instruction and more on provision of specific information seems to be appropriate. Further, as one proxy reported, "being sent to check the *Monthly Catalog* to find out about the use of camels by the Army in the American West" (question 1) is an excuse for lack of knowledge about documents reference service—not a demonstration of the importance of instruction over provision of information. A new philosophy, appropriate for today's academic depository collection, that stresses telephone services, information services, quick answers, and referral, is necessary.

The literature is profuse on how to establish an I&R center in the context of a public library setting.[31] These writings stress the importance of providing special reference sources that are easily accessible for "quick-fact" reference work, maintaining special files or lists of names and agencies where specific types of referrals can be sent, and developing interview skills especially appropriate for telephone reference work to encourage effective I&R services. Documents librarians should consider the development of I&R activities for depository collections, integrating such services into general reference services, or at least developing the I&R reference skills and techniques for everyday reference services.

A key concept of the I&R model is the importance of users and their information needs. The "bottom line" is to provide the specific answer to the question immediately when it is asked, or to be able to refer the question to another source that will be able to provide an answer. Emphasis on immediacy, accuracy, referral, and importance of the user are factors that must be integrated into documents reference services.

Indeed, the concept of "client-centered librarians" best describes a new professional role that might be especially appropriate for documents reference services. This approach attempts to develop the personal esteem and self-provider life styles of "clients" and encourages a "customized," helping relationship with clients in their search for information.[32] Academic libraries that continue a philosophy of "general instruction" instead of information provision, ignorance instead of referral, and user frustration and intimidation instead of being "client centered" are not likely to increase the quality of documents reference services. Research is needed to investigate the appropriateness of an I&R model that stresses client-centered services and "maximum" reference philosophy for depository collections as a means for improving the quality of documents reference services.

Administrative Factors Related to Effective Reference Service

The preceding section emphasized factors directly related to the quality of the reference process and suggested strategies to affect or improve these areas which are largely controlled by the reference librarian and, thus, are a primary means to improve overall quality of reference services. Another area, however, requires administrative skills, such as planning, personnel management, making decisions, establishing goals and objectives, and budgeting. It is here that documents librarians must be able to work effectively with other members of the library staff, become involved in library decision making, and obtain adequate resources to support documents reference services. Indeed, administrative strategies are necessary to integrate reference services for government documents with other services in the library and increase overall library awareness of the importance and utility of government documents.

These factors and strategies are discussed in this section in the context of assumed competencies held by the documents staff. For administrative strategies to be effective, professional documents librarians should be respected by other library staff for their knowledge of government reference sources, their ability to work effectively with a broad range of individuals during the reference process, and their ability to develop innovative search strategies that exploit all types of reference sources to answer documents questions. Finally, documents personnel are assumed to radiate an attitude of quality professional service and a positive sense that government documents *are* important resources for resolving information needs. Competencies in these areas, as well as those discussed in the preceding section, are prerequisites for the following strategies to be effective.

Development of Policy Statements and Plans

A number of proxies commented on the broad range of reference services obtained within the same library but from different individuals. Indeed, significant differences appeared between the reference "policy" at the main reference desk and that at the documents area. This finding suggests that a number of libraries (as a whole) and documents departments (in particular) have not carefully considered the type of reference service they expect to provide. For instance, the following issues or questions drastically influence the end product of the reference service:

> Will document and reference librarians work in each other's areas on a regularly scheduled basis?

What degree of bibliographic instruction is expected in the documents or reference areas?

How much time is expected to be used for "typical" reference questions?

Will paraprofessionals serve at the general reference desk, and if so, what types of duties are they expected to accomplish vis-à-vis the reference process?

Are reference staff (documents and general reference) expected to direct patrons to appropriate sources or assist them in obtaining the information requested?

How much has been budgeted in direct support of reference sources and indexes for government documents?

In what instances are referrals to occur and where are such referrals to be sent?

These are but a few of the major issues that can be addressed in a policy statement on reference services; additional issues have been covered elsewhere.[33] The point, however, is that a formal written policy of expected "standards" or guidelines for reference services is needed for each library setting, if for no other reason than to formalize and define the relationship between the depository collection and the rest of the library.

Although the authors of this book wish to emphasize the importance of developing reference policies that define the expectations of the organization for reference services, other policy statements are necessary as well. Areas such as collection development, organization and physical location of documents, bibliographic control, and use of technology (to name a few) also require policy statements. Examples of collection development policy statements have been provided by Peter Hernon and Gary Purcell,[34] and useful information regarding policy for areas of technology (as well as collection development) has been provided by Bruce Morton and J. Randolph.[35]

Once policies have been agreed upon, the development of goals and objectives is necessary. Specific objectives can be derived from these policy statements and serve as a basis to set priorities for the forthcoming year or another specific time period. A key concern for most documents depository collections is to *set priorities* and not continue to try to do all things for all people.[36] Setting priorities assumes that some activities are more or less important than others; further, that excellence on the "more important" activities has greater "payoff" than excellence on "less important" activities. Specific planning techniques and strategies to implement planning in a government documents depository collection are detailed elsewhere and need not be repeated here.[37] However, "up-front" time, committed to planning and setting priorities, saves significant amounts of time later by not having to "redo" the task, take into account situations or factors not considered at first, or reorganize and coordinate the project to meet endless "contingencies" that have just occurred.

Involvement in Organizational Decision Making

Although the specific strategies for decision making are important, a more intangible factor that impacts on the quality of reference services for government documents is the extent of personal power and the ability to affect organizational decisions.[38] Document librarians must be active in the library power structures and affect decisions if they expect to obtain adequate resources for the support of document reference services and to increase the awareness of other staff members about the value of documents.

As an example, documents librarians (assuming separate documents collection) must have some direct control over a budget for that department. Some administrators mistakenly believe that because documents are "free," no additional budget is necessary. However, budget control in areas such as purchase of nondepository documents, reference sources from private publishers, equipment, as well as support for continuing education of staff, are critical factors that will affect the overall quality of reference services. If microfiche readers cannot be purchased for the department and readers from other areas of the library must be used, the quality of reference service *in the documents area* is injured. The documents librarian is the person best able to allocate resources and make decisions about where the limited resources should be spent in the documents area. Without a regular budget and some direct control over that budget, the documents librarian is effectively hamstrung and must rely on "handouts" from the administrative offices or other departments (typically the reference department) for support.

There are a number of subtle techniques by which documents librarians can become involved in the library as a whole and better integrate themselves into total library services. First, they must become active on library committees or study groups. For example, by serving on a search committee for another librarian, documents librarians can help ensure that the new staff member has some basic knowledge about government documents and is not "scared to death" of documents. Similar analogies can be made with other committees. The case for financial support and promotion of government documents in the library must be carried by the documents librarian; further, other librarians must be made aware of such needs.

Another approach is to *initiate* participation in policy development or long-range planning for the documents department. Documents librarians can ask for assistance from other librarians and administrators and involve library staff in project planning or policy development. An assertive stance is required, but such a strategy can provide needed administrative assistance for the documents area, promote the area to other departments, and educate library staff concerning the problems and issues currently affecting the documents area. This strategy is especially useful when it is combined with demonstrating an interest and participating in issues and problems affecting other library areas. In short, one cannot adopt a provincial view of the documents area as an area unto itself. The documents librarians must "tie in" documents-related problems and issues (especially issues such as the quality of reference service) into a context of the library as a whole and foster participation from other library staff.

Integrated Bibliographic Control

The ongoing argument over the "best" approach for the organization of government publications has become nonproductive. As clearly pointed out in a review of the literature on this topic,[39] opinion dominates the thinking; proponents of every approach make assumptions to justify their particular stance. Obviously, no general rules of thumb are appropriate for all depository library collections. Yet, due to lack of research on the topic, it is likely that the argument will continue, with neither side becoming a clear winner and personal opinion dominating the discussion.

In the context of the quality of reference service for government documents, the issue is less one of separated or integrated physical location of government documents (i.e., whether documents are interfiled with other materials or filed separately). Instead, the issue relates to the degree to which government documents are bibliographically accessible by the professional reference staff, the degree to which these personnel are knowledgeable about document reference sources, and the degree to which they resolve the information needs of patrons who request government publications. In the experience of the authors, the unique situations of individual depository libraries preclude general statements about integrating or separating government documents. The key issue is the ability of documents and reference staff to provide access to information.

Bibliographic integration of government publications in a library setting can occur regardless of the documents' being integrated with or separated from the other materials physically. In recent years the importance of the argument regarding separate versus integrated collections has been reduced, due largely to the existence of more government document indexes (mainly from the private sector), availability of many government publications in online bibliographic data bases, and improved bibliographic control over government publications by the federal government. Further, it is unlikely that depository libraries will switch to either integration or separation without exceptionally good justifications.

Thus improved bibliographic access to government publications as a means for better reference service is largely an issue of staff training, knowledge of government reference tools and indexes, and exploiting new technologies to increase bibliographic control, *regardless* of the existing method of collection organization. Whether the documents collection is separated with its own classification scheme or integrated into the library's main collection, with Dewey or Library of Congress classification, bibliographic integration can occur. The primary factor that affects the degree of bibliographic integration is *not* separated or integrated collections; it is the ability of the documents and reference staff to exploit individual competencies and develop mechanisms to integrate documents bibliographically with the rest of the library.

Examples of such bibliographic integration are physical integration of key government reference sources with the main reference areas or the purchase of duplicate copies, online data base searching of the numerous government document data bases as part of a normal reference search,[40] inclusion of government documents in the OCLC archive tape for the individual library, entering government documents into OCLC,[41] inclusion of government documents in the library's automated circulation systems, exploiting documents bibliographic utilities such as the Guelph system,[42] and providing adequate staff training to ensure that all library staff are knowledgeable about these mechanisms.

Bruce Morton has provided excellent examples of integrating government documents bibliographically into the library and the larger bibliographic community.[43] He has clearly demonstrated that regardless of the separate or integrated argument, in-house automated information systems can provide an integrated mechanism for circulation, collection development, and bibliographic control for government documents. Advances in information-handling technology have made the argument over separate versus integrated collections obsolete. The new issue is the degree to which depository librarians and library staff can exploit these technologies for integrated bibliographic control and improved reference services.

Physical and Organizational Location of Documents

Identification of where the depository collection is located, physically and organizationally, can be a telling factor on the quality of reference services. Organizationally, the documents collection needs to be aligned with, or part of, a department in the library that is both powerful and involved in decision making. In many instances, depository collections are placed on the organization chart as a separate department, and "out of sight" becomes "out of mind." Careful analysis of the organizational structure and where the depository collection should be located is important and can contribute to better reference services. It can also enhance integration with other library collections, depending on the political and organizational constraints in that library.[44]

Under some organizational options, depository personnel report through either the director for public services, the director for technical services, or a department head, such as head of reference. Although it is difficult to predict where the depository can best be supported and best integrated in the library, the authors suggest that an organizational structure that clearly relates the depository collection to the reference department is in order. These two areas must be closely coordinated for overall effective service, and—typically—such close coordination will not occur at an assistant director for public services level, given the broad range of responsibilities already present at that level.

Organizational structure does not have to predict physical locations within the library, although such is possible. In short, the depository collection can be physically located three floors distant from the reference department, yet both could have the same department head. However, a more effective solution (assuming available space) is to consider a physical location that places the reference areas for government documents and the reference department together, or at least in immediate proximity.

The problem, once again, is "out of sight" and "out of mind." Because most key reference sources for government documents are not duplicated for placement at both the main reference desk and the documents desk, patrons are not exposed to these potential sources. Further, general reference librarians lose existing skills related to documents reference work, and so the reference interaction between the two areas is minimized. The converse of this problem occurs when important and "high-visibility" document reference sources are taken out of the documents depository area and placed either in the general stacks or in the main reference area. Their relocation limits the effectiveness with which patrons and staff in the depository collection can utilize government documents.

For depository collections that totally integrate all government publications into the general stacks and reference area, the physical problem of location is replaced by one of providing adequate bibliographic control. Physical integration and listing documents in the card catalog *does not* replace the need to use the various specialized reference tools and indexes produced by private publishers to gain access to government publications. Thus these tools must be physically integrated into the main reference area and utilized as an intermediary step to identify the necessary document.

When this occurs, a person would have to go to the card catalog to obtain a call number for that item.

Government publications can resolve a broad range of reference questions. By locating the depository collection next to the reference department, both areas can profit from the resources of the other; reference staff are easily accessible when referral is necessary, and patrons are not "bounced" back and forth between the two areas. Further, the depository collection may have a greater political impact because it can associate itself directly with the reference department, rather than be ignored or considered an entity unto itself.

Continuing Education

Competent staff that are knowledgeable about government publications and have professional attitudes about service are critical for improving the quality of reference services for government documents.[45] Such competency is likely to result from a *program* of education for the documents depository staff, as well as a program that develops learning opportunities for other library staff members.[46] The entire library staff must become knowledgeable about those aspects of government documents services which are appropriate for their particular position in the library.

Of some concern is the level of knowledge and formal training related to government publications that documents and reference staff currently possess. Results from this study suggest that (1) some staff at the documents reference desk have had little formal training or coursework related to documents, (2) a number of the depositories have either a part-time or no professional to oversee the operation of the depository collection, and (3) when proxies were referred to the main reference desk, reference librarians might have little knowledge about government documents.

Formal library school coursework and training in government documents are a minimum prerequisite for library staff at either the documents or reference desk. The notion that brief "on-the-job" experience can replace formal coursework is *not supported,* given the level of competencies identified in this study. Further, individuals who plan on administering a documents collection should incorporate a formal program of study in public administration, political science, American history, and information handling technologies. Intern programs in federal agencies, depository collections, or other institutions/agencies with significant collections and high-quality services also should be encouraged.

When continuing education programs encompass government publications, they often confine themselves to an introduction to basic resources and current developments affecting publishing programs. Continuing education needs of depository librarians must stress additional exposure to nondocument subject areas, such as

Automation of library processes
Administration and management
Collection development
Reference services and methods
Nonprint media
Interpersonal skills
Systems analysis.

Many staff members may require "training" in the documents field for topics such as

Online bibliographic and numeric data base searching of government
    documents
Collection organization
Gaining access to nondepository publications
Use of unique reference sources and basic government publications
Collection evaluation
Microforms
Cataloging, processing, and record keeping.

Formats and structure of continuing education opportunities would depend on the programs, the needs of the participants, costs, and other factors.

One value of unobtrusive testing is that it might identify a topic that merits greater attention than has been previously thought. Clearly, library schools have a role to play in improving the quality of documents librarianship. However, the role is often confined to formal degree programs (the master's and doctorate) or the provision of continuing education programs that will have the broadest appeal. Most of the concentrated attention of many accredited library schools falls on the master's program and preparation of students to enter the profession. In this regard, librarians hold diverse views concerning what library schools should try to accomplish. In some cases, they prefer additional course offerings devoted entirely to government publications (e.g., one for state publications), more coverage of source material in existing courses, more opportunities for a practicum, and practical understanding of the assorted routines and duties performed by documents librarians.

Professionals must be concerned about the major issues and trends that confront the field and demand that library education prepare students for the future and not for the past or even the present. The ability to think critically and to engage in problem solving should be more highly prized than technical competence. Yet little is known about the current status of documents education, librarians' expectations of it, or the feasibility of implementing their expectations.

Professionals should expect that those who teach documents librarianship, be they library educators or practitioners, be at the forefront of the field, actively participating in professional activities, publication, and research.[47] Nonetheless, the following points should be kept in mind in examining the present and potential role of library educators and schools in educating master's level students:

Teaching load

Importance of documents course in curriculum (assuming there *is* such a course)

Frequency with which the course is taught

Variations in quality of the teaching

Student and instructor expectations—course goals and objectives

Variations in teaching approach

What one course can be expected to accomplish

Number of course contact hours and length of class period

Number of documents courses offered (enrollment potential for more than one course may not justify assignment of a full-time faculty member)

Students' familiarity with topic

What one course can accomplish (how much information can students absorb and reasonably be taught)

Relationship of documents course to entire curriculum (e.g., pertinent insights might be derived from courses dealing with online data base searching, literature of the sciences, administration of libraries, collection development, and research methods)

Extent to which students should specialize

Role of library schools in providing *graduate-level,* professional education

Characteristics of job market.

Discussion of the role of library schools must take into account the full range of factors, and not "isolate" only a few. Obviously, master's level, professional education may not adequately prepare one for the first professional position. Although it provides a basis, one documents course in a master's degree in library science should not be regarded as the only education and training necessary for documents librarianship.

Library educators, students, and librarians must work together to provide the best theoretical and practical foundation possible within the limits of one degree program. At the same time, greater efforts should be undertaken to develop continuing education opportunities which concentrate on skills suggested earlier in this section. Such programs can be sponsored by individual libraries, library schools, library associations (local, state, regional, and national), and the GPO itself. The GPO has a clear obligation to ensure that the public, when searching for government information potentially available in depository collections, receives the highest and most professional service possible. When such programs are available, library staff should be encouraged to attend; perhaps attendance should be made mandatory, and credit given during the GPO inspection.

Clearly, however, significant improvement of reference services for government documents can be accomplished simply by increased education and training of the professionals who administer depository collections, by library staff participation in ongoing programs of graduate training that allow for specialization in appropriate areas related to documents, and by the host institution providing adequate numbers of trained reference staff to provide documents reference services. In addition, increasing awareness and training of other library-related constituencies regarding government publications is necessary.

Figure 14 is a contingency table that assists the planning of continuing education related to documents for specific constituencies. The column on the left suggests some types of constituencies likely to be found in a library, while the row across the top identifies typical skills or competencies which are potentially important for increasing the quality of reference services. The cells of the matrix can be completed by developing learning objectives appropriate for a specific constituency in a particular skill area. For instance, learning objectives related to the first category, "reference interview and search," might be appropriate for continuing education for the documents staff. Similar objectives, at a *different level,* might be appropriate for the reference staff; these skills may not be appropriate for "administrative" continuing education. On the other hand, such skills, from a *different perspective,* may be appropriate for users of the collection. In each instance the learning objectives are likely *to be different* for each group. In short, continuing education related to government documents must consider the following contingencies: (1) the constituencies appropriate for that library to be involved in such learning, (2) the appropriate skills or competencies, given the nature of the collection, its organization, and relationship with the library, and (3) the level of learning that needs to be accomplished for each constituency.

While everyone agrees that continuing education is important, appropriate education must be targeted to the required group at an appropriate level.

Thus the skills the documents library staff may need for reference interviewing and search techniques are likely to be more sophisticated than the skills required by the general reference staff. Therefore, the learning objectives must be modified for each group. Documents librarians must recognize the importance of targeting learning opportunities on key topics for specific audiences rather than holding or promoting general learning opportunities "for everyone."

Formats, types of workshops, and the vast array of possible occasions for obtaining continuing education opportunities have been covered elsewhere.[48] However, the documents librarian can orchestrate much of the "learning" by using in-house training sessions for other library staff members and library users. But to stay up to date on topics such as online data base searching, applications of microcomputers to depository collections, and how to conduct research and needs assessment, the documents library staff will need to attend outside workshops and seminars, as well as receive formal classroom instruction. Continuing education should not be seen as a "one-shot" attempt to improve one's skills; rather, it is an *ongoing program* of setting and accomplishing learning objectives by both the documents staff and other constituencies related to the depository collection. By using figure 14 as a guide, appropriate skills and constituencies can be identified as a basis for developing specific learning objectives in order to achieve appropriate levels of understanding.

Related to continuing education is the need for formally developed training sessions for all personnel who begin work in a depository collection. An excellent general outline for such staff training, geared toward paraprofessionals, has been reprinted in a recent book by Richard Boss.[49] New staff members in the depository collection should not be "dumped" into the collection without considerable training in the sources, manner in which that collection is organized, places and persons for referral, knowledge of how to operate the various viewing and reproductory equipment, and a host of other topics. Included in such training sessions for new employees are sessions related to attitudes and interpersonal skills, which can best be taught by example. A program of staff training for all new employees (documents paraprofessionals and nondocuments professionals), combined with a carefully planned program for continuing education, will greatly contribute to improved reference services for government documents.

Improving Referral Capabilities

The strategies delineated in this chapter can be applied to improving both the quality of service provided from the immediate collection as well as the ability of staff members to offer effective and efficient referral services.

SKILL/COMPETENCY AREA

	Knowledge of Documents Sources	Reference Interview and Search Skills	Interpersonal Skills and Attitudes	Documents Collection Development
CONSTITUENCY				
DOCUMENTS STAFF				
REFERENCE LIBRARIANS				
OTHER LIBRARIANS				
ADMINISTRATIVE STAFF				
USERS				

Explanation: In each cell specify learning objectives, level of competency required, and strategies to accomplish those objectives for each constituency.

Figure 14. Contingencies for Government Documents Continuing Education

SKILL/COMPETENCY AREA

Government Document Online Data Base Searching	Documents Planning and Decision Making	Use of Microform and other Equipment	Other Skills/Competencies

Documents collections held by depository institutions should not be viewed as able to meet all the present and potential demands placed upon them. Only 51 depository libraries have regional status and receive all GPO publications available for depository distribution; the overwhelming majority of depository libraries (over 1,300) are selective and decide what percentage they want to receive, which ranges from under 10 to over 90 percent. Further, a depository library, even a regional, is likely to need government publications issued by private publishers as well as clearinghouses and agencies other than the GPO. Given this situation and the extent of government publishing (see chapter 6), depository collections are not totally self-sufficient. Referral activity therefore is an integral part of reference service and demonstrates the interrelationship between depository libraries and other information providers.

Documents staff members need to recognize situations in which their clientele might benefit from referral activity. To aid in determination of these situations, it should be noted that referral takes place when

> Staff members do not know, or are unsure of, the answer
> Staff members suspect that the information they are disseminating is not completely correct or up to date
> Staff members do not know how to find the needed information in an efficient manner
> Staff members believe or find that the collection does not support the resolution of the information need; however, they believe that the information need can be resolved—the necessary information exists
> Patrons appear dissatisfied or disappointed with the information and service provided; they want information in addition to that provided by sources within the immediate collection.

Identification of these situations is not always easy. Further, for a variety of reasons, staff members might not always be willing to admit that referral (either to another member of the staff or library department, or external to the institution) is necessary. Clearly, the following list of research questions appears to deserve careful attention:

> What is referral and how can a referral be defined?
> Are there generalized "stages" or "components," common to the referral process?
> What institutional variables, if any, affect the frequency and accuracy of referrals?

What interpersonal and technical skills are required to provide "quality" referral services?

What factors encourage or discourage patrons from following up on a suggested referral?

What criteria can be identified as a basis of assessing the effectiveness and efficiency of referral services?

What factors determine the point during a reference interview when reference staff decide to refer a question rather than continue working on it or terminate the interview?

Other topics and areas for investigation can be identified. The sample questions are suggested only as an impetus to encourage research in the area of referral services. These studies should go beyond the use of unobtrusive methods and explore other ways for collecting data, including obtrusive testing of reference personnel as well as interviewing and surveying reference personnel and library clientele.

Until such research has been conducted, reference staff should be encouraged to look for weaknesses in the service they provide. In this regard, they might ask themselves such questions as the following:

Is there another member of the staff who is better at finding information on this topic? (In such cases, it might be helpful to discuss the question with that staff member and to expand one's ability to implement effective and efficient search strategies.)

How much time and effort are the client and the library staff willing to put into answering the question?

Is the information in the documents collection the most current and reliable? (Also, does the client need the most current and reliable information?)

What specific referral resources within the area, the state, and the nation can be drawn upon for assistance in obtaining government information, and what procedures must be followed to obtain information from those resources?

Staff members might identify the most appropriate referral site from among those depicted in figure 7 and encourage clientele to follow through on the referral suggestion(s). In order to identify possible referral sites, staff members should develop referral files, listing local information providers, the services provided, and the names and telephone numbers of key personnel. Depository libraries within a specific geographical area might work together to develop cooperative referral files. In addition, they might develop an extensive collection of directories so that, whenever necessary, referral could be extended to a state, regional, or national level.

It would be helpful to organize continuing education programs that focus on search strategies and the role of referral service. Reference personnel need to recognize the importance of such programs and be willing to attend. Since these programs relate to the quality of reference service provided and can attack the types of problems that this study has so dramatically documented, library administrators should be willing to pay registration and travel expenses so that at least one staff member can attend. This person could later brief the rest of the staff on the program.

Library staff members might also monitor the reference questions asked and use some of them to role-play referral options and strategies. They could even follow through on some of the suggestions and determine the strengths and weaknesses of various information providers. An interesting variation of this present study would be to develop a set of reference questions similar to those administered in this study and to test them on different information providers (e.g., GPO bookstores, Federal Information Centers, and depository libraries). In this way, the accuracy rate of 37 percent, discovered in this study, could be placed in a broader context—the quality of service offered by different, official providers of government information.

Regardless of the specific strategies and approaches to improve referral skills, it is critical that an attempt be made to improve both the frequency and the accuracy of referrals. The strength of government information sources lies more in the *system* (i.e., the collective formats, sources, and reference tools) than in the individual library. Effective reference services for government publications must rely upon the broad array of providers of government information. Individual reference librarians must learn how to exploit those providers, how to recognize that the patron's information need cannot be met by sources and/or information contained only in their particular library, how to assess their own ability to provide effective referral services, and how they can serve best as a "link" between the information needs of the patron and the government information sources, wherever their location.

Evaluation and Information for Decision Making

Depository librarians cannot be mere observers of organizational development and change; they must *participate* in assessing the factors that contribute to or limit the quality of reference services for government documents, design strategies to improve the quality of reference services, and implement those strategies effectively. But to accomplish these tasks, documents librarians must be able to evaluate the various factors affecting the quality of reference services and collect empirical information as a basis for decision making. As this study has shown, commonly held assumptions regarding the quality of documents depository reference services available in academic libraries, referrals, and the relationship between institutional variables and the quality of documents reference service, simply are inaccurate. Until these assumptions are evaluated and tested in an individual depository collection and library, a *rational* basis for change and improvement cannot be made.

Greater emphasis must be placed on *thinking* about what is currently happening in the documents department, the relationship of government documents to other areas of the library, and the effectiveness with which the depository collection meets library goals, GPO guidelines, and information needs of users. In this regard, the following questions might be considered:

> Does collecting greater percentages of depository material result in improved overall access to the collection?
>
> How accurate are the responses of reference librarians, documents librarians, and paraprofessional staff members regarding government documents?
>
> How can the depository collection best exploit library automation and integrate new technologies for improved user services?
>
> What can be considered "core collections" of government documents reference sources for various types of libraries?
>
> What are the information requirements of the collection's user community vis-à-vis government publications?
>
> What are the costs and benefits of obtaining duplicate copies of "key" government document reference sources for other areas of the library?

These are but a few topics that beg for evaluation and adequate information as a basis for rational decision making.

Assessment of a particular depository collection can utilize and modify (as needed) methodologies appropriate for other areas of the library. An excellent example of one approach to assessing the quality and type of reference service provided from a specific library has been reported by Paul Kantor;[50] a summary of key definitions related to libraries in general and reference in particular has been produced by the National Center for Higher Education Management Systems (NCHEMS);[51] summaries of library evaluation techniques which have appropriateness for documents collections have been provided by Lancaster[52] and by John Martyn and Lancaster;[53] and a useful summary of statistical skills and data-gathering techniques has recently been written by Charles Busha and Stephen Harter.[54] These are but a few of the many sources available to assist in the self-assessment and evaluation of the documents collection. Specific methods for evaluation and assessment related to depository collections can be obtained by examining some of the publications cited in table 1, which summarizes selected recent research and writings related to government publications.

An adequate basis for decision making implies the regular collection and maintenance of valid and reliable data related to the depository collection. Such data are critical if rational decisions are to be made, if the documents librarian is to make a case effectively for one decision as opposed to another, and if the decisions are to have credibility and include the justifications, views, and suggestions of the documents librarian. Broad areas where ongoing statistical information is necessary include:

> *Services:* use, quantity, description, quality
> *Collections:* availability, circulation, arrangement
> *Staff:* competency, activities, scheduling
> *Bibliographic control:* adequacy, techniques, weaknesses
> *Budget:* analysis of costs, cost-effectiveness ratios, benefits
> *Physical facilities and equipment:* use of floor space, costs and reliability of equipment, justification for new or replacement facilities
> *User community:* educational, social, and demographic characteristics.

These are given only to provide a general idea where data elements must be available for rational decision making. In short, library decision making must include data elements especially appropriate for depository collections. This is essential if the overall effectiveness of depositories is to be improved.

A number of recent publications have identified potential data elements appropriate for inclusion in a library management information system.[55] These sources can assist the documents librarian in identifying data elements appropriate for the depository and in developing data collection and analysis strategies by which such data can be utilized for decision making. Indeed, the planning model (and the appendixes of certain data-collection instruments) developed by Vernon Palmour for public library planning has great potential for application to depository collections.[56] More recently, a list of specific performance measures, produced by Douglas Zweizig and Eleanor Rodgers, can be modified for use in depository collections.[57]

Use of criteria suggested in *Guidelines for the Depository Library System* (see appendix D) or the depository inspection program may serve as a catalyst to identify appropriate data elements and potential performance measures. But currently, the GPO has provided no encouragement to depositories to engage in meaningful self-assessment, and its existing program of inspections does more harm than good by *de facto* acceptance of inadequate services, collections, and support in many depositories (see chapter 6). Depository librarians must strengthen their administrative skills, develop decision support systems to assist in the self-evaluation of depository collections, and develop a valid information base for rational decision making. They must also utilize planning, performance measures, and existing techniques from management information systems in order to improve the quality of documents reference services.

Cooperation and Resource Sharing

Paradoxically, the depository library *system* suggests a structure by which interdependent parts are united through common goals and objectives to accomplish a broad mission of providing access to information sources of the federal government. But the reality of that structure is more akin to separate entities that go about their daily chores with minimal shared objectives, minimal strategies for resource sharing, and minimal coordination of programs and activities. Although regional depository libraries have responsibilities for providing leadership and assistance to the selective depositories, few are able to assume such responsibilities fully.[58] Indeed, as this study has demonstrated, the regionals have little involvement (as do other selective depositories) in the referral of questions—to say nothing of other areas of cooperation and resource sharing.

Clearly, the relationship, responsibilities, and roles of the regional and selective depositories must be defined as a prerequisite for effective cooperation and resource sharing.[59] Selective depositories can no longer attempt to be all things for all patrons; they must be able to rely on a "backup" system for referral, obtaining specific documents through interlibrary loans, and receive training and advice on how to improve their effectiveness. Although much of the structure is in place to encourage cooperation and resource sharing, the rewards and support for engaging in such activities are not.

Specific areas where cooperation and resource sharing among the regionals and selective depositories are appropriate include:

Information and referral services, perhaps with certain depositories responsible for specific topics, or subject areas

Group training, continuing education, and joint sponsorship of workshops, seminars, etc.

Coordinated collection development strategies

Computer conferencing, utilizing traditional online data base vendors, or even utilizing the vendors' servicing microcomputers

Union lists of "key reference sources, periodicals, or special documents collections" unique to the various member depositories

Shared cataloging and bibliographic control, and development of archival tapes to produce computer-output microfilm (COM) catalogs for member depositories.

Obviously, the list can be extended. Additional areas for cooperation and resource sharing are limited only by one's imagination.

Currently, the depository library system is less a system and more a collection of separate entities, each attempting to utilize local resources so as best to accomplish an incredibly wide range of ill-defined objectives foisted on it by the federal government, the local institution, and the depository users. The depositories must begin to differentiate and share responsibilities within their various member-groups. They must also concentrate available resources to provide *quality* services in chosen areas of responsibilities and refer more services to other depositories. Further, they must develop structures that encourage and reward depositories for cooperating and sharing resources, rather than "going it alone." Little assistance, other than moral support, can be expected from the GPO in the immediate years ahead. Thus the responsibility for organizing, designing, and implementing cooperative and shared responsibilities among the depositories is likely to fall to individual depository libraries. But clearly, cooperation and resource sharing have great potential for the improvement of reference services for government documents.

Encouraging Change

This book has suggested that a primary factor contributing to the quality of documents reference services is the individual competency of the documents librarian. This finding suggests that improvement of documents reference services must rely on self-assessment and improvement by the individual. If change is to occur, such impetus must either come internally (self-directed by the documents reference librarian) or externally (from library administrators or outside governing boards).

Strategies for accomplishing changes to improve reference services have been suggested in this chapter. It was noted that two conceptual considerations affecting documents reference services should be analyzed before strategies are developed. The first was the process of integration and the second was identification of constraints affecting the dimensions of integration. Knowledge of these two considerations will assist the documents and reference staff in designing, implementing, and evaluating appropriate strategies to improve reference services.

The first broad area in which to develop strategies deals with factors directly related to the reference process itself. Here, the library staff must increase their knowledge of sources and types of publications available from the federal government, as well as exploit nontraditional reference sources such as online data base searching and microforms. Building skills in the reference interview process also is important, and a method to self-assess the interview techniques for both documents and reference librarians was described. Increasing search strategy skills for government document reference services is an integral component of the reference process. Although techniques will vary between the general reference and documents areas, the need to develop innovative search strategies and self-analysis, by use of the criteria suggested by Bates (see figures 12 and 13), will assist the library staff in resolving the information needs of users more effectively.

Increased attention to information and retrieval services is also needed. Academic librarians may wish to borrow from the strategies and ideas developed by public librarians to improve the referral process and, in more instances, provide specific information to patrons. Finally, it was noted that interpersonal skills and attitudes also play an important role in the quality of reference services. Given the fact that many patrons and general reference librarians are "afraid" of documents, staff members must present a positive attitude of being able to assist them, finding the appropriate material, and projecting an attitude of caring about the specific information need of the patron.

The other broad area of strategies for improving the quality of reference services for governmental documents relies on administrative factors. Administrative strategies will be most effective when the skills directly related to the reference process are of high quality. Developing policy statements and implementing a formal planning process that integrates documents and general library services is of primary importance. Further, documents staff members ought to become involved in library decision making and obtain a broad base of power within the organization. Bibliographic integration and the organizational and physical arrangement of the depository collection were discussed as potential factors affecting the quality of documents services. Recommendations were made to associate the depository collection with the reference department, if possible. The need for continuing education was noted and a matrix was suggested as a means of identifying which library-related constituencies require specific skills or competencies at specific levels of knowledge (see figure 14). Different skills are necessary for each of the constituencies, and thus a needs assessment will be necessary to determine which continuing education techniques will be appropriate to accomplish the learning objectives for each group.

Quality of documents reference services cannot be improved without

self-assessment, measurement, and maintenance of a management information system that organizes reliable and valid statistical information in support of decision making. The depository collection must be included in any
such library management systems, or must establish at least a rudimentary
system to support decision making. Specific areas for data elements and
performance measures were suggested. And last, exploitation of cooperative
and resource sharing techniques among regionals and selective depositories
was noted as having great potential to increase the quality of reference
services provided by depository libraries.

These reference and administrative-related factors comprise primary
areas where strategies can be developed to improve the quality of reference
service for government documents. Given the breadth of these areas, comprehensive review and presentation of all potential strategies is impossible.
However, documents librarians and other library staff can "pick and
choose" from these strategies and develop a formal long-range plan to
improve reference services by relying on the suggestions made throughout
this book. Clearly, the improvement of documents reference service is related to a number of factors; depending on the individual library situation,
special combinations of these strategies, or inclusion of other strategies, may
be appropriate.

The question that remains, however, is desire and a reward structure to
encourage change. Many documents librarians perceive the documents collection as "underutilized" and relegated to a place of nonimportance in the
library. Further, many depository collections, apparently, are administered
by less than full-time professionals—a number of whom apparently have
had no formal training in government documents.

Indeed, from some of the descriptions given by the proxies who administered the test questions, some of the documents library staff who assisted
them have the symptoms of professional "burnout"—"a syndrome characterized by certain physical symptoms and emotional conditions that affect
job performance."[60] Some symptoms identified by David Ferriero and
Kathleen Powers, in a recent article about "burnout" at the reference desk,
include:[61]

> *Exhaustion:* personal energy is depleted; it is hard enough coping with
> coming to work, let alone dealing with library users and other staff
> members
> *Attendance:* either sporadic attention to the job or working longer
> hours with perceived sense that "nothing is getting accomplished"
> *Inflexibility:* the unique problems of a user are dealt with by the
> "letter" of existing procedures; making individual decisions
> becomes very threatening; personal judgment is replaced with rigid
> following of procedures

Feedback: lack of positive feedback from other library staff; a sense of being alone, without recognition for one's work

Expectations: the librarian feels that he or she is not measuring up to high personal standards; dissillusionment and frustration set in; a feeling of being "out of control" in the situation; and conflicting demands between user and institution make the librarian feel "caught in the middle"

Awareness: disparity between the burnt-out librarian's perceptions and those of others; the librarian may not recognize the cumulative effect of the symptoms, and feels worse because he or she "can't cope."

While all these symptoms could not be identified during the course of conducting this unobtrusive study, a number of proxies commented on behaviors and attitudes of documents staff members which, one might speculate, appear to be very similar to the symptoms described above.

A number of strategies can be implemented to deal with burnout:[62]

Recognize the symptoms.

Examine the function of your staff meetings.

Take a hard look at working conditions.

Examine and understand the psychological environment in which you work.

Foster a sense of teamwork among the staff.

Work toward an ongoing system of evaluation.

Attend and participate in workshops, conferences, etc., as a means of "recharging one's batteries."

Use physical exercise as a means of working out tension accumulated on the job.

Reduce the user-to-librarian ratio.

Shorten the work hours spent with the public.

Make certain you are not making the library your life.

Share the reference responsibilities.

Recognize impossible job demands and time constraints.

If professional burnout is a factor affecting documents and reference librarians, the above suggestions may be useful to deal with the situation as a means of improving the quality of reference services. But should no individual attempt be made to improve reference services or deal with personnel problems, such as burnout or incompetent staff, external strategies may be called for to encourage change in depository collections that provide inadequate reference services for government documents.

Such external encouragement could take a number of forms. One possibility is development of some form of certification process whereby libraries must show evidence of meeting specific criteria, and the person who is directly responsible for the depository collection must meet specific *performance-related* criteria in order to direct the collection. Although certification has been an ongoing issue for information professionals, the situation regarding certification of government documents librarians has unique factors that encourage such a process.

The primary factor is involvement of the federal government in the depository library operation. Given the cost-cutting climate in Washington, D.C., and the likely ongoing effort to improve the "effectiveness" of government operations, the costs and subsidies for maintenance of the depository library system will surely come under review. Because the effectiveness of the depository library program rests largely on the individual competencies of documents librarians and the degree to which documents are integrated into the library as a whole, librarians with depository responsibilities may find themselves facing a certification process to maintain (or obtain) professional depository positions.

Such certification might be one method to "encourage" librarians to improve reference skills and administrative conditions, discussed in this chapter. Further, given the impotence of the depository inspection program to promote meaningful change, ongoing certification and renewal would provide a means by which continuing education, maintenance and expansion of skills, and greater control over the depository program by a certification agency could be obtained. A key question, however, is who or what would determine the requirements, criteria, and procedures for such certification, and who or what would administer the process?

Regardless of the impetus for change—internal and self-directed by librarians or externally directed by the GPO, a certification agency, or a professional association—the future of reference services for government documents in academic depository libraries is unclear. As this study has demonstrated, the quality of reference services in some academic depository libraries simply is unacceptable and is contributing to what others have referred to as "the impending crisis in government publications reference service."[63] Only time will tell if the profession, through individual documents librarians and reference staff, will take responsibility for improving the quality of reference services for government documents—or if external organizations or agencies will force changes to take place by control devices such as certification. Implementation of the strategies suggested in this chapter will assist librarians who want to improve the quality of documents reference services while, at the same time, demonstrating the profession's concern—and priority—for increasing access to government information.

6

Reference Services and the Depository Library System

Previous chapters have reported on the unobtrusive testing of staff members from academic depository libraries and have shown that these staff members frequently are unsuccessful in (1) meeting user requests for factual data and bibliographic citations, (2) providing referral services, and (3) utilizing innovative interview and search strategies. Given the preoccupation of many documents librarians with improving bibliographic inputs for the depository system (e.g., enhancing the value of the *Monthly Catalog* as a tool for bibliographic control over government publishing, improving the utility of OCLC and the accuracy of unit records for government publications contained in that data base, and encouraging the complete identification of government publishing programs),[1] this book has called attention to another area: reference service and the outcomes of requests for information from depository libraries. Extensive and well-organized collections of government publications are ineffective if staff members are unable to utilize fully the resources in their collections.

Although some documents librarians, including those at the institutions tested, might attempt to argue that *their* staffs provide high-quality reference service, this study shows that accurate reference service is not always provided and that instances in which incomplete and inferior service occur must be identified and resolved. This is all the more necessary since, beginning in 1982, the GPO implemented a marketing program designed to alert the general public that the depository library program exists and can resolve the public's information needs. If this marketing program is successful and generates increased awareness of depository collections, what are the implications when the public *does* consult staff members at these institutions, but encounters service such as that experienced in this study? In this regard, it should be noted that all but three of the test questions (1, 11, and 12) could have been answered from titles listed in appendix A of *Guidelines for the*

Depository Library System, as constituting "a basic collection," one that should be common to all depository libraries.[2] If many documents staff members are not fully aware of the potential for even these basic titles, what is the quality of the service for questions that require other, more complicated titles, microfiche, or bibliographic data base searching?

The remaining part of this chapter discusses themes previously identified and focuses on their implications with the following topics: the number of publications entering the depository library program, the importance of performance measures, *Guidelines for the Depository Library System,* the inspection program, state plans, cost-effectiveness of the depository library program, and the depository program as an interlocking network. After making specific recommendations, the chapter concludes with a discussion of issues relating to the management of the depository library program.

Number of Publications Entering the System

At present, the Reagan administration, which regards information as a priced commodity, is attempting to curtail government expenditures and the size of publishing programs. In fact, it has placed a moratorium on initiation of new periodicals, pamphlets, and audiovisual products. The Office of Management and Budget then directed the executive agencies to review all existing periodicals, pamphlets, and audiovisual products, as well as those planned for fiscal years 1981 and 1982, so that those that are duplicative and wasteful can be identified and eliminated.[3] As a consequence of fiscal constraints, agencies are reducing or eliminating the free distribution of documents and are cooperating in bibliographic control and the distribution of government publications. Congress is also reexamining programs, slashing budgets, and trying to control "unnecessary" publication. As a consequence of these governmental actions, some excellent and important publications (e.g., *Selected U.S. Government Publications* and *Statistical Reporter*) have been discontinued, while the cost of the *Federal Register* has increased from $75 to $300. To minimize the amount of duplication in congressional hearings, the GPO, in cooperation with the Joint Committee on Printing, is trying to detect previously published material and to advise congressional committees against republication.[4]

Viewed against this political and economic background, the findings of this study raise serious questions about the effectiveness of a program intended to provide the citizenry with access to published government information. For example, has the depository library program grown too large to be effective and efficient? And are many libraries receiving more titles than they can integrate, physically as well as intellectually?

Table 21 shows the number of titles shipped each year to depository libraries. From 1979 through 1981, almost 181,000 separate titles entered the depository system—which far exceeds the American book publication trade for the same period. Further, the table indicates that microfiche has become the preferred format for depository distribution. During 1981, more than 27,000 titles were converted to microfiche. "This represented a 14½ percent increase over titles converted and distributed to depository libraries during the previous year."[5] Even libraries that selected a minimum of 25 percent of the available item numbers would have received a substantial number of titles. Clearly, public access must be assessed in terms other than number of depository libraries, number of titles eligible for selection in a given year, efficiency of the GPO in distributing depository publications, and the efficiency of individual libraries in placing source material into their collections. Instead of emphasizing only collections, adequate attention must be given to reference service and staff performance.

Importance of Performance Measures

No existing criteria have been developed to determine the effectiveness and efficiency of the depository program. Thus any analysis of the depository program must take into account the need for clear criteria to determine its effectiveness and efficiency (see figure 15). Poorly constructed and non-measurable objectives, such as those in *Guidelines for the Depository Library System,* exacerbate the problem.

A "measure" is a means with which to quantify an object or process in accordance with a rule or procedure that can be used consistently. Without measures, especially those covering performance (see figure 16 for examples of areas for which performance measures can be applied), no valid basis exists to change or restructure a process. Development of such measures calls for concentrated research. Further,

> whether we can measure something depends, not on that thing, but on how we have conceptualized it, on our knowledge of it, above all on the skill and ingenuity which we can bring to bear on the process of measurement.[6]

Regardless of perceived difficulties related to establishing performance measures for the depository program, such measures are critically needed.

Performance measures are quantitative indicators of a system's ability to accomplish objectives and respond to the needs of individuals who use the system. They provide a basis upon which to evaluate the system and its components and to develop an ongoing planning process to improve the

TABLE 21. Number of Titles Distributed to Depository Libraries

Year	Paper	Microfiche	Total
1979	43,705	14,028	57,733
1980	43,379	23,438	66,817
1981	29,152*	27,240	56,392
1982	15,866	27,974	43,840

*Congressional bills were converted to microfiche

Efficiency: How well are we using the resources we
               have?

   For example,

      What is the average use of the depository col-
      lection per staff member?

      How much of the budget goes for materials?

      How many of the depository publications are
      actually used and how often are they used?

Effectiveness: How well are we doing what we say
                  we are doing?

   For example,

      How many documents that users want can they
      find?

      What percentage of the depository collection
      meets institutional goals and user information
      needs?

      What degree of duplication and uniqueness can
      be identified between reference materials in
      the documents area and other areas of the
      library?

Only representative examples are provided. Numerous
other examples can be developed depending on the
nature of each collection and library.

Figure 15.   Dimensions of Performance Measures

system (see figure 17). Research into the development of performance measures for the depository library program is nonexistent, but despite the
dearth of information about how to evaluate the program, there has been
no shortage of suggestions for how it can be changed or modified.

   Systems thinking provides a powerful basis by which one can develop
performance criteria for the depository library program. Figure 18 presents
a summary of nine open-system characteristics, their definitions, and potential areas for performance measures applicable to the depository program.
This listing of possible areas for performance measures is only cursory;

Community Penetration

Designed to measure the extent to which members
of the community are aware of the library services
available and how much use they make of these
services.

Example: Users as a percentage of the
population

User Services

These measures relate to user behavior: requesting
materials, asking questions, and checking out
materials.

Example: Title fill rate*
Attendance at programs per target
audience

Resource Management

Designed to reflect internal management decisions
about how funds are allocated, e.g., choices made
regarding materials, facilities, and staff.

Example: Collection turnover rate
Library square footage per capita

Administration and Finance

These measures reflect the decisions made by the
library director. It is recognized that some of
these measures may not be controlled directly by
the director.

Example: Per capita support
Local library funds as a percentage
of total

---

*See Douglas Zweizig and Eleanor J. Rodger, *Output
Measures for Public Libraries* (Chicago: ALA, 1982).

Figure 16.   Areas in Which Library Performance Measures Can Be Applied

Typically, each performance measure emphasizes one facet only.

An assessment of a library service or operation must be made in light of the library's objectives as well as its performance on other measures.

There are no "right" or "wrong" scores on the performance measures; the local library, the regional depository, and/or the Government Printing Office/Joint Committee on Printing set "adequacy."

A primary use of the performance measures is to identify areas where change is desired, and, by continued use of the measure over time, determine if change has, in fact, been accomplished.

Conditions can be manipulated to improve the performance on a particular measure without always improving the quality of the service or the operation, e.g., increase materials turnover rate simply by heavily weeding the collection.

By carefully defining the performance measures and the data elements necessary for each measure, libraries may be able to compare their performance to other similar libraries.

Performance measures should suggest now only what is happening but also be able to assess how good it is.

Figure 17. Potential Impact from Performance Measures

additional measures can be suggested for all of the characteristics identified. As the figure indicates, performance measures for the depository program can be developed. In fact, a number of other areas in library and information science have progressed significantly in developing such performance measures: public library services by Ernest DeProspo[7] and Alvin Schrader,[8] evaluation of information systems and services by Lancaster[9] and Colin Mick,[10] and networking by William and Sandra Rouse[11] and J. G. Williams[12] (to name but a few).

Open-systems characteristics are especially important in evaluating the depository library program because they suggest not only areas for performance measures but structures that will enable the program to better

OPEN SYSTEM CHARACTERISTIC	AREAS FOR PERFORMANCE MEASURES
1. Importation of energy—a system functions by importing energy (information, products, materials, etc.) from the larger environment.	Resource Allocation Techniques Relationship between Resources and Goals
2. Throughput—systems move energy through them, largely in the form of transformation processes. These are often multiple processes (decisions, material manipulation, etc.)	Efficiency of processes Decision Analysis Cost/Benefit of Alternatives
3. Output—systems send energy back to the larger environment in the form of products, services, and other kinds of outputs that may be intended or not.	Accomplishment of Objectives Impact of outputs on Environment Appropriateness of Outputs
4. Cycles of events over time—systems function over time and thus are dynamic in nature. Events tend to occur in natural repetitive cycles of input, throughput, and output with events in sequence occuring repeatedly.	Trend data of outputs Flowcharting Degree of Programmed Decision Making
5. Equilibrium seeking—systems tend to move toward the state where all components are in equilibrium, where a steady state exists. When changes are made that result in an imbalance, different components of the system move to restore the balance.	Impact of component on System at large Comparisons among system components

their output to regulate their input and transformation processes. These informational connections also exist between system components, and thus changes in the functioning of one component lead to changes in other system components (second-order effects).	and Formative Evaluation System Change over Time Self-Assessment Methods
7. Increasing differentiation—as systems grow, they also tend to increase their differentiation; more components are added, with more feedback loops and more transformation processes. Thus as systems get larger, they also get more complex	Political relationships among System Components Cooperation/Coordination among system components
8. Equifinality—different system configurations may lead to the same end point, or conversely, the same end and state may be reached by a variety of different processes.	Ability of match individual strength to system requirements Comparisons with Depository Competitors
9. System survival requirements—because of the inherent tendency of systems to "run down" or dissipate their energy, certain functions must be performed (at least at minimal levels) over time. These requirements include: (a) goal achievement and (b) adaptation (the ability to maintain balanced successful transactions with the environment).	Interaction with governing board/institutions Response to Environmental demands Ability to identify and obtain new resources

*From Edward Lawler III et al., Organizational Assessment (New York: Wiley, 1980), p. 267.

Figure 18. Depository Evaluation Criteria from Open-System Characteristics

achieve its objectives as a system. Still, evaluation of the depository system based on open-system characteristics contains certain assumptions: first, the system is comprised of interdependent parts, each of which has an effect on the other parts; second, the sum of the parts is more than the whole—there is an intangible "essence" of the system that results from the interaction of these parts; and third, system components respond to the environment on a logical and orderly basis—although we may not know what that basis is.[13] Although systems thinking has been present for quite some time, its use as a conceptual basis for formal evaluation of the depository library program appears not to have been explored.

In answer to the question, On what basis can performance measures be selected to evaluate the depository program as a system? figure 19 is suggested. The specific criteria (appropriateness, informativeness, validity, reproducibility, comparability, practicality, and input for decision making), which suggest what one can expect from the measures, can assist researchers in analyzing a list of candidate measures and can identify those measures that appear to have the greatest potential to evaluate accurately the current operations of the depository system.

By combining figures 17 and 18, an important first step can be made in developing meaningful performance measures for the depository library system. Until such measures are developed, depository librarians cannot know the specific levels of performance that they are expected to fulfill, the GPO cannot enforce regulations and guidelines realistically, researchers cannot meaningfully evaluate the overall success of the system, and inspection of the depository libraries cannot serve as a catalyst to improve the overall effectiveness of the system or access to information in that system.

Guidelines for the System

Although this book emphasizes the quality of reference service, it should be recognized that the various factors suggested in the *Guidelines* (see appendix D) combine to impact upon that quality. Each factor therefore cannot be viewed in isolation. The GPO must now determine its specific responsibilities relating to public access and take steps to ensure the effectiveness of the depository operation. Next, it must decide upon the strategies to accomplish these responsibilities. The first step in this process, however, is to review basic documentation (the *Guidelines,* inspection report, etc.) and make sure that they accomplish their intended purpose.

This study has shown that library users may not be able to predict the quality of response they will receive from a given depository library to their questions and that significant variations occur on an institutional basis. No library delivered the correct answers all the time, while a few of the libraries

Appropriateness: Will it do what I want it to do?
   e.g., "Is it possible to compare the measure
      across depository libraries?"

Informativeness: Will it tell me what I need to know?
   e.g., "Will comparing depository libraries of
      similar size on circulation per capita show
      which libraries need assistance?"

Validity: Does it mean what I think it means?
   e.g., "Is percent of library budget allocated
      to the documents department a measure of
      library effectiveness or departmental
      effectiveness?"

Reproducibility: Would someone else get the same
                 answer?
   e.g., "Would two depository librarians reporting
      on the same library come up with the same
      score for per capita use of depository
      materials?"

Comparability: Are we all measuring the same thing?
   e.g., "Do depository libraries in Oklahoma use
      the same procedures and definitions to
      count circulation as those in California?"

Practicality: Can we afford the time, money, and
              effort to gather data for this measure?
   e.g., "Is the information gained from the data
      worth the effort required to determine it?"

Input for Decision Making: Will it provide data to
                           assist decision makers?
   e.g., "Is the information likely to identify spe-
      cific services or operations that can be
      improved and suggest strategies for their
      improvement?"

Adapted from R. H. Orr, "Measuring the Goodness of
 Library Services: A General Framework for Considering Quantitative Measures," *Journal of Documentation,* 29 (September 1973): 315-332.

Figure 19. Criteria for Selecting Measures

could not even answer one of the questions correctly. These findings, combined with the infrequent number of referrals, suggest that the *Guidelines* must be revised so that the quality of reference service becomes a central concern for the successful operation of the depository library system.

A most important beginning point in reformulating the *Guidelines* should be to analyze the goals and objectives of the depository library program. A critical problem is that the *Guidelines* do not differentiate between goals and objectives. Goals are long-range guidelines or aspirations which chart those general areas of high priority. Objectives, on the other hand, are short-term statements which operationally attempt to fulfill goals; they are therefore accomplishable and measurable statements that describe specific activities to be done during a given time period.[14]

Goals can usually be equated with explanations of purpose. The *Guidelines,* therefore, state that the goal is making "U.S. Government publications easily accessible to the general public" and ensuring "their continued availability in the future." Two other statements explain that availability will be achieved through the depository library program and that "the *Guidelines* are to be considered [as a] recommended level of conduct by all depositories." Unfortunately, this goal of public access is mistakenly labeled as an objective. In reality, this document does not contain objectives; it skips from the goal statement to specific points around which objectives could be developed.

The library staff members who were tested accepted requests from the general public (the proxies) and provided reference assistance. In this regard, they might be considered "in compliance" with the *Guidelines.* Consequently, the issue becomes the *quality* of service provided and the willingness and competency of staff members to engage in referral. The depository library program, as reflected in the *Guidelines,* states a goal of public access but does not offer specific objectives to achieve it. Basing an inspection program upon these *Guidelines,* which are treated as principles that carry the weight of administrative law, is inappropriate. The GPO, the JCP, and the Depository Library Council to the Public Printer must give serious and immediate consideration to revising the basic documentation upon which the program operates.

Currently, any method to determine the effectiveness of the depository program will be limited because there are no objectives upon which to judge the program's effectiveness. The *Guidelines* and the "Minimum Standards" are so broad and ill defined that they can be interpreted to fit a host of different situations; and statements so open to many interpretations are meaningless.

Neither the *Guidelines* nor the accompanying "Minimum Standards for the Depository Library System" define terms or assign quantitative levels of performance. Further, they assume that what is "good" for one depository library is "good" for all other libraries in the program.[15] They also fail to recognize situations and constraints unique to individual depositories. One section of the *Guidelines,* labeled "Service to the General Public," has most relevance to this book; it notes that (except for the highest appellate court libraries) depository libraries should make their "depository publications available for the free use of the general public." These libraries should also "provide to all users reference assistance with regard to depository publications." In addition, library clientele should expect to receive "answers to reference questions or a referral to a source or place where answers can be found." The "Minimum Standards for the Depository Library System," which reinforces these points, notes that "each depository library will assign sufficient staff to select, organize and provide reference service to the collection." But key terms such as "sufficient staff" or "reference service" are neither defined nor placed in the context of goals and objectives.

With the exception of the highest appellate court libraries, all libraries are required to make depository publications available for the use of the public. This applies whether the library was designated by law or a member of Congress. Academic depository libraries may not forbid anyone from gaining access to the depository materials housed in their collections. One study, exploring public access to depository collections, discovered instances where the public was not admitted to the depository collection; the depository materials were held for the exclusive use of academic clientele.[16] The present study found similar instances where the proxies were not admitted to the depository collection because they were not enrolled at that institution. Only after intervention by the authors (in such a way as not to bias data collection) were the proxies granted special permission to use the collections. Contrary to the *Guidelines* and the inspection program, some libraries *do* inhibit use of depository collections, limit the effectiveness of reference service, and minimize the extent to which library personnel are familiar with resources in the collection. Additional unobtrusive testing could identify specific problems the general public might experience in trying to gain access to the depository collections of some academic institutions.

Although it is beyond the scope of this book, it might be helpful to note briefly some other problems with the *Guidelines.* There is a lack of (1) reference to effective interaction between depository collections and the rest of the library and (2) precise delineation of responsibilities for regional depositories in terms of duties, support, and encouragement. Further, it is assumed that 25 percent should comprise a minimal level of selection (actually, 40% of the depositories take less than the recommended percentage)[17] and that the core titles depicted in appendix A of the *Guidelines* should be common to all collections. *Historical Statistics of the United States,* for example, may be unnecessary for certain federal and law school depository libraries. The emphasis of the *Guidelines* is on resources and inputs rather than outputs—performance and services. The most important weakness, however, relates to the previous discussion of goals and objectives and to the fact that the *Guidelines* are based upon a "general consensus" of opinion rather than research.

Inspection Program

The inspection program, which has been critiqued elsewhere,[18] does not operate within clearly defined and identifiable objectives. It attempts to implement the *Guidelines* but is hindered by the lack of adequate goals and objectives for the depository library program. Further, individual inspectors have great latitude in their interpretation of individual questions, have differing experiences and competencies, and can grant libraries additional points as they see fit. Since subjectivity enters the scoring, it is not likely that outside evaluators would assign identical scores. In addition,

> All topical areas covered in the report are given equal weight, a practice that can be questioned.
>
> Terms are not adequately defined.
>
> The appropriateness of certain questions and category options provided is questionable.
>
> Category intervals for specific questions are generally unequal and therefore complicate statistical analysis.
>
> Comparisons among depository collections are not valid.
>
> The emphasis is on resource inputs.
>
> Questions are reworked and are not comparable over time; questions may not be useful for ongoing trend data, and this limits their usefulness for the decision-making process.

Section 6 of the inspection report, "Service to the General Public," would have greater validity if the questions were tied to a means of ongoing evaluation (see appendix E for a copy of the entire inspection form). Figure 20 lists the seven questions in this section of the "Inspection Visit Form" and raises fundamental questions about each of them. In spite of the weaknesses outlined here, the depository inspection program is proceeding as if the *Guidelines* and the inspection form did not contain major weaknesses.

More discussion must center on the need for the inspection program to establish performance measures and to improve the quality of reference, as well as other service provided. Some librarians might question how much weight should be accorded to testing the ability of staff members to answer a set of predetermined questions. A more important issue, however, centers on the purpose for which the data derived from the testing might be used. Would they be used for placing libraries on probation, excluding them from the program, administering a "certification program" (see chapter 5), or merely for encouragement of self-improvement and involvement in continuing education programs? A further issue relates to the method by which testing would be accomplished. It might be performed obtrusively, with staff awareness of the testing procedure, or unobtrusively, as was done in this study. However, valid unobtrusive testing would be difficult to conduct because it would substantially increase the cost of the inspection program and because depository staff members would come to anticipate testing at the time of the inspection.

Given these concerns, it might be more feasible for the GPO to support further research on the accuracy and quality of reference service by depository staff members. If additional research substantiates the findings of this study and investigations in the general reference field, the GPO should provide incentives for staff members to take part in continuing education programs. The GPO, perhaps through the regional depositories, could establish workshops devoted to reference service or could, independently of the regional depositories, encourage the Government Documents Round Table (GODORT) of the American Library Association and the accredited library schools to become more involved in improving the quality of reference service. Some of these training sessions might be made mandatory for staff members, and ample credit given on the inspection report for those who participated in such training sessions. The inspectors might also examine the nature and extent of the training programs that libraries initiate for paraprofessional personnel who handle public service positions for government publications.

Enhancing the quality of reference service will require a formal, extensive commitment by both the GPO and depository library staff. The cost of the depository library program to both the government and individual libraries might increase, but rewards in terms of increased access to government information will be far greater.

State Plans

The importance of planning can only be recognized in the context of a meaningful definition of planning. For the purposes of this chapter, planning is the process of identifying goals and objectives of the system, developing programs or services to accomplish these goals and objectives, and

VI. SERVICE TO THE GENERAL PUBLIC

A. The depository makes available for free use in the library by the general public all Government publications.

 ____(1) yes. ____(2) no.

> **Observations and Analysis**
>
> How can we tell if the response is indeed accurate?
> How is "free use" defined?
> The term "all Government publications" is too broad; it should refer only to the depository collection

B. For reference-type questions about Government publications, the depository library maintains reference stations.

 ____(1) one. ____(2) more than one. ____(3) none.

> **Observations and Analysis**
>
> The question should specify only depository publications
> A general question such as this should be followed up with indications of quality; the number of stations should not be equated with quality

C. In the library at one or more points of inquiry, it is possible for a user to find:

 ____(1) resources in the Federal documents collection including specific titles.
 ____(2) location of wanted publications.
 ____(3) answers to reference questions or referral to a source or place where answers can be found.

Figure 20. Analysis of Section from "Inspection Visit Form"

_____(4) guidance on the use of the collection, including the principal available reference sources/catalogs/abstracts/indexes/aids.

_____(5) availability of additional resources in the region.

_____(6) assistance in borrowing documents from a Regional or from other libraries.

_____(7) user privileges extended to all patrons.

Observations and Analysis

On the basis of this study, the validity of responses in the affirmative might be questionable
Differences among bibliographic identification, physical availability, borrowing, and copying (especially of microfiche) should be taken into account

---

D. The policy to circulate or not to circulate depository materials outside of the library is chiefly determined by

_____(1) the depository staff.
_____(2) the depository staff and administration.
_____(3) the administration alone.
_____(4) the professional staff as a whole.
_____(5) the circulation department.
_____(6) another department (_____).

Observations and Analysis

What is the significance of this question?
Are all types of depository materials available for circulation?
How can adequate access be provided to users without circulation?

Figure 20. (Continued)

E. The library provides facilities for

_____ (1) using depository documents.
_____ (2) making copies from documents.
_____ (3) reading microforms.
_____ (4) making copies from microforms.

Observations and Analysis

Look at the number and quality of the facilities
Are the facilities in working condition?
What is the definition of "facilities"?
Should the focus be on the broad term "microforms" or the narrower "microfiche," after all the GPO distributes in microfiche format? If the question gets at distribution by the private sector, this should be so noted and addressed.

F. The depository collection is publicized through

_____ (1) displays.
_____ (2) announcements or titles/bibliographies.
_____ (3) orientations/tours, classes.
_____ (4) radio/television/other means.

Observations and Analysis

"Other means" should not be grouped with radio/television
There should be an opportunity to specify "other means"
Why focus on these specific methods; are they presumed to be effective? (the questions should be tied to an objective and ongoing methods of evaluation)

G. Reference-type assistance with regard to depository publications is available to

Figure 20. (Continued)

___(1) all who request it.
___(2) the institution's members only.
___(4) no one at present.

```
┌─────────────────────────────────────────────┐
│           Observations and Analysis          │
│                                              │
│ Are both telephone and in-person questions   │
│ accepted (should both types be accepted)?    │
│ Is service really offered to "all who        │
│ request it"?                                 │
│ The question does not get at the quality     │
│ of the assistance                            │
│ Is the answer to this question based on      │
│ what documents librarians say, and if so,    │
│ is this "valid"?                             │
└─────────────────────────────────────────────┘
```

Figure 20. (Continued)

evaluating the success of those programs vis-à-vis the stated objectives.[19] The primary emphasis of planning is on effectiveness: the ability of the system to accomplish its goals and objectives. However, efficiency, or accomplishment of a task with as few resources as possible, is also addressed. Both questions, Are we doing things which need to be done? (effectiveness) and How well are we doing them? (efficiency), must be addressed.[20]

The Depository Council to the Public Printer has endorsed the development of state plans in which depository libraries delineate their responsibilities and address the following points:[21]

Collections
Service
Bibliographic access (depositories must know what the others collect)
Communication among state-plan participants
Financial responsibility
Goals
Review and evaluation mechanism
Signed agreement among participants
Approval by state library agency or other designated body
Other considerations (e.g., staff training and publicity).

Presumably, areas such as technology and equipment have been placed under "other considerations," an area denoting lesser importance. The listing, which does not identify the range of appropriate categories for each area, assumes that all of the areas are of equal concern to every depository library. Once a state plan has been implemented, it assumes a formal, ongoing evaluation process—better than the existing inspection program—for determining the degree to which each objective has been achieved.

Recognizing the value of better coordination of the depository program in individual states, the GPO has encouraged states in need of such plans to undertake them. Ironically, the GPO does not believe that it can require states to engage in planning. State planning is proceeding in spite of the fact that (1) the depository library program lacks formal objectives to which specific activities can be tied and (2) many academic depository libraries have not formulated written collection development policies covering their own institutions.[22] Further, the depositories are called upon to plan on an inter-institutional basis. In fact, there is even discussion of taking common features from the various state plans and merging them into a national information policy that covers federal government publications!

At present, drafts of two state plans are in existence; however, they differ significantly in approach, conceptualization, and detail. Figure 21 reprints relevant sections from each plan and shows the substantial variation between them. Both plans would benefit from methods of ongoing evaluation, the drafting of measurable objectives, and a determination of how well individual points have been met. Plan A emphasizes specific responsibilities of depository libraries within the state, while the other plan takes a larger perspective and attempts to make the *Guidelines* operational. However, Plan B assumes that the depository library program has articulated formal goals and objectives and that the *Guidelines* provide a sufficient definition of key terms. As already shown, such assumptions are incorrect.

The authors encourage planning; in fact, planning can no longer be considered a luxury. The overall importance of planning is suggested by these benefits, in which planning

provides a rational response to uncertainty and challenge
focuses attention on goals and objectives
establishes priorities for resource allocation
determines organizational, departmental, program, and individual accountability
facilitates control of organizational activities by collecting information to evaluate those activities
disseminates information to the GPO about intended depository activities and thus coordinates individual depository activities with other institutional and systemwide activities
forces informational input into the organization from the clientele,

and the environment at large, as a basis for improved decision making
orients the organization to identify opportunities in the future rather than continually responding to daily problems.

During the next decade, survival and improvement of depository collections and the system at large will depend in no small part on librarians' ability to recognize these benefits from formalized planning and clearly demonstrate their effectiveness to the immediate institutions, the government (the GPO and the Joint Committee on Printing), and society at large.

The usefulness of state plans for depository librarians, as well as advocacy of those plans by the GPO and the Depository Library Council, is of some concern. While thirty-five states, as of summer 1982, have designated "contact persons" to assist in the development of such plans, specific expertise, resources, guidelines, and tangible support have not as yet appeared to assist in the process. Given the inadequacy of the existing *Guidelines,* the need for performance measures, other problems noted in this volume, and the amount of research necessary *before* meaningful state plans can be developed, one cannot be optimistic as to the likelihood of success from such efforts. As LeRoy Schwarzkopf has pointed out, "Instead of alleviating problems for regionals—or helping them—the Council has ended up by piling more work on regional depositories."[23]

One lesson which is clear for those who wish to embark upon the planning process is to identify the reasons why the organization intends to plan. The following is a partial list of possible reasons for planning:

Establish library and system goals and objectives
Serve political justifications of the larger institution
Prove/disprove the value of the library or a specific program
Provide a place for staff
Improve library services
Justify the need for increased financial support
Evaluate the performance of library staff members.

Each of these has its own set of assumptions and its own procedures, and, perhaps most importantly, encourages a unique set of expectations from the library staff, administration, government agencies overseeing the depository program, and the community as to likely outcomes from the planning process.[24]

Before planning begins, all the constituencies involved in the planning process must know clearly the purpose for planning, the expected outcomes, and the role of each individual throughout the planning process. A constant criticism of library planning is that, after completion of its first cycle,

---
Plan A

The following depository libraries agree to provide
interlibrary loan and reference services to all
libraries . . .

The . . . State Library, the Documents Committee of
the . . . Library Association, and other documents
librarians have participated in a variety of training opportunities in the state. The following libraries agree to give special attention to this
activity . . .

Plan B

To assure that a high quality of service to the public is offered by every depository library in the
state, there should be adequate provision of funding,
staffing, and continuing education for depository
library personnel

To increase the value and visibility of the depository program, depository libraries should develop
information programs and materials that will increase the public's knowledge of the documents and
services available through the program

Patron should expect documents reference to be
available at all hours that the Depository Library's
usual reference service is available
   a. All reference librarians should be knowledge-
      able of the documents collection
   b. Provide appropriate reference tools to access
      the depository's documents collection
   c. Equal reference service to all users of
      depository collections
   d. Depository should aid non-depository libraries
      in the locale by providing reference and infor-
      mation for their patrons

Patron should expect document location information
at least on a par with normal reference services
offered at the holding library, not to exceed one day

Regional depository system to be reinforced to insure holdings in the state . . . , at . . . Public
Library, with State funding increased to supplement

Figure 21. Relevant Sections from the Two State Plans

existing reference referral system and provide for increased storage facilities and necessary hardware

To serve the Nation, interstate service should be satisfied through a two-step process: (1) the libraries within state boundaries should first attempt to locate documents within their own state and/or at their own Regional Depository; and (2) if it has been determined that the state does not have a copy, contact should be made with the Regional Depositories within their larger geographic district . . .

Libraries shall be encouraged to form and join regional groups for collection coordination

Current listing of depository library selections shall be made available and updated regularly to all depository libraries

Consider development of a retrospective listing of depository library selections

There should be an ongoing program of continuing education for depository and nondepository libraries to improve the librarians' ability to provide the services called for in the state plan. This program should include:
1. Consultative service: Advice and assistance provided by the regional library, the State Library and other members of the depository system
2. Cooperation with professional organizations
   . . .
3. Statewide coordination/information exchange on workshops and programs relating to federal documents through a professional newsletter
4. Insure the development and presentation of programs relating to federal documents and their use for depository and nondepository libraries

All libraries should accept responsibility for providing release time for staff participation in documents workshops, training, etc.

Figure 21. (Continued)

participants are disappointed because it did not meet their expectations—or rather, the outcomes or impact did not meet their expectations. Planning is no place for administrative "hidden agendas." At the outset, purposes, outcomes, and expectations should be clearly set forth.

Because large amounts of time, energy, and resources are required for planning, it is not unlikely that participants will expect significant changes to result from the planning process. Where the purposes were clear and expectations specified, the participants developed planning skills, group skills, and improved the planning process as a continuing organizational activity. On the other hand, where false expectations are raised but not met, where the planning process does not result in meaningful change, or where the process is more an academic exercise than a carefully orchestrated process to improve library and depository services, the likely result will be disappointed participants with little interest to continue future attempts to plan.

As briefly sketched, planning must be regarded as a formalized and ongoing activity, which recognizes the value of research and critically examines all underlying assumptions. Planning, which is an important and necessary activity in which libraries and the depository program must engage, should take into account differences that might emerge between the goals and objectives of the overall program and those of individual depositories. For example, certain accredited law school depositories may not want to make their collections accessible to the public.[25] Planning must also involve more than a few people from each state. It must be recognized as a legitimate activity of depository status.

The quality of reference service provided by depository libraries, the problems associated with public access, and the avenues by which referral services can be accomplished should be of vital concern to those engaged in planning depository services. Activities of the depository library program should include assisting selective depository libraries in better integrating the documents collection into the library as a whole, in developing collections of frequently needed source material, in building a prompt and reliable document delivery system for the exchange of materials among cooperating libraries, and in using collections to maximum advantage.

Without an effective document delivery and referral system, libraries cannot develop a limited body of material that will meet a large percentage of their information requests. Exhaustiveness in provision of material on a topic should not be the goal, but selection of what is most essential and useful to a library's clientele. The accumulation of large numbers of non-used or little-used publications has implications beyond the context of a particular library. It has an impact on printing, distribution, and library costs, as well as upon the efficiency by which library staff members can gain access to resources within their collections.

Cost Effectiveness of the System

Over the years, the number of depository libraries has increased dramatically. For example, there were 1,054 depositories in fiscal year 1971, 1,084 in 1972, 1,121 in 1973, and 1,186 in 1975. By mid-1978 the number had expanded to 1,217, and by 1982 had reached 1,365. Of these, approximately two-thirds are academic libraries, ranging from universities to small liberal arts and community colleges. They include private as well as public institutions.[26]

The cost of the depository library program increases annually, due to the increase in the number of depositories and the number of titles distributed. Conversion to microfiche distribution represents an attempt to hold down part of the costs. Public access, it would seem, is equated with the number of depositories and titles distributed. The assumption appears to be that the more depositories and titles distributed, the better the public access.

One estimate, made in the late 1970s, is that "it cost the Congress an average of $11,000 per year for each library in the depository program, excluding the cost of classifying and cataloging the publications for the *Monthly Catalog.*"[27] Maintenance of a depository collection also involves expenditures for individual libraries. These costs relate to factors such as staffing, collection space and needs, equipment, and the number of commercial reference aids needed. Given the costs involved and the findings of this study, it is imperative that the cost/benefit as well as the cost-effectiveness of the depository library program for both the government and individual libraries be determined.

A critical problem for documents librarianship is the need for research studies analyzing the costs and benefits of depository status and services. Unfortunately, the variables reported in existing studies, as well as the assumptions their authors make, are based on personal opinion and individual case studies, rather than on empirical research.[28] Their conclusions, therefore, are not likely to be valid.

Without the formulation of meaningful objectives for the depository library program, cost-effectiveness cannot be computed for the program as a whole. Instead, individual libraries would have to develop their own method of computing cost-effectiveness, which in turn minimizes the ability to make comparisons to depository libraries across the nation. However, with the development of valid performance measures, such comparisons could be made among the various depository libraries.

It is essential that the depository program demonstrate its utility to the widest segments of the American population. The current budget-cutting climate in Washington and the viewing of public access to government information in terms of the number of depository libraries and the distribution of depository publications in the most economical terms makes such demonstration of utility even more critical. If depository libraries are not viewed as cost-effective, government agencies may question the necessity of providing their resources for depository distribution. They might demand that funds be better spent in order to enhance public access to the information they disseminate. After all, one objective behind government publishing is communication with the public. If the role of depository libraries as a communication link is seen as ineffective, agencies will seek (and rightly so) alternative methods of public access.

If depository libraries are currently experiencing problems in absorbing the publishing output of the government, more effective ways to accommodate the total number of titles distributed each year must be studied. In this regard, it should be recognized that bibliographic control and depository distribution are not synonymous concepts. Comprehensive distribution of all government publications, however, is questionable, especially since many of these publications may be little used and costly in terms of retention and storage.

Finally, the exploration of ways to enhance the cost-effectiveness of the depository library program, while at the same time coping with problems relating to bibliographic control, document delivery, and the need for new technology, suggests that the depository program requires restructuring. Such a consideration, which is beyond the scope of this book, has been dealt with elsewhere.[29] Suffice it to say, the overall organizational structure of the depository program requires investigation. Librarians should not focus on improving or altering *one* aspect of the program; instead, they should examine how various parts fit together and how the entire network can accommodate future technology.

The Depository Program as an Interlocking Network

A network consists of two or more independent libraries or other information-providing organizations joining in a common pattern of information sharing, with mutually acceptable network goals and objectives. Since there must be both a regular sharing and a contractual arrangement, networking is a coordinated effort to solve a common problem(s). But this study has shown that staff members from many of the tested libraries view their collections in isolation from the rest of the depository libraries. If they cannot answer a reference question, they most likely do not engage in referral to another depository or to an outside agency. Clearly, the depository library program is not viewed as an interlocking network, in which there would be extensive referral of unanswered questions and the prompt, reliable delivery of needed source material. There may be specific reasons why library staff members do not always view their depository collection in a larger perspective. Perhaps the rural depository libraries place restrictions on expenditures for telephone calls, or certain regional depository libraries provide less than full service. Whatever the reasons, they merit investigation and immediate correction if the depository library program is to serve as an interlocking network.

On the whole, depository librarians are little involved in online searching of government document data bases, have limited access to online terminals, and have not received much training in the use of online data bases.[30] DIALOG now offers *LABSTAT,* which provides annual, quarterly, and monthly data collected by the U.S. Bureau of Labor Statistics. Within this file, users have access to resources such as the *Consumers' Price Index* and the *Producer Price Index.* There is also a file entitled *U.S. Exports,* which contains data collected by the U.S. Bureau of the Census. Files such as these not only permit the answering of factual questions (e.g., the number and rate of unemployment by occupation) but also the manipulation of data for statistical comparisons. This online capability has great potential appeal to faculty members and their students at academic and other types of institutions. It may also appeal to documents librarians who want to enhance their access to government information. As these examples illustrate, depository libraries must gain access to technology of the future, either directly or through networks, so that they can make new information readily available and/or provide referral to centers able to manipulate machine-readable data.

Much of the information generated and disseminated by the federal government does not appear in published (paper or microfiche) format. Instead, it is available in machine-readable form. Many libraries may not want to acquire these data files, but nonetheless should attempt to assist patrons in gaining access to needed data files. In this regard, Kathleen Heim believes that librarians should function as brokers of machine-readable information:

> As librarians come to recognize the growing impact of good social sciences research on governmental policy, the provision of machine-readable data, a key resource for the social sciences, becomes an important service to develop. While librarians may have to accommodate the service they can provide . . . and perhaps opt for a moderate rather than activist stance in acquiring and aiding in the exploitation of these data, it is imperative that librarians choose to take some action.[31]

Given the availability of numerous government, numeric data bases, it is all the more essential that documents staff members become better informed about possible referral sites and that they more actively engage in referral.

Numerous suggestions have been proposed for dealing with future needs of depository libraries as a network and with structural deficiencies within the system. The Depository Library Council to the Public Printer, for example, has requested that regional depositories need only to select and retain material for their own region "when that material is offered in a series by geographic breakdown."[32] Other proposals for change advocate cooperative or shared regional responsibilities, greater flexibility in the disposition of dated material, creation of an additional tier (e.g., a lending library of last resort), more rigorous deselection policies, increased distribution and retention of microfiche, establishment of special regionals (which collect by format, e.g., audiovisual material), and "on-demand" distribution of low-use series and titles.

Some of these suggestions require minor readjustments in the depository program while others are more far reaching in their implications. Structural defects, coping with an overload of distributed documentation and with libraries sharply reducing the percentage of item numbers received, and managing 1,365 depositories that adhere to divergent goals and objectives cannot be adequately resolved by such recommendations. Instead of focusing on specific aspects within the system, greater attention should be given to the network as a whole and to interrelationships among the various parts. Research and development studies can guide the emergence of a truly *national* network, able to exploit technological advances fully and provide the general public with access to needed government publications through the provision of high-quality reference service.

Prospects for the Future

This chapter conjures up issues and questions relating to library management and the administration of the depository library program. First, documents librarians, in many instances, are resource oriented; they appear to focus on decision making relating to purchase of sources, bibliographic control, and the arrangement of materials, aids, etc., rather than on the quality of their service and other factors that directly impact upon the user community. All of us must be concerned with the fact that library staff members with access to large depository collections may be providing limited access to the resources in their collections, as well as to the universe of government information.

Perhaps depository librarians are trying to do too much. Since some of their responsibilities and activities may be more routine and of lower priority, they should reexamine the assorted duties they perform and demonstrate more concern with the efficiency and effectiveness of the service that they and their staffs provide. At the same time, they must examine the relationship of their collections and services to the general reference department and the library as a whole.

Given current funding levels, how long can depository libraries devote so much collection space and money for staff, facilities, and reference aids to support massive documents collections that have limited use and are poorly serviced? Documents librarians will be (and in some cases are being) asked to justify the need for all of those expensive, commercially produced bibliographic retrieval tools for government publications. This is especially true where monies for documents collections must compete against the need for other library acquisitions. Funds cannot always be diverted from other budgetary categories to meet the alleged needs of depository collections, especially where documents receive limited use and reference services are less than adequate.

Evidently, some documents librarians have used the inspection visit as an attempt to pressure the library administration into increased support (financial, facilities, and staff) for the depository collection and services. Such strategies suggest a lack of concern that some library administrations may have toward depository status and collections. However, the present level and type of use of the depository collection may not warrant additional support. Obviously, the GPO and the Joint Committee on Printing must investigate the feasibility of requiring institutions to provide "adequate" resources and properly trained staff to maintain and service the depository collection. Over the years, the government and individual libraries have made a substantial investment in the depository program—and the return on this investment must now be scrutinized and, obviously, improved.

In demanding equal treatment for government publications, in comparison to other library materials, documents librarians must demonstrate the value and importance of documents as a means for resolving a broad range of information needs. Further, they must work closely with other librarians and administrators to make known the needs and requirements of the depository collection. However, they cannot be effective spokespersons for government publications if they have limited knowledge of documents and provide unsatisfactory service to users of the depository collection. One might question (1) if depository collections need to contain so many titles, especially those that receive little or no use, and (2) if libraries should make large financial expenditures for a variety of reference aids produced by the private sector, especially if staff members cannot fully exploit basic resources received free through depository distribution (e.g., the *Publications Reference File,* the *Federal Register,* and the *Code of Federal Regulations*).

Public access to government publications encompasses more than their bibliographic control and physical availability in libraries. It also requires knowledgeable reference service about information sources in depository collections and how to gain access to additional source material—be it in published or unpublished form. Where depository libraries are understaffed and unable to put professional staff members in public service positions during all the hours that documents reference service is provided, they need to further encourage paraprofessional staff members to obtain in-house training and make referrals to professional personnel. Libraries must ensure that all users of the depository collection receive quality assistance.

This study questions the validity of gathering and reporting reference statistics that merely identify the number of reference questions answered by documents staff members on a daily, weekly, monthly, and annual basis. It would be more meaningful to determine how well information needs are being met by utilizing performance measures and to revise the *Guidelines for the Depository Library System* and the inspection report so that both can take into account program goals and objectives.

It would seem that 37 percent is a low overall average for correct responses, especially since the tested documents staff members infrequently provide referral service. Library users can experience great variation in the quality of reference service, depending on the nature of the questions asked. These findings suggest that depository libraries must decide:

What types of reference questions they should attempt to address
Whether they should attempt to answer any question involving a request for government information
What degree of referral, if any, is to be provided, and to which sources
Whether they can provide the same level of service for all questions asked
Whether they are responsible for the accuracy and up to dateness of the information they disseminate.

The GPO must determine the answers to these questions, as well as to such questions as:

What are the implications for the depository library program as an interlocking network when users experience divergent levels of service and are not referred to better-equipped depositories to handle certain requests?
What is an acceptable level of correct responses to representative questions?

Should depository libraries be held responsible for the answers provided to clientele?

Should documents staff members be required to participate in continuing education programs and to receive advanced training?

Is the depository library program cost-effective? (If it is not, should the GPO make a financial commitment toward improving the quality of reference service?)

Can a national program to promote the collections and services of depository libraries be successful if, upon consulting libraries, citizens encounter undistinguished reference service?

Should a program of "certification" be initiated to improve the quality of depository library service?

Improving the quality of documents reference service has implications beyond the immediate depository. It is reflective of the institution, the depository library program, and the goals and objectives of the GPO and JCP. Further, it raises questions about the appropriateness of maintaining a system unable to provide better than 37 percent accuracy to reference questions that call largely for "basic" resources listed in the *Guidelines*. As taxpayers and librarians, we all have an interest in ascertaining the quality of reference service provided by depository libraries and in wanting to see improvements made wherever they might be necessary.

As a first step, a formal evaluation of the effectiveness of the depository library program must be initiated and funded by an appropriate government agency or consortia of depository libraries. Decisions cannot be made regarding specific strategies, resources required for change, and appropriate goals and objectives to address without a basis of factual information regarding the program. At this time, such information does not exist. Further, until depository librarians assume responsibility for improving the quality of reference services, rather than emphasizing collection building and sources, and until other library administrators and librarians recognize the value and importance of information resources in government publications, the quality of documents reference service is not likely to improve.

The recommendations suggested throughout this book can provide stop-gap measures which individuals can implement to improve services. But short-term patchwork of the depository program will not solve the long-range problems of providing quality access to government publications through the depository library system. Formal, funded, and valid evaluation of the effectiveness of the depository library program and better access to government publications, provided by participants in that program, are necessary *immediately*.

It is vitally important that the research literature on documents reference service grow substantially during this decade and assist in developing the potential role of depository staff members as effective mediators of the government information environment. In this regard, further studies might find it profitable to compare test results not only by delivery method (telephone and in person) but also by format (paper and microfiche) and type (map, etc.). Since microfiche is now the primary format for depository distribution, future testing might explore what problems, if any, this causes. Large-scale testing might also compare the service provided by general reference staff members and documents personnel, and stratify academic institutions by highest degree offered as well as by selected library variables (e.g., the percentage of item numbers selected). Testing might also extend into other types of depository libraries (e.g., public, special, and federal) and make comparisons concerning the quality of service provided. Comparisons might also be made between the services of regional and selective depositories.

As Thomas Childers did with his testing of the Suffolk Cooperative Library System in 1977 and 1978, there might be testing of the willingness of library staff members to negotiate a question. The purpose would be to determine if they will negotiate a general question ("Where can I find your books on poetry?") in order to arrive at the specific information need ("Could you give me a definition of 'concrete' poetry?"). In addition, whenever referral service is offered, that named source could be checked in order to determine its appropriateness.[33]

If the purpose of testing is to compare service between general reference and documents librarians, the type of questions depicted in appendixes A and B of this book could be stripped of any reference to the fact that a government was the publisher. For some questions, the concern might not be whether the correct answer is provided, but if the staff member recognized the question as one involving government publications. Such testing would be appropriate since this study, as well as those in the general reference field, has discovered many instances in which library staff members conduct inadequate or incomplete question negotiation. The documents field would also be well served by having studies develop and test models covering collections, services, and organizational structure. Further, studies can focus on the marketing of government publications as an information resource and on strategies to develop effective staff training programs.

Awareness of the role of research, combined with implementation of research results and development studies, will enable documents librarians to adapt better to new environments and situations, as well as to better serve the information needs of their clientele, present and potential. At the same time, existing values, beliefs, and practices must be reviewed, evaluated, and challenged. It is our belief that the positive aspects of such research far outweigh the difficulties. The ability and willingness of librarians, government officials, and others interested in access to government information to adjust to change, exploit the strengths of the system, and utilize new technologies and techniques can significantly improve the quality of reference service for government documents.

Appendixes

A. Reference Questions Used in the Study

1. For a term paper in history, I am studying the army's use of camels in the 19th Century. It is my understanding that there is a government document, from the 1850s, on the topic. Please help me find it.

    If the library does not own this 1857 document, obtain Sudoc or Serial Set number.
    Answer: Serial Set Number 881.
    Sources: Benjamin Perley Poore's *A Descriptive Catalogue of the Government Publications of the United States* (1885), *Tables of and Annotated Index to the Congressional Series of United States Public Documents* (1902), and *Checklist of United States Public Documents, 1789–1909* (1911).

2. I understand that during World War II the Japanese sent balloons over the ocean to drop bombs on the U.S. By chance, is there a document on the subject? If yes, is it still in print and what is the cost?
    Answer: Japan's World War II Balloon Attacks in North America (Smithsonian Annals of Flight, No. 9, 1973). It is still in print and sells for $2.75.
    Sources: Monthly Catalog and *Publications Reference File.*

3. I understand that the Caffeine Study Review Panel submitted its final report to the Food and Drug Administration on May 15, 1981. The report contains information pertinent to the FDA's review of the safety of added caffeine. I would like to know if the final report is available, what is the purpose of the panel, and can you help me find a summary of the panel's main findings and recommendations?

Answer: The report is available. For answers to all the questions see *Federal Register,* June 23, 1981, p. 32453.

*4.   Who is the head of the Justice Department's civil rights division?
Answer: William Bradford Reynolds.
Sources: Newspapers, popular periodicals, and Federal Information Center. His name may be too recent to appear in sources such as the *U.S. Government Manual, Washington Information Directory, Congressional Directory,* and *Federal Regulatory Directory* (Congressional Quarterly).

*5.   I understand that there is a government publication entitled *Overland Migrations: Settlers to Oregon, California, and Utah,* which deals with the Oregon Trail. Do you have it? Is it in print? What is the cost?
Answer: Still in print, this 1980 publication sells for $3.95.
Sources: Monthly Catalog and *Publications Reference File.*

6.   In the mid 1970s, the Department of Commerce issued *Clamshell Commerce,* a publication on the origins of the seafood industry in the United States. Does the library have a copy? If not, what is the Sudoc number and how can I get a copy?
Answer: Clamshell Commerce: How Seafood Started in the States [Dept. of Commerce, National Oceanic and Atmospheric Administration (Rockville, MD, 1976?)] C55.14/a:527.
Sources: Monthly Catalog, April 1980.

*7.   Did the Department of Education Organization Act of 1979 (HR 2444 and S210) go through conference? If so, when did the House and the Senate pass the conference report?
Answer: Yes; House on September 27 and Senate on September 25, 1979.
Sources: Congressional Index, Congressional Record, National Journal Reports, CQ Almanac, CIS Index, and *House Calendar.*

8.   In June 1981, President Reagan set up a President's Commission on Housing. Is the commission supposed to review all existing federal housing policies and programs? Where can I find out exactly what the commission is supposed to do?
Answer: Yes, the executive order was issued June 16, 1981.

*Questions preceded by an asterisk indicate that the question is to be asked by telephone. All other questions are to be asked in person.

Sources: Federal Register, June 18, 1981, p. 31869.

*9. In February 1978, there was an FTC (Federal Trade Commission) staff report on television advertising to children, by Ellis M. Ratner and others. It recommended the elimination of "harms arising out of television advertising to children." Is it still in print? What is the cost?
Answer: It is still in print and costs $6.00.
Sources: Monthly Catalog and *Publications Reference File.*

10. I am planning to get a license for flying as a private pilot. Is there a written test guide?
Answer: Yes, Dept. of Transportation. Federal Aviation Administration. *Private Pilot Airplane—Written Test Guide* (1979).
Sources: Monthly Catalog.

11. I have heard that in the coming years immigrants may comprise 45 percent of the growth in the U.S. labor force. Can you help me find an article on this topic?
Answer: David S. North and Phillip L. Martin, "Immigration and Employment: A Need for Policy Coordination," *Monthly Labor Review* (October 1980).
Sources: Index to U.S. Government Periodicals and *American Statistics Index.*

*12. From the 1970 census, I would like to know the number of males and females 80 years and older who were born in Massachusetts (or Oklahoma). Has this type of information been released yet from the 1980 census? If not, when will it?

Answer:	*Males*	*Females*
Massachusetts	15,156	34,504
Oklahoma	3,734	6,093

1980 data will not be available until 1982.

Sources: Census of Population (Massachusetts, Vol. 1); Table 140, p. 420, *Characteristics of the Population* 1970, Vol. 38 (Oklahoma); and contact Bureau of the Census or State Data Center for 1980 information.

*13. What is the percent of illiteracy for Massachusetts (or Oklahoma) from 1950 to 1970? I just need ten-year intervals for my term paper.

Answer:	1950	1960	1970
Massachusetts	2.8	2.2	1.1
Oklahoma	2.5	1.9	1.1

Sources: Statistical Abstracts, 1980, p. 150.

14. I would like the revenues and expenditures of the Post Office Department for all available years during the 20th Century. Where can summary statistics be found?
Sources: Historical Statistics of the US, Part II, p. 1120 and 1123.

*15. I am considering graduate studies in history and would like to know the number of master's and doctoral degrees awarded for 1978.
Answer: Master's: 3033 Doctoral: 813
Sources: Statistical Abstracts, 1980, p. 175; and *Digest of Education Statistics.*

*16 Who chairs the Senate Committee on Small Business, and who are on the Committee:

Answer: Weicker is the chair.

Members:	Packwood	Huddleston
	Hatch	Bumpers
	Hayakawa	Sasser
	Boschwitz	Baucus
	Gorton	Levin
	Nickles	Tsongas
	Rudman	Dixon
	D'Amato	
	Nunn	

Sources: Congressional Record (May 19, 1981), *Congressional Directory, Congressional Index,* etc.

17. Where can I get a detailed breakdown of the distribution of federal funds for research and development by agency?
Answer: Found in *Federal Funds for Research and Development,* an annual publication (NS1.18:yr.).
Sources: American Statistics Index and a "source" reference in *Statistical Abstracts.*

18. I need a map showing population density in various parts of Hon-

duras. Since the atlases that I checked do not show sufficient detail, I was wondering if there was anything in government maps?
Answer: Yes, CIA map of Honduras (PrEx3.10/4:H75).
Sources: This map series can be located through the *Monthly Catalog,* but this source does not indicate that specific feature. The feature is provided in an insert map of the country.

*19. Where can I find a description of regulations about the Indian Arts and Crafts Board of the federal government, specifically standards regarding the selling of silver and turquoise products?
Sources: Code of Federal Regulations, title 25, Chapter II (1980 ed.).

*20. Where can I obtain a copy of President Reagan's toast made in honor of President Sadat at a dinner/reception at the White House, sometime in August 1981?
Sources: Weekly Compilation of Presidential Documents (August 10, 1981), pp. 856–858.

B. Additional Test Questions

1. I found a footnote reference to a resolution pertaining to a commission to investigate the condition of, and progress of, Black people of the U.S. since 1865. The resolution was sponsored by H.W. Blair, a U.S. Senator from New Hampshire and member of the Committee on Education and Labor. Does the library have this document, which was issued in the 1880s?

   Answer: Serial Set 2175.

   Sources: CIS US Serial Set Index, John G. Ames' *Comprehensive Index to the Publications of the United States Government* (1905), *Tables of and Annotated Index to Congressional Series of United States Public Documents* (1902), and *Checklist of United States Public Documents, 1789–1909* (1911).

2. I was told that, during the 1970s, the Federal government issued a book on the history of music machines in America and that it covers the player piano and other equipment. Is this true?

   Answer: (Yes) Cynthia A. Hoover, *Music Machines American Style* (Smithsonian Institution, 1971).

   Sources: Monthly Catalog and *Publications Reference File.*

3. I understand that there is a book of essays giving the views of John Adams on American foreign policy. Can you help me find this government document, which was published fairly recently?

   Answer: Library of Congress. *Letters from a Distinguished American: Twelve Essays by John Adams on American Foreign Policy, 1780* (GPO, 1978). LC1.2:L56.

   Sources: Monthly Catalog.

4. I am studying labeling requirements for certain dyes used in food products. What kind of labeling information does the Food and Drug Administration require for the color additive FD&C Yellow, Number 5? Also, as of what date was the labeling requirement made mandatory for food products?
    Sources: Federal Register (September 12, 1980), p. 60419; 21 *CFR* 74.705; or CCH *Food Drug Cosmetic Law Reports.*

5. Who is the chairman of the Nuclear Regulatory Commission and what is his business address?
    Answer: Nunzio J. Palladine
    Nuclear Regulatory Commission
    1717 H Street, NW
    Washington, D.C. 20555
    Sources: Federal Information Center, newspapers, *Facts on File,* popular periodicals, *Federal Regulatory Directory* (Congressional Quarterly), etc.

6. I am preparing for certification as an airframe mechanic. Is there a handbook providing basic information on the principles and technical procedures on topics relating to airframe ratings? The book should address differences in airframe components and systems.
    Answer: Department of Transportation, Federal Aviation Administration. *Airframe and Powerplant Mechanics: Airframe Handbook* (rev. ed. 1976).
    Sources: Monthly Catalog and *Publications Reference File.*

7. I would like to know the percentage of young adults between the ages of 18 and 25 that have ever used marijuana and that currently use it. This information is needed for a term paper for an English class.
    Answer: Ever used it: 68.2 percent
    Currently do so: 35.4 percent
    Sources: Statistical Abstract, 1980, p. 129.

8. For a seminar paper in U.S. history, I would like to know how large membership was for the labor union in the textile industry from 1920–1934. Can I have the statistics for each year?
    Sources: Historical Statistics of the United States, Part I, p. 178.

9. I am considering a career in library science and would like to know how many master's and doctoral degrees were conferred in 1978.
    Answer: Master's: 6,914

Doctoral: 67
Sources: Digest of Education Statistics and *Statistical Abstract,* 1980,
p. 175.

10. Richard B. Morris edited *The American Worker,* a Department of
Labor publication issued in the 1970s. Do you have it? Is it still in
print? What is the current cost?
Answer: This 1977 history costs $5.00.
Sources: Monthly Catalog and *Publications Reference File.*

11. From the 1970 census, I would like to know the median school year
completed by males and females 18 years and over, in Massachusetts
(or Oklahoma), having incomes $8,000–9,999. Has this information
been released yet from the 1980 census? If not, when will it?

Answer:	*Males*	*Females*
Massachusetts	12.3	13.6
Oklahoma	12.5	13.0

Sources: Census of Population (Massachusetts, Vol. 1, Table 197).
Census of Population (Oklahoma, PC(1), Table 197).
For 1980 information contact the Bureau of the Census or State
Data Center.

C. Reference Question Tabulation Sheet

SHEET NUMBER: _____

Library Name _____ Dates Administered _____ Person(s) Administering Questions _____

Total Library Volumes _____ Total Budget _____ Government Doc FTE Professionals _____

Total Library Professional Staff _____ Percent of Items Selected _____ Government Doc FTE Paraprofessionals _____

					If Incorrect or No Answer						Referral						
Reference Question	Time Question Asked	Total Time of Reference Interview	Phone or in Person	Correct Answer	Partial Answer	Wrong Data	Don't Know	Don't Have Sources Needed	Other (Describe)	To Another Librarian Inside Same Library	To Gov't Agency	To GPO Bookstore	Regional Depository	"Come back when Documents Librarian is on duty"	Census Bureau or State Data Center	To Another Documents Librarian Outside Library	Patron Asked to Return at Later Date for Answer	Other (Describe)

COMMENTS OR ADDITIONAL EXPLANATION:

Guidelines
for the Depository Library System
as adopted by the Depository Library Council to the Public Printer, October 18, 1977

Minimum Standards for the Depository Library System
as adopted October 22, 1976

**United States
Government
Printing Office**

Washington, D.C. 20401

OFFICE OF THE PUBLIC PRINTER

<u>FOREWORD</u>

For over a century the depository library program, operating
under various Federal statutes, has provided the general public
with access to publications of the United States Government.
Congressional designation of selective and regional depository
libraries has made this program national in character and scope.

Currently, the depository library program is distributing more
than 3,800 classes of Government publications to a broad range
of libraries. The 1,217 designated depositories include libraries of Federal and State Governments, colleges and universities,
special and public libraries.

In operating the depository library program, the Public Printer
and the Superintendent of Documents have had the excellent
professional advice of the Depository Library Council to the
Public Printer. Council members have generously given of their
time and thought to help the program better serve the public
and the libraries which implement it. Their recommendations
have now brought forth specific guidelines designed to make
the program even more effective.

To all connected with the shaping of these guidelines, let me
extend the thanks of the Public Printer and the Superintendent
of Documents. They represent a remarkable effort from their
genesis within the Council in 1974, and the creation of a
Committee on Standards chaired by a most patient and persistent
documents librarian, Catharine Reynolds. Many others worked
with her subsequently in disseminating drafts through <u>Public
Documents Highlights</u> to the large community of documents
librarians. The thoughtful responses of hundreds of librarians
working daily with documents were integrated into this final
document. It bears the stamp of participatory professionalism
in the finest sense, and will go far in making the publications
of our Federal Government more readily accessible to all citizens
through the depository library program.

JOHN J. BOYLE
Public Printer

DEPOSITORY LIBRARY
THIS LIBRARY IS A CONGRESSIONALLY DESIGNATED
DEPOSITORY FOR U.S. GOVERNMENT DOCUMENTS

GUIDELINES FOR THE DEPOSITORY

LIBRARY SYSTEM

as adopted by Depository Library Council
October 18, 1977.

1. OBJECTIVES OF THE DEPOSITORY LIBRARY SYSTEM.

1-1 The purpose of depository libraries is to make U.S. Government publications easily accessible to the general public and to insure their continued availability in the future.

1-2 The purpose shall be achieved by a system of cooperation wherein depository libraries will receive free Federal public documents in return for making them accessible to the general public in their areas.

1-3 The guidelines are to be considered a recommended level of conduct by all depositories unless otherwise specified by statute or regulations thereunder.

2. SUPERINTENDENT OF DOCUMENTS, U.S. GOVERNMENT PRINTING OFFICE.

2-1 Obtain new Federal publications and forward free of expense to depository libraries without delay in accordance with Chapter 19, Title 44 U.S.C.

2-2 Provide all issues of series in the <u>List of Classes of United States Government Publications Available for Selection by Depository Libraries</u>, including those issues not printed at the Government Printing Office.

2-3 Actively gather and distribute in paper or microformat all Federal publications of public interest or educational value not printed at the Government Printing Office which are within the scope of 44 U.S.C. 1902.

2-4 Provide samples and/or annotations for new titles offered to depositories, and return cards for selection purposes.

2-5 Subdivide item numbers as necessary to insure that libraries need receive only wanted documents.

2-6 Supply shipping lists containing item numbers, titles of documents, classification numbers, information on classification changes, corrections to previous lists, and price information (if available) for sales publications.

2-7 Supply forms for claiming items selected but missing from the shipment, damaged or incomplete.

2-8 Offer choice of format: paper, microform or other; however, the Government Printing Office, in consultation with depository libraries, should have the option of providing only one format when the nature of the material warrants it.

2-9 Provide a timely and comprehensive system of catalogs, bibliographies and indexes to Federal publications.

2-10 Provide a standard classification system for Federal documents and related aids such as lists of subject headings.

2-11 Provide assistance to libraries on problems of using the Sudocs system of classification.

2-12 Cooperate with the National Archives that the Archives may acquire and preserve a comprehensive collection of Federal publications.

2-13 Issue instructions for the selection, claiming, retention, and withdrawal of depository documents and other activities related to depository libraries.

2-14 Allocate funds for the evaluation of depository libraries through questionnaires, surveys, and inspections at intervals considered necessary by the Superintendent of Documents, to insure compliance with the depository law.

2-15 After advance notice to the library concerned, investigate conditions in depository libraries by personal visits.

2-16 Provide written notice to a library about unsatisfactory conditions, and if not corrected within six months, consider deletion of the library from the list of depositories.

2-17 Announce new policies and changes on a regular basis to all depositories.

2-18 Cooperate with publication projects which contribute to use of Federal documents.

2-19 Consult at regular intervals with the Depository Library Council to the Public Printer on matters related to depository libraries, including the development of standards and bibliographic aids, changes in the Sudocs classification system and the selection of materials for micropublication.

2-20 Collect, compile, analyze and publish pertinent statistics on a regular basis.

2-21 Provide sufficient copies to fill claims for publications missing from depository shipments.

3.   DESIGNATION OF NEW DEPOSITORY LIBRARIES.

3-1   There may be up to two depositories in each Congressional district
      to be designated by Representatives, not more than two others within
      the state designated by Senators, and other depository libraries
      specifically provided for in Chapter 19, Title 44 U.S.C.

3-2   The library shall be open to the general public for the free use of
      depository publications, as provided in Chapter 19, Title 44 U.S.C.

3-3   The library shall have the interest, resources and ability to provide
      custody of the documents and public service.

3-4   The library should possess at least 15,000 titles other than government
      publications.

3-5   The library should be prepared to keep its documents collections open
      the same hours as other major parts of the library, when the library
      is open for full range of services.

3-6   When a new vacancy occurs through redistricting or by the resignation
      or deletion of an existing depository, this fact should be made known
      by the Superintendent of Documents to the state library authority,
      the regional depository, if any, and the state professional associations.

3-7   Eligible libraries shall apply to the state library authority for
      evaluation and recommendation, with notice of the application to the
      regional depository, if any. The library should be prepared to offer
      statistics on the size and character of its collection, population
      served, budget, and if an academic library, the size of the student
      body, and need for research materials.

3-8   The evaluation should relate to community interests and indicate
      staff, space and budget to be allocated to the collection and the
      number, scope and character of the items to be selected. The state
      library authority after consulting with other libraries, the regional
      depository, if any, and representatives from the professional
      associations, will make a recommendation to the Senator or Representative
      based on location in relation to other depositories, the need for an
      additional depository and the ability of the library to provide custody
      and service.

3-9   Libraries of independent agencies and additional libraries in
      executive departments may be designated depositories upon certification
      of need according to the provisions of 44 U.S.C. 1907.

4.   DEPOSITORY COLLECTIONS.

4-1   Each depository library should maintain a basic collection available
      for immediate use consisting of all titles in Appendix A (attached).

4-2   Each library should acquire and maintain the basic catalogs, guides
      and indexes, retrospective and current, considered essential to the

reference use of the collection. This should include selected non-governmental reference tools.

4-3   Each depository should select frequently used and potentially useful materials appropriate to the objectives of the library.

4-4   Each depository should select materials responsive to the needs of the users in the Congressional district it serves.

4-5   Selection of at least 25% of the available Item Numbers on the Classified List is suggested as the minimum number necessary to undertake the role of depository library. A prospective depository intending to select fewer than 25% should provide additional justification for its designation as a depository.

4-6   Depository libraries should coordinate selections with other depositories in the district to insure adequate coverage within the area.

5.   ORGANIZATION OF THE DEPOSITORY COLLECTION.

5-1   The library should check all daily shipping lists to insure that items selected are received, and if not, promptly claimed.

5-2   Each publication in the shipment should be marked to distinguish it from publications received from other sources. Each publication should be marked with the date of the shipping list or the date of receipt.

5-3   The library should record its depository accessions.

5-4   The minimum record for a depository library should show the library's holdings and the call numbers or locations where they may be found.

5-5   A method of classification should be adopted for precise identification and location of materials requested by library users.

5-6   The method of classification adopted shall be optional with the library; however, it is suggested that libraries which integrate their documents should maintain a shelf list by Sudocs number showing disposition of the publication.

5-7   Whenever possible documents should be available for public use within 10 days after receipt; they should be retrievable even if cataloging information is not yet available.

5-8   The library should maintain statistics of the collection needed for the Biennial Survey.

5-9   The library will retain one set of item cards, both items selected and not selected.

6. MAINTENANCE OF THE DEPOSITORY COLLECTION.

6-1 Collections should be maintained in as good physical condition as other library materials, including binding when desirable.

6-2 Lost materials should be replaced if possible.

6-3 Unneeded publications should be made available to other libraries in accordance with Chapter 19, Title 44 U.S.C.

6-4 Libraries served by a regional depository may withdraw publications retained for a period of at least five years after securing permission from the regional library for disposal in accordance with the provisions of 44 U.S.C. 1912.

6-5 Depository libraries within executive departments and independent agencies may dispose of unwanted Government publications after first offering them to the Library of Congress and the Archivist of the United States, in accordance with the provisions of 44 U.S.C. 1907.

6-6 The provisions of 44 U.S.C. 1911, disposal of unwanted publications, do not apply to libraries of the highest appellate courts of the states   (see 44 U.S.C. 1915).

6-7 Superseded material should be withdrawn according to <u>Instructions to Depository Libraries</u> (latest edition).

6-8 Depository publications should be protected from unlawful removal as are other parts of the library's collections.

7. STAFFING.

7-1 One person should be designated by the library to coordinate activities and to act as liaison with the Superintendent of Documents in all matters relating to depository libraries.

7-2 This person should be responsible for
   a) selection, receipt and claiming of depository distributions
   b) replies to correspondence and surveys from the Superintendent of Documents
   c) interpreting the depository program to the administrative level of the library
   d) performance and/or supervision of stated aspects of service, or in an integrated collection, a knowledge of persons to whom responsibilities are delegated, such as:

      (1) organization for use
      (2) maintainance of records of the collection
      (3) physical maintenance of the collection
      (4) establishment of withdrawal procedures
      (5) maintainance of reader services
      (6) promotion of use of collection
      (7) preparation of budgets
      (8) submission of reports.

7-3   The liaison person should be a professionally qualified librarian.

7-4   The liaison person should be directly responsibile to the administrative
       level of the library.

7-5.   Additional professional staff should be added depending on the size
       and scope of the library and the methods of organization of the
       collection.

7-6   Professional staff should be assisted by support staff. A suggested
       proportion is 1 professional to 3 support staff.

7-7   Librarians and such support staff as indicated by their responsibilities
       should keep up to date on new developments through participation in
       professional societies, attendance at document workshops, and
       professional reading.

8.   SPACE STANDARDS.

8-1   Space for depository operations should be of the same quality as other
       areas of the library. It should be attractive, comfortable and have
       acceptable levels of lighting, temperature, ventilation and noise
       control. It should be functional, flexible and expandable.

8-2   The space should contain well planned areas for services provided,
       reference, circulation, loan and other public service activities as
       well as adequate space for the processing of new materials and
       housing of the collection.

8-3   It should include private work areas for staff members and the
       administrator.

8-4   All parts of the collection should be readily accessible, preferably
       open shelf, but in all circumstances, should be located so that
       materials may be retrieved in a reasonable period of time.

8-5   If documents are maintained in a separate division of the library,
       the space provided should be conveniently located to encourage use
       of the materials.

8-6   The library should abide by the recommended standards for access by
       handicapped users.

8-7   Tables and/or carrels should be provided for in-library use of
       documents.

8-8   Microform readers and reader/printers for the principal types of
       microforms should be provided.

8-9   Microform storage should be located convenient to the documents
       area.

9. SERVICE TO THE GENERAL PUBLIC.

9-1 Libraries shall make depository publications available for the free
    use of the general public. Highest appellate court libraries of the
    states are exempt from the provisions of 44 U.S.C. 1911 (see 44 U.S.C.
    1915).

9-2 In each depository library, there should be recognized focal points
    for inquiries about government publications. At this point it should
    be possible to find:

    a) resources in the collection, including specific titles
    b) location of wanted publications in the library
    c) answers to reference questions or a referral to a source or
        place where answers can be found
    d) guidance on the use of the collection, including the principal
        available reference sources, catalogs, abstracts, indexes and
        other aids
    e) availability of additional resources in the region
    f) assistance in borrowing documents from a regional or other
        libraries
    g) user privileges for other libraries, educational agencies,
        culturally deprived, disadvantaged, handicapped, retired users
        and the community at large.

9-3 The library should have the option of establishing its own circulation
    policies for use of depository materials outside the library.

9-4 The library should provide facilities for using materials within
    the library, including copying facilities and equipment for reading
    microforms.

9-5 The library should publicize the depository collection through displays
    and announcements of significant new titles.

9-6 The library should provide to all users reference assistance with
    regard to depository publications.

10. COOPERATION WITH THE GOVERNMENT PRINTING OFFICE.

10-1 Depository library staff should familiarize themselves with the
     depository instructions and abide by their conditions.

10-2 Claims should be submitted within stated time limits.

10-3 Depository library staff should use correct address when corresponding
     with the Government Printing Office.

10-4 Questionnaires and surveys submitted by the Superintendent of
     Documents to depository libraries should be completed and returned
     promptly.

11. INTERLIBRARY COOPERATION.

11-1 All depository libraries should be considered as part of a network of libraries consisting of selective, regional, and national.

11-2 Selective depositories should cooperate in building up the collections of the regional depositories.

11-3 Selective depositories should cooperate with the regional depositories in the redistribution of documents not needed in their own organizations

11-4 All depository libraries should cooperate in reporting to the Superintendent of Documents new Federal documents not listed in the Monthly Catalog.

11-5 All depository libraries should cooperate in the development of tools for the identification and location of documents in other libraries.

11-6 Depository libraries borrowing documents from other libraries should verify bibliographic information as completely as possible.

11-7 All depository libraries should provide material on interlibrary loan at least for the regional depository.

11-8 All depository libraries should have a policy of providing photocopies of depository materials to other libraries no less liberal than for other library materials.

12. REGIONAL DEPOSITORIES.

12-1 Eligibility to become a regional depository library:

    a) There may not be more than two regional depositories in one state. A regional library may serve two or more states, or regional status may be shared by more than one library.
    b) A regional library must be an existing depository.
    c) A regional depository should be conveniently located to serve the largest number of libraries possible.
    d) The library selected for regional status should have an adequate retrospective collection, space, personnel and a continuing basis of financial support sufficient to fulfill the obligations of a regional depository.
    e) The selection of a regional depository should be agreed upon by the state library authority and a majority of depository libraries within the region.
    f) Designation of the regional must be made by one of the U. S. Senators of the state.

12-2 Responsibilities of regional libraries include:

    a) receiving and maintaining permanently all depository publications in either printed or microform as provided in the depository instructions

b) attempting to complete their retrospective collections of major serials, annuals and other research materials by means of gift, exchange or purchase, including microforms
c) screening all lists of documents withdrawn from selective depositories to insure their future availability in the region
d) acquiring additional copies where necessary
e) assisting selective depositories with reference questions, interlibrary loans and photocopies
f) granting permission to selective depositories to dispose of unwanted documents according to the Instructions to Depository Libraries (latest edition)
g) providing guidelines to selective depositories for preparing disposal lists of unwanted documents
h) contributing to the effectiveness of the depository network through workshops, training sessions and consultive services within their region.

12-3 The regional depository may authorize the transfer of depository material within the state between depositories to insure maximum use. Transfer of material is not to be regarded as disposal.

12-4 The initial receiving depository library remains responsible and accountable for the documents during the period required by law.

Appendix A

Budget of the United States Government
Catalog of Federal Domestic Assistance
Census Bureau Catalog
Census of Housing (for State of Depository only)
Census of Population (for State of Depository only)
Code of Federal Regulations
Congressional Directory
Congressional District Data Book
Congressional Record
County-City Data Book
Federal Register
Historical Statistics of the United States
Monthly Catalog
Numerical Lists and Schedule of Volumes
Publications Reference File
Slip Laws (Public)
Statistical Abstract
Statutes at Large
Subject Bibliographies (S.B. Series)
Supreme Court Reports
United States Code
United States Government Manual
Weekly Compilation of Presidential Documents

MINIMUM STANDARDS FOR THE

DEPOSITORY LIBRARY SYSTEM

as adopted by Depository Library Council

October 22, 1976

1. The Superintendent of Documents will be responsible for distribution
    of documents to depository libraries in accordance with the provisions
    of Title 44 of the United States Code.

2. The Superintendent of Documents will provide a comprehensive system
    of catalogs, bibliographies and indexes to U.S. Government publications.

3. There should be at least one depository accessible to the public in
    each Congressional district. The designated library shall have the
    interest, resources and ability to provide custody of the documents
    and public service. The library must contain at least 10,000 books
    other than government publications.

4. Each depository shall select and maintain a collection responsive
    to the needs of the users in the geographic area it serves and
    promote their use by the general public.

5. The collection in a depository library shall be organized to insure
    quick and easy access by library users. The library will promptly
    open shipments and claim publications selected but not received.

6. The collection shall be maintained in as good physical condition as
    the other collections in the library.

7. Each depository library will assign sufficient staff to select,
    organize and provide reference service to the collection.

8. Each depository will provide sufficient space of a quality which
    conforms to ALA standards for the type of library.

9. The depository will be open to the public for free use of depository
    publications.

10. Each depository library will cooperate with the instructions issued
    by the Superintendent of Documents, respond promptly to the Biennial
    Survey and to other communications from the Public Documents Office.

11. All depository libraries shall be considered part of a national
    system to make Government documents available.

12. All selective depositories should be served by a regional depository.
    The regional depository libraries will retain at least one copy of all
    Government publications either in printed or microfacsimile form
    (except those authorized to be discarded by the Superintendent of
    Documents) and within the region served will provide interlibrary
    loan, reference service, and assistance for depository libraries in
    the disposal of unwanted Government publications.

E. U.S. DEPOSITORY LIBRARY

INSPECTION VISIT FORM

LIBRARY: _____

City/State: _____

Staff: _____

Depository No.: _____

Designation Year: _____

Title: _____

Date of Visit: _____

TYPE OF LIBRARY

_____ Town Library

_____ City Library

_____ City/County Library

_____ County/Regional Library

_____ County Law Library

_____ State Library

_____ (Selective Depository)

_____ (Regional Depository)

_____ (Commission)

_____ (Historical Society)

_____ (Law)

_____ (2 years)

_____ (4 years/undergraduate)

_____ (4 years/graduate)

_____ (graduate)

———— Junior College Library
———— Community College Library
———— College Library
———— University Library

———— (Agriculture)
———— (Law)
———— (Medicine)
———— (Mines/Mining)
———— (Technology)
———— (Vocational/Technical)

———— State Court Library
———— Federal Court Library

———— (Academy)
———— (Agency)
———— (Commission)
———— (Department)
———— (University)

———— Federal Government Library

———— (Contracted)

———— Other: _____

POINT SCORES

———— I.   Depository Collections
———— II. Organization of the Depository Collection
———— III. Maintenance of the Depository Collection
———— IV. Staffing
———— V.   Space Standards
———— VI. Service to the General Public
———— VII. Cooperation with the Government Printing Office
———— VIII. Interlibrary Cooperation
———— IX. Regional Depository

I. DEPOSITORY COLLECTIONS

A.₁₈ **The depository library maintains a basic collection for immediate use which includes titles in "Appendix A" of Guidelines for the Depository Library System.**

_____ ₁₈ (1) all 23.   _____ ₁₂ (3) 16–20.   _____ ₆ (5) 6–10.   _____ ₀ (7) none.

_____ ₁₅ (2) 21–22.   _____ ₉ (4) 11–15.   _____ ₃ (6) 1–5.

Budget of the United States Government
Catalog of Federal Domestic Assistance
Census Bureau Catalog
Census of Housing (for State of Depository)
Census of Population (for State of Depository)
Code of Federal Regulations
Congressional Directory
Congressional District Data Book
Congressional Record
County-City Data Book
Federal Register
GPO Sales Publications Reference File

Historical Statistics of the United States
Monthly Catalog
Numerical Lists and Schedule of Volumes
Slip Laws (Public)
Statistical Abstract
Statutes at Large
Subject Bibliographies (S.B. Series)
Supreme Court Reports
United States Code
United States Government Manual
Weekly Compilation of Presidential Documents

(4–1)

B.₁₆ **The depository library has acquired and maintains basic Federal document publications catalogs and indexes which are**

_____ ₄ (1) current.   _____ ₄ (3) governmentally issued.

_____ ₄ (2) retrospective.   _____ ₄ (4) commercially produced.

(4–2)

C.₋₁₇ **The depository library has carefully selected items of potential use for this library.**

_____ ₁₇ (1) yes, all being offered.   _____ ₉ (3) yes, some being offered.

_____ ₁₃ (2) yes, most being offered.   _____ ₀ (4) no, because _____

(4–3)

D.₋₁₇ The depository library selects materials responsive to the needs of users in the Congressional district being served.

—— ₁₇ (1) yes, carefully.

—— ₁₇ (2) yes, in relation to neighboring depository collections.

—— ₁₇ (3) yes, automatically, as we select 100% or near it.

—— ₀ (4) not as yet.   (4-4)

E.₋₁₆ Current selection of the available Item Numbers on the Classified list is:

—— ₁₆ (1) 100%

—— ₁₆ (2) 75%–99%

—— ₁₆ (3) 50%–74%

—— ₁₆ (4) 25%–49%

—— ₁₃ (5) 15%–24%

—— ₁₀ (6) 10%–14%

—— ₇ (7) 9% or less.   (4-5)

F.₋₁₆ The depository library coordinates selections (formally or informally) with other depositories in the Congressional district (or relevant region) to insure adequate coverage within the area.

—— ₁₆ (1) yes, carefully.

—— ₁₆ (2) yes, we are beginning to do so.

—— ₁₆ (3) no, as the district (or region) lacks other depositories.

—— ₁₆ (4) no, as we select 100% or near it.

—— ₁₆ (5) no, as this does not apply to our type of depository.

—— ₀ (6) not as yet.   (4-6)

Does the Depository Library Inspector wish to call special attention to anything relating to *Depository Collections?*

—— (1) yes.   —— (2) no.

Special Merit/Demerit:

—— (1) +10

—— (2) + 5

—— (3) – 5

—— (4) –10

Inspector's Initials: ——————

II. ORGANIZATION OF THE DEPOSITORY COLLECTION

A.$_{22}$ Shipping lists are checked

$_{22}$ (1) within one working day of receipt.
$_{15}$ (2) within two working days of receipt.
$_{8}$ (3) within three working days of receipt.
$_{1}$ (4) within a longer time period.
$_{0}$ (5) seldom or never.   (5-1)

B.$_{5}$ Each publication in the depository shipment

$_{8}$ (1) is marked "depository" or "depository item."
$_{8}$ (2) is distinguished "depository" in another manner.
$_{0}$ (3) is not clearly distinguished as a depository item.   (5-2)

C.$_{8}$ Each publication is dated

$_{8}$ (1) with the shipping list date.
$_{8}$ (2) with date of processing.
$_{5}$ (3) in a special manner.
$_{0}$ (4) seldom or never.   (5-2)

D.$_{8}$ A depository record (holdings/check-in/accessions) is

$_{8}$ (1) kept for all documents.
$_{5}$ (2) kept for most documents.
$_{2}$ (3) kept for some documents.
$_{0}$ (4) not kept.   (5-3)

E.$_{8}$ The depository record shows

$_{2}$ (1) the library's holdings.
$_{2}$ (2) call numbers.
$_{2}$ (3) location where documents may be found.
$_{2}$ (4) additional information (number changes, etc.).   (5-4)

F.₈ The classification adopted by the library for the precise identification of depository documents is

₈ (1) Sudocs . . . . (_____%).
₈ (2) LC . . . . (_____%).
₈ (3) Dewey . . . . (_____%).
₈ (4) another system . . . . (_____%).
₀ (5) not used.

(5-5)

G.₈ A shelf list for depository material

₈ (1) lists documents integrated in the general collection.
₈ (2) is arranged by SuDocs number.
₅ (3) is not arranged by SuDocs, but has SuDocs numbers.
₂ (4) is kept, but lacks SuDocs numbers.
₀ (5) is not kept.

(5-6)

H.₂₂ After documents have been received in the library, they are retrievable for public use

₂₂ (1) within one working day of receipt.
₁₅ (2) within two/ten working days of receipt.
₈ (3) within eleven/twenty working days of receipt.
₁ (4) within more than twenty-one working days of receipt.

(5-7)

I.₈ The depository library maintains a record of item numbers selected.

₈ (1) yes.   _____ ₀ (2) no.

(5-9)

Does the Depository Library Inspector wish to call special attention to anything relating to *Organization of the Depository Collection?*

_____ (1) yes.   _____ (2) no.

Special Merit/Demerit:

_____ (1) +10
_____ (2) + 5
_____ (3) − 5
_____ (4) −10

Inspector's Initials: _____

223

III. MAINTENANCE OF THE DEPOSITORY COLLECTION

A.₋₁₄ Physical condition of the depository collection is   (6–1)

   ₋₁₄ (1) as good as (or better than) other library materials.
    ₀ (2) poorer than other library materials.

B.₁₄ A binding policy for documents   (6–1)

   ₋₁₄ (1) exists and is equal to (or better than) library binding policy.
   ₋₁₀ (2) exists but is inferior to library binding policy
   ₋₁₄ (3) exists and it is a decision not to bind.
    ₆ (4) doesn't exist; arbitrary decision governs binding.
    ₀ (5) doesn't exist; there is no binding.

C.₋₁₄ A replacement policy for lost documents   (6–2)

   ₋₁₄ (1) exists and is equal to (or better than) library binding policy.
   ₋₁₀ (2) exists but is inferior to library replacement policy.
    ₆ (3) exists and it is a decision not to replace.
    ₆ (4) doesn't exist; arbitrary decision governs replacement.
    ₀ (5) doesn't exist; there is no replacement.

D.₋₁₆ Discards are made available to other libraries   (6–3)

   ₋₁₆ (1) regularly.
   ₋₁₂ (2) occasionally.
   ₋₁₆ (3) as lists processed by us as Regional.
   ₋₁₆ (4) not as yet, since depository is less than 5 years old.
   ₋₁₂ (5) not as yet, primarily because there is no Regional.
    ₀ (6) not as yet, although obvious need exists.
   ₋₁₆ (7) doesn't apply, except as law governing Federal libraries.

E.₋₁₄ Regional library service for discarding is

   ₋₁₄ (1) being used by us.
   ₋₁₄ (2) provided by us as a Regional.
   ₋₁₀ (3) not available.
   ₋₁₄ (4) not used as we strive for completeness.

224

—14 (5) not used since depository is less than 5 years old.

—0 (6) not used because of our lack of staff/time.

—10 (7) not used because of Regional's problems.

—NA (8) not applicable to us as a Federal library.

(6-4)

FEDERAL LIBRARIES

F.-14 As an executive department/independent U.S. agency library we offer discards to the Library of Congress and/or the Archivist of the United States

—14 (1) regularly. ———10 (2) occasionally. ———0 (3) not at all. (6-5)

G.-14 As an appellate court library we

—14 (1) offer discards to other libraries.

—14 (2) use other means to discard. ———14 (3) do not discard. (6-6)

H.-14 Superseded publications are withdrawn according to *Instructions to Depository Libraries* (latest edition).

—14 (1) yes.

—14 (2) no, but kept for reference/Regional use. ———0 (3) not at present. (6-7)

I.-14 The depository collection is adequately protected from unlawful removal of publications

—14 (1) as well as (or better than) the rest of the library's collection.

—0 (2) poorer than the rest of the library's collection. (6-8)

Does the Depository Library Inspector wish to call special attention to anything relating to *Organization of the Depository Collection?*

—— (1) yes. —— (2) no.

Special Merit/Demerit:

—— (1) +10
—— (2) + 5
—— (3) – 5
—— (4) –10

Inspector's Initials:____

IV. STAFFING

A.-10 A person has been designated to coordinate depository activities and act as liason with the Superintendent of Documents.

—10 (1) yes. —0 (2) no. (7–1)

B.-10 This person has or shares responsibility for each of the following aspects of depository distributions:

—2 (1) selection of items.
—1 (2) receipt of items.
—1 (3) claiming of items.
—1 (4) replying to correspondence/surveys.
—2 (5) interpreting program to library administration.
—1 (6) performing and/or supervising service to the public.
—2 (7) knowing to whom documents responsibilities are delegated. (7–2)

C.-10 The position of the person responsible for depository documents is classified as

—10 (1) professional librarian.
—3 (2) library technician.
—3 (3) library assistant.
—2 (4) clerical.
—1 (5) another category (_____). (7–3)

D.-10 The person responsible for depository documents

—10 (1) holds a doctoral library degree.
—10 (2) holds a master's library degree.
—10 (3) holds the equivalent of a master's library degree (_____).
—4 (4) holds a bachelor's library degree.
—3 (5) holds a doctoral degree in another field (_____).
—2 (6) holds a master's degree in another field (_____).
—1 (7) holds a bachelor's degree in another field (_____).
—1 (8) holds a certificate in a field (_____).
—0 (9) holds no degree.
—3 (10) has (_____) years of library experience. (7–3)

E.-10 The person responsible for depository documents

—10 (1) is the head of the library.
—10 (2) reports directly to the head of the library.
—10 (3) reports to an intermediate level of administration.
—0 (4) does not report. (7–4)

non-librarians

— 10 (1) equivalent to more than 3 full-time positions.
— 10 (2) equivalent to 3 full-time positions.
— 9 (3) equivalent to 2½ full-time positions.
— 8 (4) equivalent to 2 full-time positions.
— 7 (5) equivalent to 1½ full-time positions.
— 6 (6) equivalent to 1 full-time position.
— 4 (7) equivalent to ½ a full-time position.
— 2 (8) equivalent to ¼ a full-time position.
— 0 (9) lacking altogether.

(7-6)

G.10 Given the size and scope of the library, as well as collection organization, additional professional staff for depository documents

— 0 (1) is needed now.
— 5 (2) will be needed soon.
— 10 (3) is not needed (staff adequate).

(7-5)

H.10 Given the size and scope of the library, as well as collection organization, additional support staff for depository documents

— 0 (1) is needed now.
— 5 (2) will be needed soon.
— 10 (3) is not needed (staff adequate).

(7-6)

I.10 Librarians connected with the depository participate in

— 5 (1) professional societies.
— 3 (2) documents workshops.
— 2 (3) professional reading.
— 0 (4) none of the above.

(7-7)

J.10 Support staff connected with the depository have, according to their responsibilities, opportunities to participate in

— 5 (1) professional societies.
— 3 (2) documents workshops.
— 2 (3) documents-related reading.
— 0 (4) none of the above.

(7-7)

Does the Depository Library Inspector wish to call special attention to anything relating to *Staffing*?

— (1) yes.   — (2) no.

Special Merit/Demerit:

— (1) +10
— (2) +5
— (3) −5
— (4) −10

Inspector's Initials:

227

V. SPACE STANDARDS

A.5 Overall space for depository operations is of

_____ 5 (1) the same (or better) quality than other areas of the library.

_____ 0 (2) poorer quality than other areas of the library. (8–1)

B.30 Overall space for depository operations appears

_____ 3 (1) clean.

_____ 3 (2) attractive.

_____ 3 (3) comfortable.

_____ 3 (4) well lighted.

_____ 3 (5) well ventilated.

_____ 3 (6) temperature controlled.

_____ 3 (7) not excessively noisy.

_____ 3 (8) functional.

_____ 3 (9) flexible.

_____ 3 (10) expandable. (8–1)

C.5 Space provided for depository public services is

_____ 5 (1) adequate.   _____ 0 (2) inadequate. (8–2)

D.5 Space for processing new depository materials is

_____ 5 (1) adequate.   _____ 0 (2) inadequate. (8–2)

E.5 Space for housing the depository collection is

_____ 5 (1) adequate.   _____ 0 (2) inadequate. (8–2)

F.6 Space in the library includes suitable private work areas for

_____ 3 (1) the person responsible for the depository.

_____ 3 (2) depository support staff.

_____ 0 (3) no depository staff members. (8–3)

G.8 All publications in the depository collection are accessible on request and can be retrieved within

_____ 8 (1) one hour (or sooner).

_____ 4 (2) one working day.

_____ 1 (3) one working week.

_____ 0 (4) more than one working week. (8–4)

H.8 Depository publications are located in the library in such a way as to provide physical facilities for the public which

_____ 8 (1) encourage use.

_____ 4 (2) are adequate.

_____ 1 (3) allow minimal use.

_____ 0 (4) are frustrating to use. (8–5)

I₆ Handicapped users (blind/in wheelchairs/deaf) will find the library

6 (1) provides them easy physical access.

3 (2) provides depository service despite obstacles.

0 (3) frustrating to use. (8-6)

J₆ Tables and/or carrels for in-house use of depository publications

6 (1) are adequate.

3 (2) will be needed in the near future.

0 (3) are inadequate. (8-7)

K₆ The principal types of microforms are serviced by

3 (1) adequate readers (minimum one).

3 (2) adequate reader/printers (minimum one).

0 (3) no equipment. (8-8)

L₅ Microfilm equipment for depository materials is

5 (1) located where documents reference service is provided.

5 (2) convenient to where documents reference service is provided.

1 (3) distant from where documents reference service is provided.

0 (4) lacking. (8-8)

M₅ Microfilm storage for depository materials is

5 (1) located where documents reference service is provided.

5 (2) convenient to where documents reference service is provided.

1 (3) distant from where documents reference service is provided.

0 (4) lacking. (8-9)

Does the Depository Library Inspector wish to call special attention to anything relating to *Space Standards?*

_____ (1) yes.   _____ (2) no.

Special Merit/Demerit:

_____ (1) +10

_____ (2) +5

_____ (3) −5

_____ (4) −10

Inspector's Initials: _____

229

VI. SERVICE TO THE GENERAL PUBLIC

A.-9 **The depository makes available for free use in the library by the general public all Government publications.** (9-1)

——— 9 (1) yes.   ——— 0 (2) no.

B.-9 **For reference-type questions about Government publications, the depository library maintains reference stations.** (9-2)

——— 9 (1) one.   ——— 9 (2) more than one.   ——— 0 (3) none.

C.-42 **In the library at one or more points of inquiry, it is possible for a user to find:** (9-2)

——— 6 (1) resources in the Federal documents collection including specific titles.

——— 6 (2) location of wanted publications.

——— 6 (3) answers to reference questions or referral to a source or place where answers can be found.

——— 6 (4) guidance on the use of the collection, including the principal available reference sources/catalogs/abstracts/indexes/aids.

——— 6 (5) availability of additional resources in the region.

——— 6 (6) assistance in borrowing documents from a Regional or from other libraries.

——— 6 (7) user privileges extended to all patrons.

D.-7 **The policy to circulate or not to circulate depository materials outside of the library is chiefly determined by** (9-3)

——— 7 (1) the depository staff.

——— 7 (2) the depository staff and administration.

——— 3 (3) the administration alone.

——— 7 (4) the professional staff as a whole.

——— 3 (5) the circulation department.

——— 3 (6) another department (———————).

E.₁₂ The library provides facilities for

    ₃ (1) using depository documents.
    ₃ (2) making copies from documents.
    ₃ (3) reading microforms.
    ₃ (4) making copies from microforms.

(9–4)

F.₁₂ The depository collection is publicized through

    ₃ (1) displays.
    ₃ (2) announcements of titles/ bibliographies.
    ₃ (3) orientations/tours/classes.
    ₃ (4) radio/television/other means.

(9–5)

G.₉ Reference-type assistance with regard to depository publications is available to

    ₉ (1) all who request it.
    ₃ (2) the institution's members only.
    ₀ (3) no one at present.

(9–6)

Does the Depository Library Inspector wish to call special attention to anything relating to *Service to the General Public?*

    (1) yes.   (2) no.   **Special Merit/Demerit:**

    ———— (1) +10
    ———— (2) + 5
    ———— (3) – 5
    ———— (4) –10

Inspector's Initials:————

VII. COOPERATION WITH THE GOVERNMENT PRINTING OFFICE

A.₂₅ The depository library staff is familiar with the *Instructions to Depository Libraries* (latest edition):

 ₂₅ (1) all staff.   ₂₀ (3) supervisory staff.

 ₂₀ (2) most staff.   ₀ (4) none of staff.

(10–1)

B.₂₅ Upon receipt of shipping lists, necessary claims are usually made within the amount of time specified.

 ₂₅ (1) yes.   ₀ (2) no.

(10–2)

C.₂₅ Sufficient statistics are kept to complete the *Biennial Report of Depository Libraries.*

 ₂₅ (1) yes, and previous *Report* sent to GPO.

 ₅ (2) yes, but previous *Report* not sent to GPO.

 ₀ (3) no, and previous *Report* not sent to GPO.

(5–8)

D.₂₅ Questionnaires and surveys received from the Superintendent of Documents are promptly considered and returned (if necessary).

 ₂₅ (1) no later than the date requested by GPO.

 ₁₀ (2) frequently after the date requested by GPO.

 ₀ (3) not at all.

(10–4)

Does the Depository Library Inspector wish to call special attention to anything relating to *Cooperation with the Government Printing Office?*

_____ (1) yes.   _____ (2) no.

Special Merit/Demerit:

_____ (1) +10

_____ (2) + 5

_____ (3) – 5

_____ (4) –10

Inspector's Initials:_____

233

VII. INTERLIBRARY COOPERATION

A.₁₅ **The depository library cooperates directly, or through a system to which it belongs, with other depositories.**

    ₆ (1) in the state.

    ₄ (2) out of state.

    ₅ (3) and with the Regional/s (unless lacking).

    ₅ (4) opportunity for cooperation does not exist.

    ₀ (5) opportunity exists, but we do not cooperate.

    (11–1)

B.₁₀ **The depository library cooperates with the Regional/s in building their comprehensive retrospective collection by offering discards/duplicates/gifts to them.**

    ₁₀ (1) yes, on a regular basis.

    ₇ (2) yes, only when called upon.

    ₀ (3) not as yet.

    ₁₀ (4) does not apply.

    (11–2)

C.₁₃ **The depository library cooperates with the Regional/s in redistributing weeded publications to depositories which can use them.**

    ₁₃ (1) yes, on a regular basis.

    ₁₀ (2) yes, only when called upon.

    ₀ (3) not as yet.

    ₁₃ (4) does not apply.

    (11–3)

D.₁₀ **The depository library cooperates in reporting new Federal documents unlisted in the** *Monthly Catalog* **to the Superintendent of Documents.**

    ₁₀ (1) yes, by actively seeking out unlisted publications.

    ₁₀ (2) yes, when such publications are encountered.

    ₀ (3) choose not to do so.

    ₁₀ (4) no such publications discovered as yet. (11–4)

other libraries.

___ 13 (1) yes, actively.

___ 10 (2) yes, but in a limited way.

___ 10 (3) we tried, but could get no cooperation from others.

___ 10 (4) no projects of this kind are being done.

___ 0 (5) projects exist, but we do not cooperate.

(11-5)

F.₋13 When the depository borrows documents from other libraries, it strives to verify bibliographic information as completely as possible.

___ 13 (1) regularly.

___ 6 (2) occasionally.

___ 0 (3) not at all.

(11-6)

G.₋13 The depository provides original documents (or copies) on interlibrary loan, if so requested.

___ 13 (1) yes, all.

___ 12 (2) yes, most (excluding reference/high demand/special collections).

___ 6 (3) yes, some.

___ 10 (4) yes, but to Regional/s only.

___ 0 (5) choose not to do so.

(11-7)

H.₋13 The depository has a policy of providing photocopies of Federal publications.

___ 13 (1) more liberal than for other library materials.

___ 13 (2) as liberal as for other library materials.

___ 6 (3) less liberal than for other library materials.

(11-8)

Does the Depository Library Inspector wish to call special attention to anything relating to *Interlibrary Cooperation*?

___ (1) yes.   ___ (2) no.   **Special Merit/Demerit:**

___ (1) + 10

___ (2) + 5

___ (3) − 5

___ (4) − 10

Inspector's Initials: _____

IX. REGIONAL DEPOSITORIES

A.-10 **The Regional depository receives and maintains permanently all depository publications in either printed or microform versions as provided in the *Instructions to Depository Libraries* (latest edition).**

——— 10 (1) yes, according to the regulations.

——— 5 (2) yes, but not able to comply with all regulations.

(PROBLEM AREAS:

_____

_____).

(12-2-a)

B.-10 **The Regional depository is attempting to complete its retrospective collections of major serials, annuals, and other research materials by means of gift, exchange or purchase, including microforms.**

——— 10 (1) yes, according to a planned program.   ——— 0 (3) not at present.

——— 5 (2) yes, randomly, as circumstances permit.

(12-2-b)

C.-10 **The Regional depository is screening lists of documents withdrawn from selective depositories to insure their future availability in the state.**

——— 10 (1) yes, all lists.   ——— 0 (3) not at present.

——— 5 (2) yes, but not all lists.

(12-2-c)

D.-10 **The Regional depository is acquiring (when available) additional copies of documents where necessary.**

——— 10 (1) yes, almost always.   ——— 0 (3) not at present.

——— 5 (2) yes, but selectively.

(12-2-d)

E.-10 **The Regional depository assists selective depositories with reference questions, interlibrary loans, and photocopies.**

——— 10 (1) yes, always.   ——— 0 (3) not at present.

——— 5 (2) yes, but not consistently.

(12-2-e)

F.₁₀ **The Regional depository grants permission to selective depositories to dispose of unwanted documents according to the** *Instructions to Depository Libraries* **(latest edition).**

_____ ₁₀ (1) yes, in written form.

_____ ₁₀ (2) yes, in oral communication.

_____ ₀ (3) not at present.

(12-2-f)

G.₁₀ **The Regional depository provides guidelines to selective depositories for preparing disposal lists of weeded documents.**

_____ ₁₀ (1) yes, regularly, according to plan..

_____ ₁₀ (2) yes, randomly, as circumstances permit.

_____ ₀ (3) not at present.

(12-2-g)

H.₂₀ **The Regional depository contributes to the effectiveness of the depository network through**

_____ ₄ (1) workshops.

_____ ₄ (2) training sessions.

_____ ₄ (3) consultive services offered.

_____ ₄ (4) outreach to non-depositories.

_____ ₄ (5) other means. (_____).

_____ ₀ (6) none of the above.

(12-2-h)

I.₁₀ **The Regional depository authorizes/oversees the transfer of depository materials within the state between depositories.**

_____ ₁₀ (1) no requests received as yet.

_____ ₁₀ (2) yes, in written form.

_____ ₁₀ (3) yes, in oral communication.

_____ ₀ (4) choose not to authorize transfers.

(12-3/4)

Does the Depository Library Inspector wish to call special attention to anything relating to *Regional Depositories?*

_____ (1) yes.   _____ (2) no.

Special Merit/Demerit:

_____ (1) + 10

_____ (2) + 5

_____ (3) − 5

_____ (4) − 10

Inspector's Initials: _____

X. GPO SALES PROGRAM

A. The library purchases documents directly from the inventory offered for sale by the Superintendent of Documents.

_____ (1) yes.   _____ (2) no.

B. The estimated number of times in a year that we order documents is: _____ .

C. The estimated dollar value of our annual orders is: _____ .

D. The name and correct address of the person most concerned with the purchase of Government documents for the library is:

_____

_____

_____

_____

_____

E. The library receives the following from GPO Sales in a timely manner:

	yes	no	sometimes
(1) Monographs.	☐	☐	☐
(2) Serials.	☐	☐	☐
(3) Renewals.	☐	☐	☐

F. The library has opened a GPO Deposit Account for purchase of sales copies.

_____ (1) yes.

_____ (2) no.

_____ (3) would you like information on advantages/procedures for this.

_____ (8) because of lost publications.
_____ (9) because of defective publications.
_____ (10) because of damage in transit.
_____ (11) because of another reason:

_____ (1) yes.
_____ (2) no.
_____ (3) relating to monographs.
_____ (4) relating to serials.
_____ (5) relating to renewals.
_____ (6) for a refund.
_____ (7) because wrong publication sent.

H. Was this matter handled by GPO in a manner satisfactory to your library?

_____ (1) yes. _____ (2) no.

I. Do you know the location of the nearest GPO Bookstore which can serve your library?

_____ (1) yes _____ . _____ (2) no.

J. Does the library use the services of the GPO Bookstore?   **K.** Does the library ever refer patrons to the GPO Bookstore?

_____ (1) yes. _____ (2) no.   _____ (1) yes. _____ (2) no.

L. If the library uses GPO Bookstore services, how does it rate them?

_____ (1) excellent.   _____ (3) satisfactory.
_____ (2) very good.   _____ (4) disappointing.

M. Is the library aware of the various subscriptions which are available through the Superintendent of Documents?

_____ (1) yes. _____ (2) no.

N. Please rank the following tools in your preferred order of use if you use any of them in purchasing sales materials from the Superintendent of Documents.

_____ (1) the "Selected U.S. Government Publications" list.   _____ (4) the *Monthly Catalog.*
_____ (2) the microfiche "Publications Reference File".   _____ (5) Price List 36 (subscriptions).
_____ (3) Depository Shipping Lists.   _____ (6) Subject Bibliographies.

O. Have you any comments on your experience with GPO Sales Service, or any suggestions for improving it?

239

XI. SPECIAL COMMENTS

A. Have you any comments on your library's experience with the *Monthly Catalog*, or any suggestions for its improvement?

B. Have you any comments on your depository's experience with Regional library services, or possible suggestions for enhancing them?

C. Do you wish to offer any elaboration on areas covered by the Inspection Visit Form?

D. Are there any other comments, questions, or areas of concern to the depository library staff?

E. Is there any message you would like to convey to the Superintendent of Documents?

F. Does the Depository Library Inspector have any particular observations to make on this inspection visit?

Inspected by: _____

Inspection date: _____

**Draft of letter from Superintendent of Documents which is sent to
Library Director (with copy to Depository Librarian) of inspected
depository (appropriate variant A/B/C paragraph selected)**

_____
_____
_____
_____
_____

Dear_____:

This letter is to certify that on_____your library's
depository collection was officially inspected by_____
representing the Office of Superintendent of Documents.

In order to let you know how your depository was perceived by our inspector
in terms of its strengths and weaknesses, a copy of the inspection visit
form is being provided for your reference.

The specific areas evaluated, which correspond to those listed in the
Guidelines for the Depository Library System, are given below with a rating
for each derived from data obtained during the inspection visit. A rating
of ''Good'' meets the minimum level of adequacy for the areas evaluated.

(A) I congratulate you and your staff on those areas of excellence achieved, and
sincerely trust that any areas falling short of excellence will see
improvement on the occasion of the next inspection visit.

(B) I congratulate you and your outstanding staff on achieving standards of
excellence in all areas relating to the Depository Library Program. This
places your library among a select vanguard of pace-setters serving as
creative models for depository documents service in the United States.

(C) I regret to inform you and your staff that in the area/areas of_____

your depository fails to meet an adequate standard maintained by most
libraries. I trust that you will take steps to correct this matter; and
that considerable improvement will be found by my representative on the
occasion of the next inspection visit.

With best wishes,

Carl A. LaBarre
SUPERINTENDENT OF DOCUMENTS

RATINGS		SCORE RANGE	
_____	I Depository Collections		
_____	II Organization of the Depository Collection	90–100	EXCELLENT
_____	III Maintenance of the Depository Collection		
_____	IV Staffing	80–89	VERY GOOD
_____	V Space Standards	70–79	GOOD (meets *Guidelines*)
_____	VI Service to the General Public		
_____	VII Cooperation with the Government Printing Office	60–69	FAIR (fails to meet *Guidelines*)
_____	VIII Interlibrary Cooperation		
	IX Regional Depositories (for Regionals only)	50–59	POOR

Notes

Preface

1. Peter Hernon, "Academic Library Reference Service for the Publications of Municipal, State, and Federal Government: A Historical Perspective Spanning the Years Up to 1962," *Government Publications Review,* 5 (1978): 31–50.

2. John V. Richardson, Jr., Dennis C. W. Frisch, and Catherine M. Hall, "Bibliographic Organization of U.S. Federal Depository Collections," *Government Publications Review,* 7A (1980): 463–480.

3. *Guidelines for the Depository Library Program* (Washington, D.C.: Government Printing Office, 1977).

4. Claire Selltiz, Lawrence S. Wrightsman, and Stuart W. Cook, *Research Methods in Social Relations,* 3rd ed. (New York: Holt, Rinehart and Winston, 1976), p. 90.

5. Bernard M. Fry, "Government Publications and the Library: Implications for Change," *Government Publications Review,* 4 (1977): 115.

6. *Guidelines for the Depository Library Program,* p. 7.

Chapter 1

1. U.S. Congress, Joint Committee on Printing, *Government Depository Libraries, The Present Law Governing Designated Depository Libraries, Revised March 1981* (Washington, D.C.: Government Printing Office, 1981), p. 6.

2. Bernard M. Fry, *Government Publications: Their Role in the National Program for Library and Information Services* (Washington, D.C.: Government Printing Office, 1978).

3. Letter from Raymond M. Taylor, Superintendent of Documents, to Peter Hernon, August 5, 1982. See also *Annual Report of the U.S. Government Printing Office Fiscal Year 1981* (Washington, D.C.: Government Printing Office, 1982), p. 30.

4. LeRoy C. Schwarzkopf, "Depository Libraries and Public Access," in *Collection Development and Public Access of Government Documents,* edited by Peter Hernon (Westport, Conn.: Meckler, 1982), p. 31; *Federal Government Printing and Publishing: Policy Issues,* Report of the Ad Hoc Advisory Committee on Revision of Title 44 (Washington, D.C.: Government Printing Office, 1979).

5. *Instructions to Depository Libraries* (Washington, D.C.: Government Printing Office, 1977).

6. *100 GPO Years: 1861–1961* (Washington, D.C.: Government Printing Office, 1962).

7. LeRoy C. Schwarzkopf, "The Depository Library Program and Access by the Public to Official Publications of the United States Government," *Government Publications Review,* 5 (1978): 155–156.

8. John V. Richardson, Jr., Dennis C. W. Frisch, and Catherine M. Hall, "Bibliographic Organization of U.S. Federal Depository Collections," *Government Publications Review,* 7A (1980): 463–480.

9. Charles R. McClure, "Indexing U.S. Government Periodicals: Analysis and Comments," *Government Publications Review,* 5 (1978): 409–421.

10. Charles R. McClure, "Technology in Government Document Collections," *Government Publications Review,* 9 (1982): 255–276.

11. Kevin L. Cook, "A Study of Varying Levels of Support Given to Government Documents Collections in Academic Libraries" (master's thesis, University of Oklahoma, 1981).

12. McClure, "Technology in Government Document Depository Collections."

13. Fry, *Government Publications,* pp. 4–19.

14. Peter Hernon, *Use of Government Publications by Social Scientists* (Norwood, N.J.: Ablex Publishing, 1979).

15. Peter Hernon and Gary R. Purcell, *Developing Collections of U.S. Government Publications* (Greenwich, Conn.: JAI Press, 1982).

16. Charles R. McClure and Keith Harman, "Government Documents as Bibliographic References and Sources in Dissertations," *Government Publications Review,* 9 (1982): 61–72.

17. Peter Hernon, "Use of Microformatted Government Publications," *Microform Review,* 11 (Fall 1982): 237–252.

18. Charles R. McClure, "Administrative Basics for Microformatted Government Documents Librarians," in *Microforms and Government Information,* edited by Peter Hernon (Westport, Conn.: Microform Review, 1981), pp. 125–145.

19. Charles R. McClure, "Online Government Documents Data Base Searching and the Use of Microfiche Documents Online by Academic and Public Depository Librarians," *Microform Review,* 10 (Fall 1981): 245–259.

20. George W. Whitbeck, Peter Hernon, and John Richardson, Jr., "The Federal Depository Library System: A Descriptive Analysis," *Government Publications Review,* 4 (1977): 1–11.

21. U.S. Congress, Joint Committee on Printing, *Federal Government Advisory Committee on Revision of Title 44* (Washington, D.C.: Government Printing Office, 1979).

22. Charles R. McClure, "Structural Analysis of the Depository System: A Preliminary Assessment," in *Collection Development and Public Access of Government Documents,* edited by Peter Hernon (Westport, Conn.: Meckler, 1982), pp. 35–56.

23. U.S. Congress, House Committee on House Administration, Subcommittee

on Printing, *The National Publications Act.* Hearings, 96th Congress, 1st Session, on H.R. 5424 (Washington, D.C.: Government Printing Office, 1979).

24. National Commission on Libraries and Information Science, *Public Sector/ Private Sector Interaction in Providing Information Services* (Washington, D.C.: Government Printing Office, 1982), p. 52.

25. Richardson et al., "Bibliographic Organization of U.S. Federal Depository Collections."

26. Fry, *Government Publications,* pp. 1–12.

27. Charles R. McClure, "An Integrated Approach to Government Publication Collection Development," *Government Publication Review,* 8A (1981): 5–15.

28. Michael Waldo, "An Historical Look at the Debate over How to Organize Federal Government Documents in Depository Libraries," *Government Publications Review,* 4 (1977): 319–329.

29. *Instructions to Depository Libraries* (Washington, D.C.: Government Printing Office, 1977).

30. *Guidelines for the Depository Library System* (Washington, D.C.: Government Printing Office, 1977).

31. American Library Association, Reference and Adult Services Division, Standards Committee, "A Commitment to Information Services: Developmental Guidelines 1979," *RQ,* 18 (Spring 1979): 277.

32. McClure, "An Integrated Approach to Government Publication Collection Development," pp. 13–14.

33. F. W. Lancaster, *The Measurement and Evaluation of Library Services* (Washington, D.C.: Information Resources Press, 1977), pp. 77–136.

34. Ibid., pp. 108–109.

35. Terence Crowley and Thomas Childers, *Information Service in Public Libraries: Two Studies* (Metuchen, N.J.: Scarecrow Press, 1971).

36. Marcia J. Myers, "The Accuracy of Telephone Reference Services in the Southeast: A Case for Quantitative Standards," in *Library Effectiveness: A State of the Art* (Chicago: Library Administration and Management Association, American Library Association, 1980), p. 229.

37. G. B. King and L. R. Berry, *Evaluation of the University of Minnesota Libraries' Reference Department Telephone Information Service, Pilot Study* (Minneapolis: University of Minnesota Library School, 1973). ED 077 517.

38. Jassim Muhammed Jirjees, "The Accuracy of Selected Northeastern College Library Reference/Information Telephone Services in Responding to Factual Inquiries" (Ph.D. dissertation, Rutgers University, 1981).

39. Thomas Childers, "The Test of Reference," *Library Journal,* 105 (April 15, 1980): 925.

40. Ibid.

41. Ibid.

42. Ronald Rowe Powell, "An Investigation of the Relationship between Reference Collection Size and Other Reference Service Factors and Success in Answering Reference Questions" (Ph.D. dissertation, University of Illinois, 1976).

43. Terry L. Weech and Herbert Goldhor, "Obtrusive versus Unobtrusive

Evaluation of Reference Service in Five Illinois Public Libraries," *Library Quarterly,* 52 (October 1982): 305–324.

44. U.S. Congress, Joint Committee on Printing, *Government Depository Libraries,* 1981.

45. *American Library Directory, 1980–1981* (New York: Bowker, 1982).

46. Eugene J. Webb et al., *Unobtrusive Measures: Nonreactive Research in the Social Sciences* (Chicago: Rand McNally, 1966).

47. D. K. Witka, ed., *Handbook of Measurement and Assessment in Behavior Sciences,* 2nd ed. (Reading, Mass.: Addison-Wesley, 1968), pp. 267–268.

48. Stephen Isaac and William B. Michael, *Handbook in Research and Evaluation* (San Diego: Edits Publishers, 1971), pp. 89–91.

49. Fred N. Kerlinger, *Foundations of Behavioral Research,* 2nd ed. (New York: Holt, Rinehart and Winston, 1973), p. 446.

50. John T. Roscoe, *Fundamental Research Statistics for the Behavioral Sciences,* 2nd edition (New York: Holt, Rinehart and Winston, 1975), pp. 134–135.

51. Jum C. Nunally, *Psychometric Theory* (New York: McGraw-Hill, 1967), p. 80.

52. Edward G. Carmines and Richard A. Zeller, *Reliability and Validity Assessment* (Beverly Hills, Calif.: Sage Publications, 1979), p. 17.

53. Nunally, *Psychometric Theory,* p. 80.

54. Kerlinger, *Foundations of Behavioral Research,* pp. 456–459.

55. McClure, "Online Government Documents Data Base Searching," p. 247.

56. Richardson et al., "Bibliographic Organization of U.S. Federal Depository Collections," p. 469.

57. Hubert M. Blalock, Jr., *Conceptualization and Measurement in the Social Sciences* (Beverly Hills, Calif.: Sage Publications, 1982).

Chapter 2

1. For examples of performance measures that may be adapted for use in government documents collections, see: Douglas L. Zweizig and Eleanor Rodgers, *Output Measures for Public Libraries* (Chicago: American Library Association, 1982).

2. F. W. Lancaster, "Evaluation of Reference Service," *The Measurement and Evaluation of Library Services* (Washington, D.C.: Information Resources Press, 1977), pp. 73–136.

3. Gerald Miller, "The Current Status of Theory and Research in Interpersonal Communication," *Human Communication,* 4 (1978): 164–178.

4. Terry L. Weech and Herbert Goldhor, "Obtrusive versus Unobtrusive Evaluation of Reference Service in Five Illinois Public Libraries: A Pilot Study," *Library Quarterly,* 52 (October 1982): 305–324.

5. Helen M. Gothberg, "Immediacy: A Study of Communication Effect on the Reference Process," *Journal of Academic Librarianship,* 2 (July 1976): 126–129.

6. Brenda Dervin (Dept. of Communication, University of Washington), telephone interview, April 21, 1982. See also Brenda Dervin, "Communication Gaps and Inequalities: Moving toward a Reconceptualization," in *Progress in Communi-*

cation Science, edited by Brenda A. Dervin and Melvin J. Voigt, vol. II (Norwood, N.J.: Ablex Publishing Corp., 1980), pp. 73–113.

7. Brenda Dervin, "Useful Theory for Librarianship: Communication Not Information," *Drexel Library Quarterly,* 13 (July 1977): 16–32.

8. G. B. King and R. Berry. *Evaluation of the University of Minnesota Libraries' Reference Department Telephone Information Service, Pilot Study* (Minneapolis: University of Minnesota Library School, 1973). ED 077 517.

9. Peter Hernon and Gary R. Purcell, *Developing Collections of U.S. Government Publications* (Greenwich, Conn.: JAI Press, 1982).

10. Marcia J. Bates, "Information Search Tactics," *Journal of the American Society for Information Science,* 30 (July 1979): 211.

11. Robert S. Taylor, "Question Negotiation and Information Seeking in Libraries," *College & Research Libraries,* 29 (May 1968): 178–194.

12. James Benson and Ruth K. Maloney, "Principles of Searching," *RQ,* 15 (Summer 1975): 316–320.

13. Mary Jo Lynch, *The Reference Interview in Public Libraries* (Ph.D. dissertation, Rutgers University, 1977).

14. Charles R. McClure, "A Reference Theory of Specific Information Retrieval," *RQ,* 13 (Spring 1974): 207–212.

15. Jeffrey St. Clair and Rao Aluri, "Staffing the Reference Desk: Professionals or Nonprofessionals," *Journal of Academic Librarianship,* 3 (July 1977): 149–153.

16. *Guidelines for the Depository Library System* (Washington, D.C.: Government Printing Office, 1977), p. 8.

17. Peter Hernon and Maureen Pastine, "Student Perceptions of Academic Libraries," *College & Research Libraries,* 38 (March 1977): 129–139.

Chapter 3

1. Terence Crowley and Thomas Childers, *Information Service in Public Libraries: Two Studies* (Metuchen, N.J.: Scarecrow Press, 1971).

2. Ibid., p. 172.

3. Ibid., p. 173.

4. Marcia Jean Myers, "The Effectiveness of Telephone Reference/Information Services in Academic Libraries in the Southeast" (Ph.D. dissertation, Florida State University, 1979), p. iii.

5. Ibid., p. 283.

6. Ibid., pp. iv–v.

7. Jassim Muhammad Jirjees, "The Accuracy of Selected Northeastern College Library Reference/Information Telephone Services in Responding to Factual Inquiries" (Ph.D. dissertation, Rutgers University, 1981).

8. Ronald Rowe Powell, "An Investigation of the Relationship between Reference Collection Size and Other Reference Service Factors and Success in Answering Reference Questions" (Ph.D. dissertation, University of Illinois, 1976), p. 152.

9. Ibid., p. 153.

10. Myers, "Effectiveness of Telephone Reference/Information Services in Academic Libraries in the Southeast," p. 287.

11. Ching-chih Chen and Peter Hernon, *Information Seeking: Assessing and Anticipating User Needs* (New York: Neal-Schuman, 1982).

12. *Guidelines for the Depository Library System* (Washington, D.C.: Government Printing Office, 1977). Nationally, over 40 percent of the more than 1,300 depository libraries select fewer than the recommended percentage. For a discussion of this, see Peter Hernon and Gary R. Purcell, *Developing Collections of U.S. Government Publications* (Greenwich, Conn.: JAI Press, 1982).

13. Lucille H. Pendell, "The Use of Federal Documents," *Wilson Library Bulletin,* 5 (April 1931): 507.

14. Edward P. Leavitt, "Government Publications in the University Library," *Library Journal,* 86 (May 1, 1961): 1741.

15. Both Spearman's rho and Kendall's tau are nonparametric correlations in which assumptions are not made concerning the distribution of cases on the variables. These correlations show whether two rankings of the same cases are similar. Kendall coefficients are more meaningful when numerous cases are classified into a few categories and the ranking of data produces a large number of tied ranks. Spearman's rho is preferred when the ratio of cases to categories is smaller and there are few ties at each ranking. See Sidney Siegel, *Nonparametric Statistics for the Behavioral Sciences* (New York: McGraw-Hill, 1956).

16. Analysis of variance permits a comparison of a number of samples at the same time in order to determine if they came from populations identical in their means. Analysis of variance also enables researchers to draw inferences about the differences between populations and the factors that produce those differences. See Clinton I. Chase, *Elementary Statistical Procedures,* 2nd ed. (New York: McGraw-Hill, 1976), pp. 177–191.

17. William C. Robinson, "Evaluation of the Government Documents Collection: An Introduction and Overview," *Government Publications Review,* 8A (1981): 113.

18. William C. Robinson, "Evaluation of the Government Documents Collection: A Step-by-Step Process," *Government Publications Review,* 9 (1982): 137.

19. Charles R. McClure, "From Public Library Standards to Development of Statewide Levels of Adequacy," *Library Research,* 2 (Spring 1980–81): 47–62.

20. Charles A. Bunge, "Professional Education and Reference Efficiency" (Ph.D. dissertation, University of Illinois, 1967).

21. See Edward B. Reeves, Benita J. Howell, and John Van Willigen, "Before the Looking-Glass: A Method to Obtain Self-Evaluation of Roles in a Library Reference Service," *RQ,* 17 (Fall 1977): 25–32. This article has identified the range of activities performed by general reference librarians, and should enable reference departments to engage in introspection.

22. Peter Hernon, *Use of Government Publications by Social Scientists* (Norwood, N.J.: Ablex, 1979), pp. 91–107.

23. Ibid.

24. For support of the thesis that resources are not related to access, either bibliographic or reference, see John V. Richardson, Jr., Dennis C. W. Frisch, and Catherine M. Hall, "Bibliographic Organization of U.S. Federal Depository Collections," *Government Publications Review,* 7A (1980): 463–480.

Chapter 4
1. Thomas Childers, "Trends in Public Library I&R Services," *Library Journal,* 104 (October 1, 1979): 2036.

2. See Ching-chih Chen and Peter Hernon, *Information Seeking: Assessing and Anticipating User Needs* (New York: Neal-Schuman, 1982), and Marcia Jean Myers, "The Effectiveness of Telephone Reference/Information Services in Academic Libraries in the Southeast" (Ph. D. dissertation, Florida State University, 1979).

3. See LeRoy C. Schwarzkopf, "Regional Depository Libraries for U.S. Government Publications," *Government Publications Review,* 2 (1975): 91–102.

4. See Chen and Hernon, *Information Seeking: Assessing and Anticipating User Needs;* Carl Orgren, "Library Schools and the Network," *RQ,* 11 (Summer 1972): 347–351; "Community Information in the '80s: Toward Automation of Information and Referral Files," *RQ,* 21 (Winter 1981): 135–155; "Resources at the Top: Answers and Referrals," *RQ,* 21 (Fall 1981): 28–42; *Toward a Federal Library and Information Services Network: A Proposal* (a report of the Intergovernmental Library Cooperation Project and a joint undertaking of the National Commission on Libraries and Information Science and the Library of Congress) (Washington, D.C.: Government Printing Office, 1982); and Marjorie E. Murfin and Lubomyr R. Wynar, *Reference Service: An Annotated Bibliographic Guide* (Littleton, Colo.: Libraries Unlimited, 1977).

5. Childers, "Trends in Public Library I&R Services," pp. 2036–2037.

6. Myers, "The Effectiveness of Telephone Reference/Information Services in Academic Libraries in the Southeast"; Lowell A. Martin, *Progress and Problems of Pennsylvania Libraries: A Resurvey,* Pennsylvania State Library Monograph No. 6 (Harrisburg: Pennsylvania State Library, 1967), p. 34; Terence Crowley and Thomas Childers, *Information Service in Public Libraries: Two Studies* (Metuchen, N.J.: Scarecrow, 1971); Thomas Childers, "The Test of Reference," *Library Journal,* 105 (April 15, 1980): 924–928; and Terry L. Weech and Herbert Goldhor, "Obtrusive versus Unobtrusive Evaluation of Reference Service in Five Illinois Public Libraries: A Pilot Study," *Library Quarterly,* 52 (October 1982): 305–324.

7. Myers, "The Effectiveness of Telephone Reference/Information Services in Academic Libraries in the Southeast," p. 138.

8. Crowley and Childers, *Information Service in Public Libraries: Two Studies,* p. 171.

9. Childers, "The Test of Reference," p. 926.

10. Chen and Hernon, *Information Seeking: Assessing and Anticipating User Needs.*

11. Peter Hernon, "Use of GPO Bookstores," *Government Publications Review,* 7A (1980): 283–301.

12. For examples of points to include in policy statements, see Mary Jo Lynch, "Academic Library Reference Policy Statements," *RQ,* 11 (Spring 1972): 222–226; Billie Bozone, "Staff Manuals for Reference Departments in College and University Libraries," in *Reference Services,* edited by Arthur Ray Rowland (Hamden, Conn.: Shoe String Press, 1964), pp. 130–134; and Kathleen Coleman and Pauline Dickin-

son, "Drafting a Reference Collection Policy," *College and Research Libraries,* 38 (May 1977): 227–233.

13. For a discussion of the terms "conservative," "moderate," and "liberal," as well as the related terms "minimal," "middling," and "maximum," see James I. Wyer, *Reference Work* (Chicago: American Library Association, 1930); Samuel Rothstein, "Reference Service: The New Dimension in Librarians," *College and Research Librarianship,* 22 (January 1961): 11–18; and Charles R. McClure, "A Reference Theory of Specific Information Retrieval," *RQ,* 13 (Spring 1974): 207–212.

14. See Peter Hernon, "Academic Library Reference Service for the Publications of Municipal, State, and Federal Government: A Historical Perspective Spanning the Years Up to 1962," *Government Publications Review,* 5 (1978): 31–50; and Michael Waldo, "An Historical Look at the Debate over How to Organize Federal Government Documents in Depository Libraries," *Government Publications Review,* 4 (1977): 319–329.

15. Peter Hernon and Maureen Pastine, "Student Perceptions of Academic Librarians," *College & Research Libraries,* 38 (March 1977): 129–139.

16. Peter Hernon, "Use of Microformatted Government Publications," *Microform Review,* 11 (Fall 1982): 237–252.

17. Hernon and Pastine, "Student Perceptions of Academic Librarians."

18. Abdul Rahman, "Philosophy of Reference Service," *Annals of Library Science and Documentation,* 8 (December 1961): 152.

Chapter 5

1. Charles R. McClure, "An Integrated Approach to Government Publication Collection Development," *Government Publication Review,* 8 (1981): 7.

2. Charles R. McClure, "Indexing U.S. Government Periodicals: Analysis and Comments," *Government Publications Review,* 5 (1978): 409–421.

3. Steven D. Zink, "The Impending Crisis in Government Publications Reference Service," *Microform Review,* 11 (Spring 1982): 106–111.

4. Charles R. McClure, "Technology in Government Document Collections," *Government Publications Review,* 9 (1982): 255–276.

5. Charles R. McClure, "Online Government Documents Data Base Searching and the Use of Microfiche Documents Online by Academic and Public Depository Librarians," *Microform Review,* 10 (Fall 1981): 245–259.

6. Kevin L. Cook, "A Study of Varying Levels of Support Given to Government Documents Collections in Academic Libraries" (master's thesis, University of Oklahoma, 1981).

7. Reviewing reference collections in another depository library is an excellent technique to learn about new or "missed" reference sources.

8. Deborah S. Hunt, "Accessing Federal Government Documents Online," *Database,* 4 (February 1982): 10–17.

9. Kathleen Heim, "Government Produced Machine-Readable Statistical Data as a Component of the Social Science Information System: An Examination of Federal

Policy and Strategies for Access," in *Communicating Public Access to Government Information,* edited by Peter Hernon (Westport, Conn.: Meckler, 1983).

10. William A. Katz, *Introduction to Reference Work Volume II: Reference Service and Reference Process* (New York: McGraw-Hill, 1982), pp. 41–65.

11. Mary Jo Lynch, "Reference Interviews in Public Libraries," *Library Quarterly,* 48 (April 1978): 119–141.

12. Nice M. de Figueiredo, "A Conceptual Methodology for Error Prevention in Reference Work" (Ph.D. dissertation, Florida State University, 1975).

13. Charles Stewart and William Cash, *Interviewing: Principles and Practices* (Dubuque, Iowa: Wm. C. Brown Co., 1974).

14. Robert S. Taylor, "Question Negotiation and Information Seeking in Libraries," *College and Research Libraries,* 29 (May 1968): 178–194.

15. Raymond, L. Gordon, *Interviewing: Strategy, Techniques and Tactics* (Homewood, Ill.: Dorsey Press, 1969).

16. Judith Mucci, "Videotape Self-Evaluation in Public Libraries: Experiments in Evaluating Public Service," *RQ,* 16 (Fall 1976): 33–37.

17. Virginia Boucher, "Nonverbal Communication and the Library Reference Interview," *RQ,* 16 (Fall 1976): 27–31.

18. Marilyn Domas White, "The Dimensions of the Reference Interview," *RQ,* 20 (Summer 1981): 373–381.

19. Ibid., p. 375.

20. Ibid., p. 376.

21. William A. Katz, *Introduction to Reference Work Volume II,* pp. 67–94.

22. James Benson and Ruth K. Maloney, "Principles of Searching," *RQ,* 15 (Summer 1975): 316–320, and Gerald Jahoda, *The Librarian and Reference Queries* (New York: Academic Press, 1980).

23. Marcia J. Bates, "Information Search Tactics," *Journal of the American Society for Information Science,* 30 (July 1979): 205–214.

24. Marcia J. Bates, "Idea Tactics," *Journal of the American Society for Information Science,* 30 (September 1979): 280–289.

25. Ibid., p. 280.

26. Mary Jane Swope and Jeffrey Katzer, "The Silent Majority: Why Don't They Ask Questions," *RQ,* 12 (Winter 1972): 161–166.

27. Helen M. Gothberg, "User Satisfaction with a Librarian's Immediate and Non-Immediate Verbal-Nonverbal Communication" (Ph.D. dissertation, University of Denver, 1974); Barron Holland, "Updating Library Reference Services through Training for Interpersonal Competence," *RQ,* 17 (Spring 1978): 207–211; W. B. Lukenbill, "Teaching Helping Relationship Concepts in the Reference Process," *Journal of Education for Librarianship,* 18 (Fall 1977): 110–120; and Gerald Egan, *Interpersonal Living: A Skills/Contract Approach to Human Relations Training* (Monterey, Calif.: Brooks/Cole Publishing Co., 1976).

28. James Rettig, "A Theoretical Model and Definition of the Reference Process," *RQ,* 17 (Fall 1978): 19–29.

29. Anita R. Shiller, "Reference Service: Instruction or Information," *Library Quarterly,* 35 (January 1965): 52–60.

30. Thomas Childers, "Trends in Public Library I&R Services," *Library Journal,* (October 1, 1979): 2036–2037.

31. Clara S. Jones, *Public Library Information and Referral Services* (Syracuse, N.Y.: Gaylord Brothers, 1978); Sadie Espar, "Building and Maintaining the Community Resources File for I&R Services," *Collection Building,* 1 (1978): 7–18; and Marta Wold, "Cooperation between Libraries and Other Agencies in Information and Referral," *Public Libraries,* 20 (Summer 1981): 61–62.

32. Patrick R. Penland, "Client Centered Librarians," *Public Libraries,* 21 (Summer 1982): 44–48.

33. Appropriate areas are discussed throughout William A. Katz, *Introduction to Reference Work,* volume II.

34. Peter Hernon and Gary R. Purcell, *Developing Collections of U.S. Government Publications* (Greenwich, Conn.: JAI Press, 1982).

35. Bruce Morton and J. Randolph Cox, "Cooperative Collection Development between Selective U.S. Depository Libraries," *Government Publications Review,* 9 (1982): 221–230.

36. Charles R. McClure, "The Planning Process: Strategies for Action," *College & Research Libraries,* 39 (November 1978): 456–466, and Charles R. McClure, "Planning for Library Services: Lessons and Opportunities," *Journal of Library Administration,* 2 (1982): 7–28.

37. Charles R. McClure, "Planning for the Future," *Government Publications Review,* 5 (1978): 511–515.

38. Charles R. McClure, *Information for Academic Library Decision Making: The Case for Organizational Information Management* (Westport, Conn.: Greenwood Press, 1980), pp. 88–123.

39. Michael Waldo, "An Historical Look at the Debate over How to Organize Federal Government Documents in Depository Libraries," *Government Publications Review,* 4 (1977): 319–329.

40. Linda Futato, "Online Bibliographic Data Base Searching for Government Document Collections," *Government Publications Review,* 9 (1982): 311–322. See also "An Untapped Resource: Government Data Bases," *Infosystems* (July 1982): 94–96.

41. Sharon Walbridge, "OCLC and Government Documents Collections," *Government Publication Review,* 9 (1982): 277–287.

42. Virginia Gillham, "CODOC as a Consortium Tool," *Government Publications Review,* 9 (1982): 45–54, and Virginia Gillham, "In-House Procedures in a Library Using CODOC," *Government Publications Review,* 8 (1981): 411–417.

43. Bruce Morton, "Implementing an Automated Shelflist for a Selective Depository Collection: Implications for Collection Management and Public Access," *Government Publications Review,* 9 (1982): 323–344, and Bruce Morton, "An Item Record Management System," *Government Publications Review,* 8 (1981): 185–196.

44. Charles R. McClure, "Administrative Basics for Microformatted Government Documents Librarians," in *Microforms and Government Information,* edited by Peter Hernon (Westport, Conn.: Microform Review, 1981), pp. 126–132, and

Charles R. McClure, "Administrative Integration of Microformatted Government Publications," *Microform Review,* 6 (September 1977): 259–271.

45. Charles R. McClure, "Personnel Development," *Government Publications Review,* 7A (1980): 341–348.

46. Beverly Lynch, "Assimilation of Government Publications in Study and Research, Final Report, July 1, 1978 through June 30, 1979" (Chicago: University of Illinois at Chicago Circle, 1979). ED 184 571.

47. For a number of views on documents education, see "Opinion: Education for Government Documents Librarians," *Government Publications Review,* 9 (1982): 231–235.

48. Publications and information can be obtained from CLENE (Continuing Library Education Network and Exchange), Box 1228, 6200 Michigan Ave. NE, Washington, D.C. 20064; Larry Nolan Davis, *Planning, Conducting & Evaluating Workshops* (Austin, Tex.: Learning Concepts, 1974), and Barbara Conroy, *Library Staff Development and Continuing Education: Principles and Practices* (Littleton, Colo.: Libraries Unlimited, 1978).

49. Richard M. Boss with Deborah Raikes, *Developing Microform Reading Facilities* (Westport, Conn.: Microform Review, Inc. 1982), pp. 147–170.

50. Paul B. Kantor, "Quantitative Evaluation of the Reference Process," *RQ,* 21 (Fall 1981): 43–52.

51. Mary Jo Lynch, ed. *Library Data Collection Handbook* (Chicago, American Library Association, 1981).

52. F. W. Lancaster, *The Measurement and Evaluation of Library Services* (Washington, D.C.: Information Resources Press, 1977).

53. John Martyn and F. Wilfred Lancaster, *Investigative Methods in Library and Information Science: An Introduction* (Washington, D.C.: Information Resources Press, 1981).

54. Charles H. Busha and Stephen P. Harter, *Research Methods in Librarianship* (New York: Academic Press, 1980).

55. Michael R. W. Bommer and Ronald W. Chorba, *Decision Making for Library Management* (White Plains: Knowledge Industry Publications, 1982), and Robert S. Runyon, "Towards the Development of a Library Management Information System," *College & Research Libraries,* 42 (November 1981): 539–548.

56. Vernon E. Palmour, Marcia C. Bellassai, and Nancy DeWath, *A Planning Process for Public Libraries* (Chicago: American Library Association, 1980).

57. Douglas L. Zweizig and Eleanor Rodger, *Output Measures for Public Libraries* (Chicago: American Library Association, 1982).

58. *Guidelines for the Depository Library System* (Washington, D.C.: Government Printing Office, 1977), pp. 8–9; see also Title 44, *U.S. Code.*

59. Ibid.

60. David S. Ferriero and Kathleen A. Powers, "Burnout at the Reference Desk," *RQ,* 21 (Spring 1982): 274.

61. Ibid., pp. 274–279.

62. Ibid.

63. Zink, "The Impending Crisis in Government Publications Reference Service," pp. 106–111.

Chapter 6

1. See Peter Hernon, ed., *Microforms and Government Information* (Westport, Conn.: Microform Review, 1981), pp. 17–28.

2. *Guidelines for the Depository Library System* (Washington, D.C.: Government Printing Office, 1977), pp. 10 and 3.

3. See U.S. Office of Management and Budget, *Bulletin* (No. 81–16), April 21, 1981, and *Bulletin* (No. 81–16), Supplement No. 1, October 9, 1981.

4. House Committee on Appropriations, *Legislative Branch Appropriations for 1982: Hearing . . .*, Part 2 (Washington, D.C. Government Printing Office, 1981), p. 880.

5. *Public Documents Highlights*, 50 (February 1982): 2 and 13.

6. Abraham Kaplan, *The Conduct of Inquiry: Methodology for Behavioral Science* (Scranton, Pa.: Chandler Publishing, 1964), p. 176.

7. Ernest R. DeProspo, Ellen Altman, and Kenneth E. Beasley, *Performance Measures for Public Libraries* (Chicago: American Library Association, 1973).

8. Alvin M. Schrader, "Performance Measures for Public Libraries: Refinements in Methodology and Reporting," *Library Research*, 2 (1980–1981): 129–155.

9. F. Wilfrid Lancaster, *The Measurement and Evaluation of Library Services* (Washington, D.C.: Information Resources Press, 1977).

10. Colin K. Mick, "Cost Analysis of Information Systems and Services," in *Annual Review of Information Science and Technology*, vol. 14, edited by Martha E. Williams (White Plains, N.Y.: Knowledge Industries, 1979), pp. 36–64.

11. William B. Rouse and Sandra H. Rouse, *Management of Library Networks* (New York: John Wiley, 1980).

12. J. G. Williams, "Performance Criteria and Evaluation for a Library Resource Sharing Network," in *Library Resource Sharing* (New York: Marcel Dekker, 1977), pp. 225–277.

13. C. West Churchman, *The Systems Approach and Its Enemies* (New York: Basic Books, 1979).

14. Charles R. McClure, ed., *Planning for Library Services: A Guide To Utilizing Planning Methods for Library Management* (New York: Haworth Press, 1982).

15. For a more complete discussion of goals and objectives for the depository library program, see Charles R. McClure, "Structural Analysis of the Depository System: A Preliminary Assessment," in *Collection Development and Public Access of Government Documents: Proceedings of the First Annual Library Government Documents and Information Conference*, edited by Peter Hernon (Westport, Conn.: Meckler, 1982), pp. 35–56.

16. Ann Armstrong and Judith C. Russell, "Public Access," *Information World*, 1 (October 1979): 1 and 11.

17. See Peter Hernon and Gary R. Purcell, *Developing Collections of U.S. Government Publications* (Greenwich, Conn.: JAI Press, 1982).

18. "Opinions: GPO Inspection Program," *Government Publications Review*, 7A

(1980): 449–452, and Carol Watts, "The Depository Library Inspection Program," *Reference Services Review* 10 (September 1982): 55–62.

19. Charles R. McClure, "The Planning Process: Strategies for Action," *College & Research Libraries,* 39 (November 1978): 456.

20. Ernest R. DeProspo and James W. Liesener, "Media Program Evaluation: A Working Framework," *School Media Quarterly,* 3 (Summer 1975): 289–301.

21. At its spring 1981 meeting, the Depository Library Council to the Public Printer adopted the following resolution:

> In order to bolster the Regional depository libraries' capabilities to serve their state missions and in order to assure that Federal documents are available throughout the United States on an equal and expeditious basis, the Depository Library Council recommends that the Public Printer investigate the feasibility of requiring each state to prepare a plan to coordinate the Federal documents depository program within that state. The plan should be developed through consultation with all designated Federal depository libraries within the state and should address all depository responsibilities outlined in the *Instructions to Depository Libraries* as well as the concerns expressed through the Regional Depository Library Council at the first afternoon session of the Spring 1981 meeting.

See "GPO Responds to Depository Library Council Resolutions," *Public Documents Highlights,* 48/49 (October/December 1981): 5. For additional coverage of the state plans, see other issues of *Public Documents Highlights, Documents to the People,* and *Minutes* of the Depository Library Council.

22. See Hernon and Purcell, *Developing Collections of U.S. Government Publications.*

23. LeRoy C. Schwarzkopf, "1982 Spring Meeting Depository Library Council to the Public Printer," *Documents to the People,* 10 (July 1982): 150.

24. Herbert J. Gans, "Supplier-Oriented and User-Oriented Planning for the Public Library," in *Public Library Purpose: A Reader,* edited by Barry Totterdell (Hamden, Conn.: Linnett Books, 1977), pp. 71–83.

25. See Armstrong and Russell, "Public Access," and Kathleen T. Larson, "Establishing a New GPO Depository Documents Department in an Academic Law Library," *Law Library Journal,* 72 (Summer 1979): 484–496.

26. See LeRoy C. Schwarzkopf, "Depository Libraries and Public Access," in *Collection Development and Public Access of Government Documents,* pp. 24–25.

27. *Federal Government Printing and Publishing: Policy Issues.* Report of the Ad Hoc Advisory Committee on Revision of Title 44 (Washington, D.C.: Government Printing Office, 1979), p. 42.

28. See Ann Bregent, "Cost of Regional Depository Library Service in the State of Washington" (Olympia: Washington State Library, 1979; Washington, D.C.: Government Printing Office, 1979), and Sandra K. Faull, "Cost and Benefits of Federal Depository Status for Academic Research Libraries," *Documents to the People,* 8 (January 1980): 33–39.

29. See Hernon, *Microforms and Government Information,* pp. 146–164, and

McClure, "Structural Analysis of the Depository System: A Preliminary Assessment," pp. 35–56.

30. Charles R. McClure, "Online Government Documents Data Base Searching and the Use of Microfiche Documents Online by Academic and Public Depository Librarians," *Microform Review,* 10 (Fall 1981): 245–259.

31. Kathleen M. Heim, "Government Produced Machine-Readable Statistical Data as a Component of the Social Science Information System: An Examination of Federal Policy and Strategies for Access," in *Communicating Public Access to Government Information,* edited by Peter Hernon (Westport, Conn.: Meckler, 1983).

32. "Resolutions Approved by the Depository Library Council to the Public Printer," *Documents to the People,* 9 (July 1981): 160.

33. Thomas Childers, "The Test of Reference," *Library Journal,* 105 (April 15, 1980): 925–926.

Bibliography

Articles

American Library Association, Reference and Adult Services Division, Standards Committee. "A Commitment to Information Services: Developmental Guidelines 1979," *RQ,* 18 (Spring 1979): 277–278.

Armstrong, Ann, and Judith C. Russell. "Public Access," *Information World,* 1 (October 1979): 1 and 11.

Bates, Marcia J. "Idea Tactics," *Journal of the American Society for Information Science,* 30 (September 1979): 280–289.

———. "Information Search Tactics," *Journal of the American Society for Information Science,* 30 (July 1979): 205–214.

Benson, James, and Ruth K. Maloney. "Principles of Searching," *RQ,* 15 (Summer 1975): 316–320.

Boucher, Virginia. "Nonverbal Communication and the Library Reference Interview," *RQ,* 16 (Fall 1976): 27–31.

Childers, Thomas. "The Test of Reference," *Library Journal,* 105 (April 15, 1980): 924–928.

———. "Trends in Public Library I&R Services," *Library Journal,* 104 (October 1, 1979): 2035–2039.

Coleman, Kathleen, and Pauline Dickinson. "Drafting a Reference Collection Policy," *College and Research Libraries,* 38 (May 1977): 227–233.

"Community Information in the '80s: Toward Automation of Information and Referral Files (A Symposium)," *RQ,* 21 (Winter 1981): 135–155.

DeProspo, Ernest R., and James W. Liesener. "Media Program Evaluation: A Working Framework," *School Media Quarterly,* 3 (Summer 1975): 289–301.

Dervin, Brenda. "Useful Theory for Librarianship: Communication Not Information," *Drexel Library Quarterly,* 13 (July 1977): 16–32.

Espar, Sadie. "Building and Maintaining the Community Resources File for I&R Services," *Collection Building,* 1 (1978): 7–18.

Faull, Sandra K. "Cost and Benefits of Federal Depository Status for Academic Research Libraries," *Documents to the People,* 8 (January 1980): 33–39.

Ferriero, David S., and Kathleen A. Powers. "Burnout at the Reference Desk," *RQ,* 21 (Spring 1982): 274–279.

Futato, Linda. "Online Bibliographic Data Base Searching for Government Document Collections," *Government Publications Review,* 9 (1982): 311–322.

Gillham, Virginia. "CODOC as a Consortium Tool," *Government Publications Review,* 9 (1982): 45–54.

———. "In-House Procedures in a Library Using CODOC," *Government Publications Review,* 8 (1981): 411–417.

Gothberg, Helen M. "Immediacy: A Study of Communication Effect on the Reference Process," *Journal of Academic Librarianship,* 2 (July 1976): 126–129.

"GPO Responds to Depository Library Council Resolutions," *Public Documents Highlights,* 48/49 (October/December 1981): 5.

Hernon, Peter. "Academic Library Reference Service for the Publications of Municipal, State, and Federal Government: A Historical Perspective Spanning the Years Up to 1962," *Government Publications Review,* 5 (1978): 31–50.

———. "Use of GPO Bookstores," *Government Publications Review,* 7A (1980): 283–301.

———. "Use of Microformatted Government Publications," *Microform Review,* 11 (Fall 1982): 237–252.

——— and Maureen Pastine. "Student Perceptions of Academic Libraries," *College & Research Libraries,* 38 (March 1977): 129–139.

Holland, Barron. "Updating Library Reference Services through Training for Interpersonal Competence," *RQ,* 17 (Spring 1978): 207–211.

Hunt, Deborah S. "Accessing Federal Government Documents Online," *Database,* (February 1982): 10–17.

Kantor, Paul B. "Quantitative Evaluation of the Reference Process," *RQ,* 21 (Fall 1981): 43–52.

Larson, Kathleen T. "Establishing a New GPO Depository Documents Department in an Academic Law Library," *Law Library Journal,* 72 (Summer 1979): 484–496.

Levitt, Edward P. "Government Publications in the University Library," *Library Journal,* 86 (May 1, 1961): 1741–1743.

Lukenbill, W. B. "Teaching Helping Relationship Concepts in the Reference Process," *Journal of Education for Librarianship,* 18 (Fall 1977): 110–120.

Lynch, Mary Jo. "Academic Library Reference Policy Statements," *RQ,* 11 (Spring 1972): 222–226.

———. "Reference Interviews in Public Libraries," *Library Quarterly,* 48 (April 1978): 119–141.

McClure, Charles R. "Administrative Integration of Microformatted Government Publications," *Microform Review,* 6 (September 1977): 259–271.

———. "From Public Library Standards to Development of Statewide Levels of Adequacy," *Library Research,* 2 (Spring 1980–1981): 47–62.

———. "Indexing U.S. Government Periodicals: Analysis and Comments," *Government Publications Review,* 5 (1978): 409–421.

———. "An Integrated Approach to Government Publication Collection Development," *Government Publication Review,* 8A (1981): 5–15.

———. "Online Government Documents Data Base Searching and the Use of

Microfiche Documents Online by Academic and Public Depository Librarians," *Microform Review,* 10 (Fall 1981): 245–259.

———. "Personnel Development," *Government Publications Review,* 7A (1980): 341–348.

———. "Planning for Library Services: Lessons and Opportunities," *Journal of Library Administration,* 2 (1982): 7–28.

———. "Planning for the Future," *Government Publications Review,* 5 (1978): 511–515.

———. "The Planning Process: Strategies for Action," *College & Research Libraries,* 39 (November 1978): 456–466.

———. "A Reference Theory of Specific Information Retrieval," *RQ,* 13 (Spring 1974): 207–212.

———. "Technology in Government Document Collections," *Government Publications Review,* 9 (1982): 255–276.

——— and Keith Harman. "Government Documents as Bibliographic References and Sources in Dissertations," *Government Publications Review,* 9 (1982): 61–72.

Miller, Gerald. "The Current Status of Theory and Research in Interpersonal Communication," *Human Communication,* 4 (1978): 164–178.

Morton, Bruce. "Implementing an Automated Shelflist for a Selective Depository Collection: Implications for Collection Management and Public Access," *Government Publications Review,* 9 (1982): 323–344.

———. "An Item Record Management System," *Government Publications Review,* 8 (1981): 185–196.

——— and J. Randolph Cox. "Cooperative Collection Development between Selective U.S. Depository Libraries," *Government Publications Review,* 9 (1982): 221–230.

Mucci, Judith. "Videotape Self Evaluation in Public Libraries: Experiments in Evaluating Public Service," *RQ,* 16 (Fall 1976): 33–37.

"Opinion: Education for Government Documents Librarians," *Government Publications Review,* 9 (1982): 231–235.

"Opinion: GPO Inspection Program," *Government Publications Review,* 7A (1980): 449–452.

Orgren, Carl. "Library Schools and the Network," *RQ,* 11 (Summer 1972): 347–351.

Pendell, Lucille H. "The Use of Federal Documents," *Wilson Library Bulletin,* 5 (April 1931): 507–509.

Penland, Patrick R. "Client Centered Librarians," *Public Libraries,* 21 (Summer 1982): 44–48.

Rahman, Abdul. "Philosophy of Reference Service," *Annals of Library Science and Documentation,* 8 (December 1961): 152.

Reeves, Edward B., Benita J. Howell, and John Van Willigen. "Before the Looking-Glass: A Method to Obtain Self-Evaluation of Roles in a Library Reference Service," *RQ,* 17 (Fall 1977): 25–32.

"Resolutions Approved by the Depository Library Council to the Public Printer," *Documents to the People,* 9 (July 1981): 160–163.

"Resources at the Top: Answers and Referrals (A Symposium)," *RQ,* 21 (Fall 1981): 28–42.

Rettig, James. "A Theoretical Model and Definition of the Reference Process," *RQ,* 17 (Fall 1978): 19–29.

Richardson, John V., Jr., Dennis C. W. Frisch, and Catherine M. Hall. "Bibliographic Organization of U.S. Federal Depository Collections," *Government Publications Review,* 7A (1980): 463–480.

Robinson, William C. "Evaluation of the Government Documents Collection: A Step-by-Step Process," *Government Publications Review,* 9 (1982): 131–141.

_____. "Evaluation of the Government Documents Collection: An Introduction and Overview," *Government Publications Review,* 8A (1981): 111–125.

Rothstein, Samuel. "Reference Service: The New Dimension in Librarianship," *College & Research Libraries,* 22 (January 1961): 11–18.

Runyon, Robert S. "Towards the Development of a Library Management Information System," *College & Research Libraries,* 42 (November 1981): 539–548.

Schrader, Alvin M. "Performance Measures for Public Libraries: Refinements in Methodology and Reporting," *Library Research,* 2 (1980–1981): 129–155.

Schwarzkopf, LeRoy C. "The Depository Library Program and Access by the Public to Official Publications of the United States Government," *Government Publications Review,* 5 (1978): 147–156.

_____. "1982 Spring Meeting Depository Library Council to the Public Printer," *Documents to the People,* 10 (July 1982): 150.

_____. "Regional Depository Libraries for U.S. Government Publications," *Government Publications Review,* 2 (1975): 91–102.

Shiller, Anita R. "Reference Service: Instruction or Information," *Library Quarterly,* 35 (January 1965): 52–60.

St. Clair, Jeffrey, and Rao Aluri. "Staffing the Reference Desk: Professionals or Nonprofessionals," *Journal of Academic Librarianship,* 3 (July 1977): 149–153.

Swope, Mary Jane, and Jeffrey Katzer. "The Silent Majority: Why Don't They Ask Questions," *RQ,* 12 (Winter 1972): 161–166.

Taylor, Robert S. "Question Negotiation and Information Seeking in Libraries," *College & Research Libraries,* 29 (May 1968): 178–194.

"An Untapped Resource: Government Data Bases," *Infosystems* (July 1982): 94–96.

Walbridge, Sharon. "OCLC and Government Documents Collections," *Government Publications Review,* 9 (1982): 277–287.

Waldo, Michael. "An Historical Look at the Debate over How to Organize Federal Government Documents in Depository Libraries," *Government Publications Review,* 4 (1977): 319–329.

Watts, Carol. "The Depository Library Inspection Program," *Reference Services Review,* 10 (September 1982): 55–62.

Weech, Terry L., and Herbert Goldhor. "Obtrusive versus Unobtrusive Evaluation of Reference Service in Five Illinois Public Libraries: A Pilot Study," *Library Quarterly,* 52 (October 1982): 305–324.

Whitbeck, George W., Peter Hernon, and John Richardson Jr. "The Federal

Depository Library System: A Descriptive Analysis," *Government Publications Review*, 4 (1977): 1–11.

White, Marilyn Domas. "The Dimensions of the Reference Interview," *RQ*, 20 (Summer 1981): 373–381.

Wold, Marta. "Cooperation between Libraries and Other Agencies in Information and Referral," *Public Libraries*, 20 (Summer 1981): 61–62.

Zink, Steven D. "The Impending Crisis in Government Publications Reference Service," *Microform Review*, 11 (Spring 1982): 106–111.

Books

American Library Directory 1980–1981. New York: Bowker, 1982.

Blalock, Hubert M. *Conceptualization and Measurement in the Social Sciences*. Beverly Hills, Calif.: Sage Publications, 1982.

Bommer, Michael R. W., and Ronald W. Chorba. *Decision Making for Library Management*. White Plains, N.Y.: Knowledge Industry Publications, 1982.

Boss, Richard M., and Deborah Raikes. *Developing Microform Reading Facilities*. Westport, Conn.: Microform Review, Inc., 1982.

Bozone, Billie. "Staff Manuals for Reference Departments in College and University Libraries," in *Reference Services*, edited by Arthur Ray Rowland. Hamden, Conn.: Shoe String Press, 1964.

Busha, Charles H., and Stephen P. Harter. *Research Methods in Librarianship*. New York: Academic Press, 1980.

Carmines, Edward G., and Richard A. Zeller. *Reliability and Validity Assessment*. Beverly Hills, Calif.: Sage Publications, 1979.

Chase, Clinton I. *Elementary Statistical Procedures*, 2nd. ed. New York: McGraw-Hill, 1976.

Chen, Ching-chih, and Peter Hernon. *Information Seeking: Assessing and Anticipating User Needs*. New York: Neal-Schuman, 1982.

Churchman, C. West. *The Systems Approach and Its Enemies*. New York: Basic Books, 1979.

Conroy, Barbara. *Library Staff Development and Continuing Education: Principles and Practices*. Littleton, Colo.: Libraries Unlimited, 1978.

Crowley, Terence, and Thomas Childers. *Information Service in Public Libraries: Two Studies*. Metuchen, N.J.: Scarecrow Press, 1971.

Davis, Larry Nolan. *Planning, Conducting, & Evaluating Workshops*. Austin, Tex.: Learning Concepts, 1974.

DeProspo, Ernest R., Ellen Altman, and Kenneth E. Beasley. *Performance Measures for Public Libraries*. Chicago: American Library Association, 1973.

Dervin, Brenda. "Communication Gaps and Inequalities: Moving toward a Reconceptualization," in *Progress in Communication Science*, vol. II, edited by Brenda A. Dervin and Melvin J. Voigt. Norwood, N.J.: Ablex Publishing Corp., 1980.

Egan, Gerald. *Interpersonal Living: A Skills/Contract Approach to Human Relations Training*. Monterey, Calif.: Brooks/Cole Publishing Co., 1976.

Gans, Herbert J. "Supplier-Oriented and User-Oriented Planning for the Public

Library," in *Public Library Purpose: A Reader,* edited by Barry Totterdell. Hamden, Conn.: Linnett Books, 1977.

Gordon, Raymond L. *Interviewing: Strategy, Techniques and Tactics.* Homewood, Ill.: Dorsey Press, 1969.

Heim, Kathleen. "Government Produced Machine-Readable Statistical Data as a Component of the Social Science Information System: An Examination of Federal Policy and Strategies for Access," in *Communicating Public Access to Government Information,* edited by Peter Hernon. Westport, Conn.: Meckler, 1983.

Hernon, Peter, ed. *Microforms and Government Information.* Westport, Conn.: Microform Review, Inc., 1981.

————. *Use of Government Publications by Social Scientists.* Norwood, N.J.: Ablex Publishing Corp., 1979.

———— and Gary R. Purcell. *Developing Collections of U.S. Government Publications.* Greenwich, Conn.: JAI Press, 1982.

Isaac, Stephen, and William B. Michael. *Handbook in Research and Evaluation.* San Diego: Edits Publishers, 1971.

Jahoda, Gerald. *The Librarian and Reference Queries: A Systematic Approach.* New York: Academic Press, 1980.

Jones, Clara S. *Public Library Information and Referral Services.* Syracuse, N.Y.: Gaylord Brothers, 1978.

Kaplan, Abraham. *The Conduct of Inquiry: Methodology for Behavioral Science.* Scranton, Pa.: Chandler Pub. Co., 1964.

Katz, William A. *Introduction to Reference Work Volume II: Reference Service and Reference Process,* 4th ed. New York: McGraw-Hill, 1982.

Kerlinger, Fred N. *Foundations of Behavioral Research,* 2nd ed. New York: Holt, Rinehart and Winston, 1973.

Lancaster, F. W. *The Measurement and Evaluation of Library Services.* Washington, D.C.: Information Resources Press, 1977.

Lynch, Mary Jo, ed. *Library Data Collection Handbook.* Chicago: American Library Association, 1981.

Martin, Lowell A. *Progress and Problems of Pennsylvania Libraries: A Resurvey.* Pennsylvania State Library, Monograph No. 6. Harrisburg: Pennsylvania State Library, 1967.

Martyn, John, and F. Wilfred Lancaster. *Investigative Methods in Library and Information Science: An Introduction.* Washington, D.C.: Information Resources Press, 1981.

McClure, Charles R. "Administrative Basics for Microformatted Government Documents Librarians," in *Microforms and Government Information,* edited by Peter Hernon. Westport, Conn.: Microform Review, Inc., 1981.

————. *Information for Academic Library Decision Making: The Case for Organizational Information Management.* Westport, Conn.: Greenwood Press, 1980.

————. *Planning for Library Services: A Guide to Utilizing Planning Methods for Library Management.* New York: Haworth Press, 1982.

————. "Structural Analysis of the Depository System: A Preliminary Assessment," in *Collection Development and Public Access of Government Documents,* edited by Peter Hernon. Westport, Conn.: Meckler, 1982.

Mick, Colin K. "Cost Analysis of Information Systems and Services," in *Annual Review of Information Science and Technology,* vol. 14, edited by Martha E. Williams. White Plains, N.Y.: Knowledge Industries, 1979.

Murfin, Marjorie E., and Lubomyr R. Wynar. *Reference Service: An Annotated Bibliographic Guide.* Littleton, Colo.: Libraries Unlimited, 1977.

Myers, Marcia J. "The Accuracy of Telephone Reference Services in the Southeast: A Case for Quantitative Standards," in *Library Effectiveness: A State of the Art.* Chicago: American Library Association, 1980.

Nunally, Jum C. *Psychometric Theory.* New York: McGraw-Hill, 1967.

Palmour, Vernon E., Marcia C. Bellassai, and Nancy DeWath. *A Planning Process for Public Libraries.* Chicago: American Library Association, 1980.

Roscoe, John T. *Fundamental Research Statistics for the Behavioral Sciences,* 2nd ed. New York: Holt, Rinehart and Winston, 1975.

Rouse, William B., and Sandra H. Rouse. *Management of Library Networks.* New York: Marcel Dekker, 1977.

Schwarzkopf, LeRoy C. "Depository Libraries and Public Access," in *Collection Development and Public Access of Government Documents,* edited by Peter Hernon. Westport, Conn.: Meckler, 1982.

Selltiz, Claire, Lawrence S. Wrightsman, and Stuart W. Cook. *Research Methods in Social Relations,* 3rd ed. New York: Holt, Rinehart and Winston, 1976.

Siegel, Sidney. *Nonparametric Statistics for the Behavioral Sciences.* New York: McGraw-Hill, 1956.

Stewart, Charles, and William Cash. *Interviewing: Principles and Practices.* Dubuque, Iowa: Wm. C. Brown Co., 1974.

Webb, Eugene J., et al. *Unobtrusive Measures: Nonreactive Research in the Social Sciences.* Chicago: Rand McNally, 1966.

Williams, J. G. "Performance Criteria and Evaluation for a Library Resource Sharing Network," in *Library Resource Sharing.* New York: Marcel Dekker, 1977.

Witka, D. K. *Handbook of Measurement and Assessment in Behavior Sciences,* 2nd ed. Reading, Mass.: Addison-Wesley, 1968.

Wyer, James I. *Reference Work.* Chicago: American Library Association, 1930.

Zweizig, Douglas L., and Eleanor Rodger. *Output Measures for Public Libraries.* Chicago: American Library Association, 1982.

ERIC Publications

King, G. B., and L. R. Berry. *Evaluation of the University of Minnesota Libraries' Reference Department Telephone Information Service, Pilot Study.* Minneapolis: University of Minnesota Library School, 1973. ED 077 517.

Lynch, Beverly. "Assimilation of Government Publications in Study and Research, Final Report, July 1, 1978 through June 30, 1979." Chicago: University of Illinois at Chicago Circle, 1979. ED 184 571.

Theses and Dissertations

Bunge, Charles A. "Professional Education and Reference Efficiency." Ph.D. dissertation, University of Illinois, 1967.

Cook, Kevin L. "A Study of Varying Levels of Support Given to Government Documents Collections in Academic Libraries." Master's thesis, University of Oklahoma, 1981.

De Figueiredo, Nice M. "A Conceptual Methodology for Error Prevention in Reference Work." Ph.D. dissertation, Florida State University, 1975.

Gothberg, Helen M. "User Satisfaction with a Librarian's Immediate and Non-Immediate Verbal-Nonverbal Communication." Ph.D. dissertation, University of Denver, 1974.

Jirjees, Jassim Muhammed. "The Accuracy of Selected Northeastern College Library Reference/Information Telephone Services in Responding to Factual Inquiries." Ph.D. dissertation, Rutgers University, 1981.

Lynch, Mary Jo. "The Reference Interview in Public Libraries." Ph.D. dissertation, Rutgers University, 1977.

Myers, Marcia Jean. "The Effectiveness of Telephone Reference/Information Services in Academic Libraries in the Southeast." Ph.D. dissertation, Florida State University, 1979.

Powell, Ronald Rowe. "An Investigation of the Relationship between Reference Collection Size and Other Reference Service Factors and Success in Answering Reference Questions." Ph.D. dissertation, University of Illinois, 1976.

U.S. Government Publications

Annual Report of the U.S. Government Printing Office, Fiscal Year 1981. Washington, D.C.: Government Printing Office, 1982.

Bregent, Ann. "Cost of Regional Depository Library Service in the State of Washington." Olympia: Washington State Library, 1979; Washington, D.C.: Government Printing Office, 1979.

Congress. House. Committee on Appropriations. *Legislative Branch Appropriations for 1982: Hearing . . .* , Part 2. Washington, D.C.: Government Printing Office, 1981.

————. ————. Committee on House Administration. Subcommittee on Printing. *The National Publications Act.* Hearings, 96th Congress, 1st Session on H.R. 5424. Washington, D.C.: Government Printing Office, 1979.

————. Joint Committee on Printing. *Federal Government Advisory Committee on Revision of Title 44.* Washington, D.C.: Government Printing Office, 1979.

————. ————. *Government Depository Libraries, The Present Law Governing Designated Depository Libraries, Revised March 1981.* Washington, D.C.: Government Printing Office, 1981.

Federal Government Printing and Publishing: Policy Issues. Report of the Ad Hoc Advisory Committee on Revision of Title 44. Washington, D.C.: Government Printing Office, 1979.

Fry, Bernard M. *Government Publications: Their Role in the National Program for*

Library and Information Services. Washington, D.C.: Government Printing Office, 1978.

Guidelines for the Depository Library System. Washington, D.C.: Government Printing Office, 1977.

Instructions to Depository Libraries. Washington, D.C.: Government Printing Office, 1977.

National Commission on Libraries and Information Science. *Public Sector/Private Sector Interaction in Providing Information Services.* Washington, D.C.: Government Printing Office, 1982.

Office of Management and Budget. *Bulletin,* No. 81–16, April 21, 1982, and No. 81–16, Supplement No. 1, October 9, 1981.

100 GPO Years: 1861–1961. Washington, D.C.: Government Printing Office, 1962.

Toward a Federal Library and Information Services Network: A Proposal. A report of the Intergovernmental Library Cooperation Project; a joint undertaking of the National Commission on Libraries and Information Science and the Library of Congress. Washington, D.C.: Government Printing Office, 1982.

United States Code (Title 44). Washington, D.C.: Government Printing Office, 1976.

Other Sources

Dervin, Brenda. Telephone Interview with Charles R. McClure, April 21, 1982.

Taylor, Raymond (Superintendent of Documents, Government Printing Office). Letter to Peter Hernon, August 5, 1982.

Index